NEW ENGLAND'S
B E S T - L O V E D
D R I V I N G
T O U R S

Ⓦ Wiley Publishing, Inc.

Written by Kathy Arnold and Paul Wade
Additional research: Lans Christensen, Gael May McKibben, Tom Arnold and Harlan Levy

Published by AA Publishing, a trading name of Automobile Association Developments Limited, whose registered office is Millstream, Maidenhead Road, Windsor, Berkshire SL4 5GD. Registered number 1878835.

ISBN 0 7495 2603 3

The contents of this publication are believed correct at the time of printing. Nevertheless, AA Publishing accept no responsibility for errors, omissions or changes in the details given, or for the consequences of readers' reliance on this information. This does not affect your statutory rights. Assessments of the attractions, hotels and restaurants are based upon the authors' own experiences, and contain subjective opinions that may not reflect the publisher's opinion or a reader's experience. We have tried to ensure accuracy, but things do change, so please let us know if you have any comments or corrections.

A CIP catalogue record for this book is available from the British Library.

Colour separation: Daylight Colour Art, Singapore
Printed and bound by G. Canale & C. s.p.a., Torino, Italy

Find out more about AA Publishing and the wide range of travel publications and services the AA provides by visiting our website at www.theAA.com

First published 1997
Reprinted and updated 1999; Reprinted 1999
Revised second edition 2001
Reprinted 2003. Information verified and updated

Cover credits: CORBIS f/cover (top), f/flap (Joseph Sohm, ChromoSohm Inc.), b/cover (top, Ric Ergenbright), b/flap (David Muench); C COE b/cover (centre top); M LYNCH b/cover (centre bottom); POWERSTOCK/ZEFA b/cover (bottom)

A01355

CONTENTS

ROUTE MAP OF NEW ENGLAND inside front and back covers

ABOUT THIS BOOK 4 – 5

MASSACHUSETTS 6 – 57
Birthplace of a Nation 8 – 9
Tour 1 Lexington & Concord 10 – 15
Tour 2 The North Shore 16 – 22
Tour 3 Cape Cod 23 – 29
Tour 4 The Berkshire Hills 30 – 37
Boston 38 – 39
Tour 5 The Boston Freedom Trail 40 – 44
Tour 6 Boston Old & New 45 – 50
Tour 7 Cambridge & Harvard University 51 – 55
Cultural Cradle 56 – 57

CONNECTICUT 58 – 83
Tour 8 Hartford 60 – 65
Tour 9 New Haven & Yale University 66 – 70
Tour 10 The Housatonic Valley 71 – 75
Tour 11 The Connecticut Shore 76 – 81
The Maritime Tradition 82 – 83

RHODE ISLAND 84 – 95
Tour 12 Providence 86 – 89
Tour 13 Newport 90 – 95

VERMONT 96 – 121
Tour 14 Bennington 98 – 101
The Fall 102 – 103
Tour 15 Southern Vermont 104 – 109
Tour 16 Central Vermont 110 – 114
Tour 17 Northern Vermont 115 – 121

NEW HAMPSHIRE 122 – 137
Tour 18 Portsmouth 124 – 127
Tour 19 The White Mountains 128 – 133
Tour 20 Around Lake Winnipesaukee 134 – 137

MAINE 138 – 157
Tour 21 The Mid-Coast of Maine 140 – 146
Tour 22 Portland 147 – 151
Tour 23 Mountains & Lakes of Maine 152 – 157

PRACTICAL INFORMATION 158 – 173

INDEX & ACKNOWLEDGMENTS 174 – 176

ABOUT THIS BOOK

This book is not only a practical touring guide for the independent traveler, but is also invaluable for those who would like to know more about New England.

It is divided into the 6 states, each with its own city and driving tours. The driving tours start and finish in those cities which we consider to be the most interesting centers for exploration.

There are special features on Boston and the American Revolution, the beauty of the fall, and the rich heritage of the arts and the surrounding seas.

Each tour has details of the most interesting places to visit en route. Boxes catering for special interests follow some of the main entries – for those whose interest is in history, or walking, or those who have children. There are also boxes which highlight scenic stretches of road and which give details of special events, crafts and customs.

The simple route directions are accompanied by an easy-to-use map at the beginning of each tour, along with a chart showing how far it is from one town to the next in miles and kilometers. This can help you to decide where to take a break and stop overnight. (All distances quoted are approximate.)

Before setting off, it is advisable to check with the information center listed at the start of the tour for recommendations on where to break your journey, and for additional information on what to see and do, and when best to visit.

Torrington, Connecticut

only cash or travelers' checks. If you have a major credit or charge card, you may be able to obtain cash from an ATM.

Currency

The American unit of currency is the dollar, consisting of 100 cents. All the notes are green, are the same size and have similar designs, so be careful. They range from one to two, five, ten, 20, 50 and 100 dollars. Coins are in demoninations of one cent, (penny), 5 cents (nickel), 10 cents (dime), 25 cents (quarter) and ... rarely, a silver dollar.

Customs Regulations

Non-U.S. residents may take in 200 cigarettes or 50 cigars, a liter of alcohol and $100 worth of gifts. Customs officials are very strict about banning any fresh meat, fruit, plants and, of course, drugs (unless on prescription).

Electricity

Standard voltage is 110–120V, 60 cycles AC, using flat two-pin plugs. Bring the right adaptor.

Emergency Telephone Numbers

If you have an emergency, telephone the police at 911 who will put you in touch with the right

---

Tour Information

See pages 165–73 for addresses, telephone numbers and opening times of the attractions mentioned in the tours, including telephone numbers of tourist offices.

Accommodations and restaurants

See pages 161–4 for a list of recommended hotels and restaurants for each tour.

Motoring

For information on aspects of motoring in New England see pages 158–60.

INFORMATION FOR NON-U.S. RESIDENTS

Banks

Banks are usually open Mon–Fri 9–3. Many have extended hours until 5pm (or 8–9pm on Thu) and on Sat from 9–2, or later.

Although foreign currency can be changed at big hotels or airports, U.S. dollar travelers' checks are recommended as they are readily accepted as cash everywhere from restaurants to gas stations.

Credit Cards

Major credit cards are accepted in New England. However, many small bed and breakfasts or remote small shops will accept service. Otherwise, dial "0" and consult the operator.

Entry Regulations

Citizens of most European countries, plus Japan and New Zealand, no longer need visas as long as they are visiting the U.S. for business or tourist purposes. For a stay not exceeding 90 days, and provided that a return or onward ticket is held, only a valid passport is required. Check with your travel agent before traveling, since American immigration officials are very strict.

Health Matters

It is essential to have adequate health insurance before traveling to the U.S. While hospitals are usually excellent, treatment can be expensive. It may be delayed or refused without proof of proper insurance. Your hotel will be able to recommend a doctor or hospital. Alternatively, call the local hospital. No special inoculations are required. See also page 159.

Post Offices

Stamps for postcards and letters are on sale in many shops and hotels; for larger packages, go to a post office. It is cheaper to send postcards and aerograms than letters. See also page 160.

Public Holidays

See page 159.

Telephones

Each state has several area codes, with new ones opening up all the time as telecommunications expand.

Pay phones require 5, 10 and 25 cent coins, so use a telephone card for convenience. To call abroad, dial 011, then the country code:
Australia 61, Canada 1, New Zealand 64, U.K. 44.

Time

New England is on Eastern Standard Time (EST), 5 hours behind the U.K., 6 hours behind mainland Europe, and 15 hours behind Sydney, Australia. Daylight Saving Time alters the time by 1 hour from March or April to October or November.

Travelers Aid Society

The Travelers Aid Society, at 17 East Street, Boston, Massachusetts 02111 (tel: 617/542 7286), is dedicated to helping travelers. Staff provide crisis intervention, counseling, referrals to community sources, and emergency financial assistance to travelers in crisis. Travelers Aid volunteers at Logan Airport (tel: 617/567 5385) and the Greyhound Bus Terminal, South Station (tel: 617/737 2880) will help you to find an address, a hospital, lost luggage, a way to get money from home, or the solution to any other travel dilemma.

Useful Addresses

As well as the listings on pages 161–4, these agencies have a selection of places to stay:
Select Registry, Distinguished Inns of North America (tel: 800/344-5244); (in U.K.) North America Travel Service (tel: 0113 243 0000); Bed and Breakfast Agency of Boston, 47 Commercial Wharf, Boston, MA 02110. Tel: (in U.K.) 0800 895128 (in U.S.A. and Canada) 800/248 9262; Nutmeg Bed & Breakfast Agency (Connecticut). Tel: 800/727-7592; National Network of Bed & Breakfast Reservation Services (tel: 800/236-6698; www.go-lodging.com).

Lobster pots at Mystic Seaport

MASSACHUSETTS

After 380 years of permanent European settlement, Massachusetts has acquired a "little history." Here, the Pilgrims landed and built their communities. A century and a half later, patriotic passion exploded in a series of events culminating in the American Revolution. Not surprisingly, that heritage has been preserved. Conservation has encompassed old houses and bridges, churches and farms, even entire villages.

Massachusetts is known as the Bay State because of the gaping Atlantic gulf enclosed by the flexed arm of Cape Cod. The shape of the state ensures a variety of landscapes. It stretches from the storm-tossed Atlantic to the rolling, wooded hills of the Berkshires, with the rich meadows of the Connecticut Valley in between.

The seasons are distinct: crisp, clear winter days melting into an explosion of spring greenery and flowers, followed by muggy, soporific summers and, finally, the fall with its dazzling multi-colored leaves (see pages 102–3).

Massachusetts, especially around Boston, was also America's cultural cradle (see pages 56–7). Artists and writers, poets and musicians have long been drawn together by the web of academia. Harvard University, founded in 1636, is the oldest American institute of higher learning, but there are numerous other colleges to be found throughout the state, as well as boarding schools (called "prep schools" because they prepare students for college).

Concord is a beautiful town with a rich and varied history

Outdoor festivals of music and drama are a bonus for visitors during the summer months.

But the region's focus always returns to history. Many of America's most treasured icons are here, from Plymouth Rock to Boston's Old North Church and Concord's historic bridge. Thanksgiving is celebrated with justifiable pride; after all, the tradition of eating turkey and pumpkin pie was "invented" here. They even have the cranberry bogs nearby to provide the accompanying sauce.

Tour 1

"Listen, my children, and you
    shall hear,
Of the midnight ride of
    Paul Revere ..."

Paul Revere is one of the best-known messengers in history, thanks to Henry Wadsworth Longfellow's poem. His ride from Boston to warn the Americans that the British were on the march has become legendary. The patriots assembled and took on the trained soldiers, first in Lexington and then in Concord. All the British wanted to do was capture the rebels' arms cache; they had no idea that the skirmishes of April 19, 1775 would spark the American Revolution. In both towns, historic sites have been preserved, while the visitor information centers provide details of "who did what and when." The route for this tour also has a literary focus. In the 19th century, Concord was the home of some of the best-known writers of the day: Henry David Thoreau, Louisa May Alcott, Nathaniel Hawthorne and Ralph Waldo Emerson.

Tour 2

Although Cape Cod has long been recognized as a playground for Bostonians, the North Shore, with its rugged, rocky outcrops is also a popular place to relax by the sea. Add to that atmospheric fishing villages and the gruesome history of witches in Salem, and this drive is fun as well as scenic. The sparkling light has long attracted artists, especially in Rockport. Castles and underwater rocks, whales, frozen peas and even clam chowder are threads in the rich tapestry of America's history which unravels along this shoreline drive.

Tour 3

Cape Cod enjoys a mystique matched by few holiday destinations. The names of its 300-year-old villages are reminders of English fishing ports, its history peopled with Indians and fishermen, whalers and sea captains. On Cape Cod Bay, the sands are sheltered and the water is warmer than on the Atlantic Ocean shore, where strong waves buffet the dunes of the Cape Cod National Seashore.

This 40-mile (60km) coastline stretches from the elbow of the peninsula up to Provincetown, known for its bohemian lifestyle. The popularity of the Cape has taken its toll: roadside development sprawls around Hyannis on the south shore and traffic can be bumper to bumper on summer weekends. Off season, it is easier to get away from it all, and find what aficionados call "the old Cape Cod."

Tour 4

Western Massachusetts has an intriguing mixture of the rural and sophisticated, the historic and eccentric. The rolling Berkshire Hills inspired authors

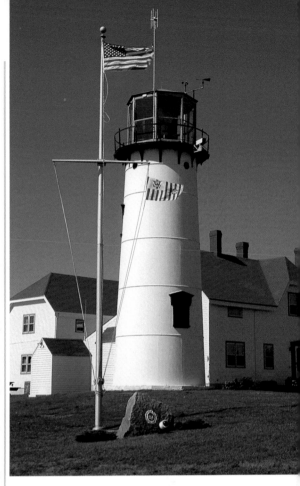

Chatham Light, Cape Cod.
Lighthouses are a unique part of
New England's heritage

such as Herman Melville and Edith Wharton, and attracted millionaires, who built vacation homes away from the seaside. Now the hills resound to summer festivals of music and theater. Attractive towns and villages range from Deerfield, with its perfectly preserved 17th-century houses, to Williamstown with its excellent college and astonishing art collection. Stockbridge thrives on its "traditional America" image, ably reinforced by *Saturday Evening Post* cover artist Norman Rockwell, whose paintings are on display here. Drive down lazy back roads to old covered bridges arching over rocky streams; there are surprises around every corner.

BIRTHPLACE OF A NATION

The American perspective of the War of Independence is simple: the Colonists were oppressed by King George III and Parliament and justifiably rebelled. The issues were a little more complex. In the early days, there were no "states" as such. The Colonies differed in population and style of government: some depended on fishing and trade, others on farming and tobacco. Although links with the Mother Country were strong for economic and cultural reasons, the Colonists had become increasingly independent-minded during the century-and-a-half since the first settlers arrived.

A turning point in American history was the defeat of the French and the Indians in the war from 1756 to 1763. This gave the New Englanders, and the colonies along the coast to the south, a vision of vast lands stretching westward and a sense of "new" country to be developed. Relations with Britain, however, became strained when Parliament decided that the colonies should help pay for the seven years of war; after all, the English reasoned, they were defending Colonial lands. Moreover, a 10,000-strong army was still needed to protect the Colonies. A monopoly on trade was proclaimed, restricting Colonists to dealing only with Britain and other British possessions (notably the West Indies). Further, a ban was issued on new settlements west of the Appalachians.

Although these restrictions rankled, what inflamed Colonial passions was direct taxation. Traditionally, Britain had raised money by customs duties on shipping; the Stamp Act in 1765 set a new precedent. This placed a charge on all contracts, deeds, newspapers and legal documents. Protests forced its repeal within a year, but other revenue-raisers followed, only to be repealed. Parliament decided to stand firm on one, however. That was the tax on tea.

After the French and Indian War, economic times were hard for the Colonists, and the new rules hurt financially. But the Colonists also protested on principle. "No taxation without representation" was the cry at public meetings and in pamphlets. Articles questioned the legality of such taxes, claiming that they infringed the charters of some of the Colonies.

Boston was an important focus of militant feelings, which periodically exploded into riots. One relatively minor event, on March 5, 1770, became a legend. A lone British sentry on duty at the Custom House was harassed by a crowd. Reinforcements arrived, but the mob continued to bait the soldiers, heckling them and throwing stones. Shots were fired; five Colonists died. This incident became known as the "Boston Massacre" and was used by leaders such as Samuel Adams to whip up emotions.

Three years later, in December, came one of the most colorful incidents of the era, the Boston Tea Party. As a protest against the tax of 3 pence per pound on tea, about a hundred men, disguised as Native Americans, boarded the newly arrived HMS *Dartmouth*. Its cargo of 300 chests of tea was thrown overboard. In response, General Gage and four British regiments were sent to Boston, and the port was closed down in 1774.

Below: the Boston Massacre, in which five Colonists died
Bottom: the "Sons of Liberty," disguised as Mohawk Indians, throw East India Company tea into the water

The scene was set for the smoldering coals of resentment to be ignited. In April, 1775, it was reported to General Gage that farmers in Concord, a small village west of Boston, were stockpiling firearms. He ordered 700 British troops to march out, confiscate and destroy the Patriots' illegal cache. On route, they skirmished with the Minute Men (locals who could be ready "in a minute" to fight) in Lexington before being outnumbered in Concord. Instead of withdrawing in an orderly manner, the British confronted the militiamen, lost three soldiers and had to beat a hasty, undignified retreat to Boston.

cost was hundreds of lives. The psychological victory belonged to the Americans. King George III replied savagely by declaring the Colonies to be in rebellion. Mercenaries were hired in Europe and transported across the Atlantic to augment the troops.

Not all the Colonists were ready for war. About one-third remained loyal to the crown and another third were neutral. The rest, however, were vociferous and demanded to sever links with the Mother Country. Further British attacks on Falmouth (now Portland, Maine) in October, 1775 and on Norfolk, Virginia in January, 1776, only

Boston, never to return. Fighting, however, continued elsewhere. In May, representatives of all 13 Colonies met in Philadelphia, Pennsylvania. Freedom was the agenda of this Continental Congress. A short document drafted by Thomas Jefferson of Virginia set out the grievances and proclaimed that "these united colonies are, and of right ought to be, free and independent states." This was the Declaration of Independence, accepted unanimously by the delegates and signed on July 4, 1776.

Liberty did not come immediately, however. War raged for five years and even after the

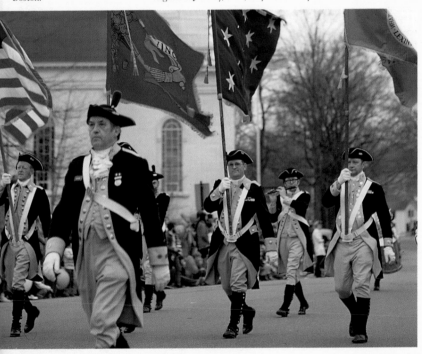

Some 20,000 Minute Men rushed to Boston, penning the British forces in. In May, 1775, artillery powder and ammunition captured at Fort Ticonderoga in New York State was hauled overland by the Colonists and used to capture Bunker Hill. Although the Redcoats soon stormed and recaptured it, the

served to fan the fury. *Common Sense*, a pamphlet written by Thomas Paine, became a best seller, with 120,000 copies sold in January, 1776 alone. Although he was an Englishman who had lived in the Colonies for only a year, he argued strenuously for independence. In March, 1776, the British withdrew from

The citizens of Lexington re-enact the events of April 19, 1775

formal British surrender in 1781, London refused to recognize the Colonies' independence. Finally, in September, 1783, a peace treaty was signed in Paris, acknowledging that a new nation had been born.

Lexington
& Concord

Concord and Lexington are two of the most famous towns in the United States, due to the skirmishes between locals and British soldiers in 1775 that triggered the American Revolution. Concord has an additional claim to fame: it was home to some of the great writers of 19th-century America. Today, Lexington feels like a residential suburb of Boston, while Concord has retained more of its historical flavor. The main themes of this route are liberty and literature, but at the end of the drive, the focus is strictly contemporary.

The Captain John Parker Statue on Lexington Green

1 DAY • 30 MILES • 49KM

ITINERARY	
CAMBRIDGE	▶ Lexington (8m-13km)
LEXINGTON	▶ Concord (6m-10km)
CONCORD	▶ Cambridge (16m-26km)

i *Cambridge Visitor Information Booth, Harvard Square*

▶ *From Cambridge, take the Fresh Pond Parkway (Routes 16 and 3) to Route 2 west. Take this for 3 miles (5km) and then exit onto Routes 4 and 225. At the first stop sign, turn left onto Massachusetts Avenue (always known as "Mass Ave"). This was the route taken by Paul Revere on his way to Lexington. At the junction with the 2A, turn left onto 2A West to reach the National Heritage Museum.*

❶ National Heritage Museum

This bright and airy museum provides a useful background to the rest of the tour. The permanent exhibition, entitled "Lexington Alarm'd!", portrays life in this farming community in the years leading up to the start of the Revolution. Entertaining and enlightening are the videos showing the "television news" in London and Boston in 1765; not surprisingly, they present two opposite views of the Stamp Act.

▶ *Return to the Massachusetts Avenue junction and turn left to reach Munroe Tavern.*

❷ Munroe Tavern

On the afternoon of April 19, 1775, this fine old pub (1695) was the site of the temporary hospital and headquarters for British soldiers retreating from the battle at Concord. Fourteen years later, George Washington dined here in an upstairs room, while on tour in New England. Today it is the headquarters of the Lexington Historical Society.

▶ *Follow Massachusetts Avenue for about a mile (1.5km), straight into Lexington to the triangular green.*

❸ Lexington

This cradle of the American Revolution is dotted with significant sites, not least of which is Battle Green. Here, a bronze statue of Captain John Parker stands on a stone cairn, facing the line of the British approach. Behind him the Lexington militia would have stood. "Ye villains, ye rebels, disperse!" ordered the arrogant Major John Pitcairn. Faced by the superior numbers and strength of the

Headquarters of the Lexington Minute Men, 1775

British, Parker wisely told his men: "Don't fire unless fired upon, but if they mean to have a war, let it begin here!"

A shot rang out, no-one knows from where. Suddenly fire was exchanged; two British soldiers and eight Minute Men were killed or wounded. Seven of them are buried under the Revolutionary Monument further along on the Green. The British, having beaten off this minor attack, marched on toward Concord.

In the nearby Visitor Center there is a diorama giving an overview of the events of that day. Next door to it is Buckman Tavern, a handsome three-story tavern (1710) where, in the early hours of April 19, 1775, several Lexington Minute Men had gathered to drink ale. Around 4am came the news that 700 British troops were just minutes from the Green. Bells rang out, drums rolled and the Minute Men, under the command of

Captain John Parker, filed out of the tavern. As the sun rose, they assembled on the Green, more as a protest than looking for a fight. The Tavern looks exactly as it did in 1775, with bar orders chalked on the tap room wall. The front door has a hole in it, allegedly from a bullet shot during the encounter.

From here go to the right of the Green and turn right on Hancock Street. Number 36 is the Hancock-Clarke House, where, at around 1am on April 19, 1775, John Hancock and Samuel Adams were awakened by a knock on the door. Paul Revere had arrived to warn these two important leaders that the British were on the march. This 1698 house is furnished as it would have been on that night. You can see Major Pitcairn's

pistols (see previous page) and the drums belonging to Minute Man William Drummond.

[i] *1875 Massachusetts Avenue or Battle Green*

▶ *Leave Lexington on Massachusetts Avenue and follow it west (where it becomes Battle Road) for 2 miles (3km). Turn right onto* **Route 2A** *and drive to the Minute Man National Historical Park.*

4 Minute Man National Historical Park

Although the actual road followed by the British troops has been largely covered over by Route 2A, a small section has been preserved in the Minute Man National Historical Park. About half a mile (800m) beyond the Visitor Center is the

SPECIAL TO...

The events of April 19, 1775 are re-enacted each year on Patriots' Day. At sunrise, latter-day Minute Men from communities around Concord march through the woods much as their ancestors did. Historically accurate 1775 uniforms are *de rigueur*, both for the "farmers" and the "Redcoats." In a brief but moving ceremony near the Old North Bridge, officials from Britain and America pay their respects to those who died, as the *Last Post* rings out. Later in the day, skirmishes are cheerfully re-enacted, with much rattling of drums and piping of fifes. Nowadays, the holiday falls on the Monday closest to April 19, to make a long weekend.

Lexington's First Parish Church

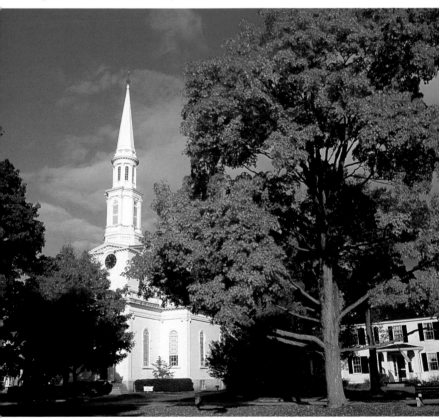

site where Paul Revere was captured by a British patrol. His fellow messenger, Dr. Samuel Prescott, eluded them and rode on to Concord. In another half mile (800m), a narrow winding section of the original Battle Road bears off to the right. This is a typical "two rod road," named because of the 32-foot (10m) distance between the stone walls on either side of the road (a rod measures 16 feet/ 5m). Here, the William Smith House and the Ephraim Hartwell Tavern all reflect the style of architecture and the methods of construction used in the buildings of Colonial Massachusetts.

[i] *Minute Man Visitor Center, Route 2A, Lexington*

▶ *Drive to the intersection of Battle Road and **Route 2A**, turn right and continue to Concord.*

Concord

Concord was founded in 1635, and is redolent with history, from its historic houses (many with date plaques) to its reminders of the Revolution, to its fine literary heritage.

The approach to the center of Concord is along Lexington Avenue, where two historic properties were once the homes of famous writers. The Wayside, with its distinctive red brick chimneys, was originally the home of the muster master, whose job was to summon the Minute Men if the British attacked. In the 19th century, it became first the residence of the Alcott family, then in 1852, Nathaniel Hawthorne bought it and changed the name from Hillside to The Wayside. He completed *Tanglewood Tales* in his study in the tower at the top of the house.

A little way farther up the street is Orchard House, to which the Alcott family moved after leaving The Wayside. It was here that Louisa May wrote much of *Little Women*. Researchers for the 1992 movie

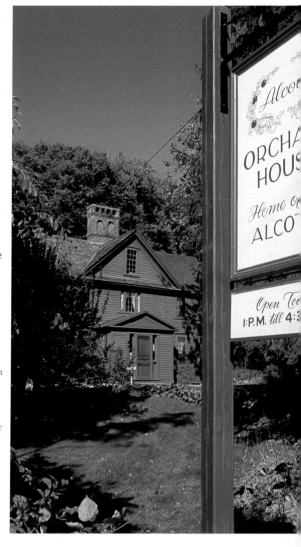

of the book took photographs and made sketches here, then built a house in Canada especially for the filming. It was not an exact replica, however, and those taking the guided tour may notice a number of differences, particularly in the bedrooms. Carefully preserved furnishings and costumes reflect the family's 20 years here.

Closer to the town center, take a left onto the Concord Turnpike for the Concord Museum. This is a fine example

Orchard House, the home of novelist Louisa May Alcott

of a small museum, and it encompasses all aspects of Concord's history in a particularly engaging way. Relics of the Revolution include Paul Revere's signal lantern and the sword that belonged to Colonel Barrett, commander of the Concord militia. Literary mementos include Louisa May Alcott's tea kettle and doll, Henry David Thoreau's bed, writing desk and rocking chair from his cabin at Walden Pond (see below), and Ralph Waldo Emerson's study, brought from his former home across the street and reconstructed here.

When Emerson's original house was destroyed by fire in 1872, the philosopher-poet's reaction was unusual, to say the least: "But isn't it a lovely blaze!" was all he said. Sent away to recover from the shock, he returned after a year to find that his home had been rebuilt by his friends and neighbors. Emerson's life here was characterized by "plain living and high thinking" but he is less remembered for his essays than for quotes such as, "If a man can write a better book, preach a better sermon, or make a better mousetrap than his neighbor, though he builds his house in the woods, the world will beat a path to his door." The reconstructed house is exactly as he left it – except for the study, of course.

Off Concord's Green, along Route 62, is Sleepy Hollow Cemetery, every bit as peaceful as it sounds. Here, on top of "Author's Ridge," are the last resting places of Louisa May Alcott, Ralph Waldo Emerson and Nathaniel Hawthorne. The grave of Henry David Thoreau is marked by a simple headstone, inscribed with only one word: "Henry."

The most famous site in Concord is undoubtedly the North Bridge on Liberty Street, the "rude bridge" where, on April 19, 1775, "... the embattled farmers stood, And fired the shot heard round the world." These words are from the *Concord Hymn*, written by Emerson in 1837 to celebrate the completion of the Battle Monument. One of the most powerful American icons, it was sculpted by Daniel Chester French, who also created the figure of Abraham Lincoln for the Lincoln Memorial in Washington D.C.

On the day of the battle, some 400 Minute Men were waiting here to confront the 700 tired and worried British Regulars. As they advanced across the bridge, the famous shot rang out. The sloping fields would have looked much as they do now, though the bridge is a modern replica. Across the river, at the edge of an open field, stands the Old Manse. It was from a window of this three-story wooden house that the parson, William Emerson, watched the bloody events. He was the grandfather of Ralph Waldo Emerson, who lived here as a little boy. In later years the house was rented to Nathaniel Hawthorne, and some of his possessions are still there, including his writing desk.

i *Concord Chamber of Commerce, 58 Main Street; North Bridge Visitor Center, Liberty Street*

▶ *Leave Concord following the sign for* **Route 2A**, *from the Green. After a short distance, turn right on Heywood Street, then left on Walden Street* (**Route 126**). *Continue for 1 mile (1.5km), crossing* **Route 2**, *to the Walden Pond parking lot.*

6 Walden Pond

Henry Thoreau came here and "lived alone, in the woods, a mile from any neighbor, in a house I had built myself, on the shore of Walden Pond." This two-year "back to nature" experience was the basis of his most famous work, *Walden*, published in 1854. Seeking the solitude that he found may be difficult in summer, when families swim and picnic at "this pond ... so remarkable for its depth and purity ... a clear and deep well, half a mile long and a mile and three quarters in circumference ..." A replica of his cabin is conveniently close to the parking lot; to avoid the crowds, walk around to the far side of the water, where a cairn marks the site of the real cabin. The pond is surrounded by the 333-acre (138-hectare) Walden Pond State Reservation.

▶ *Follow* **Route 126** *south for a short distance to Baker Bridge Road and turn left. At No. 68 is the Gropius House.*

7 Gropius House

This is the home of the German architect Walter Gropius, founder of the Bauhaus Movement, who moved to the U.S. in 1937 and lectured at Harvard for 14 years. The house was far ahead of its time, combining traditional architecture with the innovative use of modern materials, such as welded steel, glass blocks, and chrome. Its furnishings are also interesting, and the house contains works of modern art.

▶ *Continue to the end of the road and turn right onto Sandy Pond Road. On the left is the DeCordova Museum.*

8 DeCordova Museum

Dedicated to the work of contemporary American artists, this museum is located in 35

The Old North Bridge, actually a modern replica

acres (14 hectares) of open fields and woods overlooking Sandy Pond. Around 80 sculptures are displayed outside in natural settings. The museum shop sells original works of art.

▶ Return to Sandy Pond Road, turn left and drive to the first

intersection. Cross Lincoln Road, and continue on Trapelo Road for 2¹/₂ miles (4km) to **Route 128**. Go north on **Route 128** to **Route 2** east, the first exit, and return to Cambridge.

SPECIAL TO...

Around 1845, Concord was the literary epicenter of America, with four of the country's most revered writers living near one another. Ralph Waldo Emerson (1803–82) was a philosopher, poet and magnetic speaker. Today, he is best remembered for the *Concord Hymn*, encapsulating the events of the Old North Bridge (see page 14). In 1837, he struck up a friendship with Henry Thoreau (1817–62). Thoreau came to live in Concord and spent two years in a small cabin that he constructed himself at the edge of Walden Pond. It was here that he wrote his most memorable book, *Walden*. The Salem-born novelist Nathaniel Hawthorne (1805–64), a Concord resident for a few years, was also part of the group. At that time, though Louisa May Alcott (1832–88) was just a child, she was already writing poems and romantic stories.

RECOMMENDED TRIPS

Canoes can be rented at the South Bridge Boathouse (on Main Street, Concord) for trips through Concord and the Great Meadows National Wildlife Refuge. Although there are 18 miles (29km) of navigable water, the paddle to the North Bridge and back is an easy two hours and is an excellent way to see parts of the town that haven't changed significantly since the Revolution.
If paddling is not your style, you can take the marked nature trail (3 miles/5km) in the wildlife refuge.

FOR HISTORY BUFFS

"March with the Corps of Grenadiers and Light Infantry ... to Concord, where you will seize and destroy all Artillery, Ammunition, Provisions, Tents, Small Arms, and all Military Stores ... but you will take care that the Soldiers do not plunder the Inhabitants, or hurt private property."
Unfortunately the orders of General Gage were leaked to patriots in Boston and, as the British prepared to cross the Charles River on the night of April 18, two lanterns appeared in the belfry of the Old North Church. A waiting Paul Revere saw the signal and set off on horseback to tell the men of Lexington and Concord to be ready.

The North
Shore

One famous seaport after another follows the curve of the coast north of Boston, from the towns of Gloucester and Marblehead, to Salem and Newburyport. There are hundreds of handsome old houses, and dozens of high-quality museums and art galleries.

ITINERARY

BOSTON	▶	**Marblehead (17m-27km)**
MARBLEHEAD	▶	**Salem (5m-8km)**
SALEM	▶	**Manchester-by-the-Sea (7m-11km)**
MANCHESTER-BY-THE-SEA	▶	**Gloucester (8m-13km)**
GLOUCESTER	▶	**Rockport (5m-8km)**
ROCKPORT	▶	**Pigeon Cove (2m-3km)**
PIGEON COVE	▶	**Essex (10m-16km)**
ESSEX	▶	**Ipswich (5m-8km)**
IPSWICH	▶	**Plum Island (21m-34km)**
PLUM ISLAND	▶	**Newburyport (11m-18km)**
NEWBURYPORT	▶	**Boston (43m-69km)**

1 DAY • 134 MILES • 215KM

Salem Custom House where Nathaniel Hawthorne worked

i *Boston Common Visitor Information Center, 147 Tremont Street*

▶ *Leave Boston via the Callahan Tunnel, and follow* **Route 1A** *to Lynn. After 8 miles (13km), pass a rotary (roundabout), and bear right onto Carroll Parkway. Follow* **Route 129** *along the sea wall to Swampscott, and bear right onto Puritan Road for 1 mile (1.5km) until it rejoins* **Route 129**. *Go right on* **Route 129** *to Ocean Avenue and turn right to Marblehead Neck.*

❶ Marblehead Neck

On the road across the causeway, look right for a view of the Boston skyline. To the left, a fleet of sailboats sits anchored in Marblehead harbor. Bear right and follow signs for the Bike Route for about 2 miles (3km) to Chandler Hovey Park and the lighthouse. From the park there are spectacular views all the way to Manchester and Gloucester harbors. Marblehead Neck itself is all quiet residential streets.

▶ *Return to* **Route 129** *and turn right to Marblehead.*

❷ Marblehead

The up-hill-and-down-dale style of Marblehead's old town reflects the West of England origins of the fishermen who settled here in 1629. On Front Street, the oldest houses cluster round the harbor of what was soon known as the "greatest Towne for fishing in New England." As the seafarers developed a thriving overseas trade, so the merchants built bigger and better houses. Jeremiah Lee Mansion is a fine example: a Georgian mansion, built in 1768 and now home to the Marblehead Historical Society. Marblehead sailors played a vital role in the Revolution, and a local boat, the *Hannah*, takes pride in being America's first warship. Today luxury yachts fill the moorings.

i *Information Booth, Pleasant and Spring streets*

▶ *Leave Marblehead on* **Route 114**, *then join* **Route 1A North** *and drive 5 miles (8km) to Salem.*

❸ Salem

One short period of hysteria in the 17th century singled Salem out from the rest of the North Shore coastal ports. Now, more than 300 years later, witchcraft trials and executions have become big business. Those wanting to relive the gruesome spectacles can visit the Witch Museum, Witch Village and Witch House, but there is much more to see in this historic town. The fine mansions were so impressive that future-president John Adams wrote in 1766: "the houses are the most elegant and grand that I have seen in any of the maritime towns." Examples can be found on Chestnut, Essex and Federal streets.

The Pioneer Village is a re-

Statue of Puritan Roger Conant, who founded Salem in 1626, outside the Salem Witch Museum

SPECIAL TO...

Salem's gloomy past inspired two authors in particular – Nathaniel Hawthorne and Arthur Miller. Born here, Hawthorne reflected the hypocrisy of Puritan Salem in *The Scarlet Letter* (the subject of a film in 1995) and set *The House of the Seven Gables* in his cousin's home, which still stands. Three hundred years later, Arthur Miller wrote *The Crucible*, where he used the hysteria of the Salem witch trials as a symbol for the McCarthy anti-Communist trials which took place in the early 1950s.

created 17th-century fishing village, complete with period homes, gardens, and live animals. Costumed guides show how the early settlers lived, and there is lots of visitor participation.

The Peabody Essex Museum, arguably America's oldest museum, was started in 1799 by a group of sea captains wishing to display their souvenirs from far-flung voyages. The richest and most impressive section is the Asian Export Art Collection which contains beautiful oriental objects that were made specifically for sale to the West.

The town's nautical traditions are portrayed in the admirable Salem Maritime National Historic Site that snakes along the harbor front.

[i] *New Liberty and Essex streets*

FOR HISTORY BUFFS

Salem comes from the Hebrew word *Shalom*, meaning peace. But the calm of Salem was shattered in 1692 when several young girls began to have fits and accused three women of casting spells on them. Panic followed, other accusations were made, and before common sense prevailed, 19 people had been hanged, and one man, Giles Corey, was crushed by rocks. The hysteria was stamped out the following year, when the governor ordered all the "witches" to be released from prison, probably because his wife had been one of the accused!

▶ *Take* **Route 1A North** *across the bridge over Beverly Harbor, and follow* **Route 127** *through Beverly for 4 miles (6km) to the Prides Crossing railroad station.*

4 Prides Crossing
When the railroad from Beverly was extended to Manchester in 1840, it crossed land once owned by the Pride family, who supposedly received the grant in the early 1700s from the King of England. The route was used by wealthy Bostonians who left the city and came out to spend the summers by the water in their large mansions. The railroad depot still has separate benches marked for use by Democrats and Republicans. Now, residents of this small village make the trip in and out of Boston every day by car.

▶ *Continue on* **Route 127** *for 3 miles (5km) into the center of Manchester-by-the-Sea.*

5 Manchester-by-the-Sea
Originally settled by Englishmen from Manchester, the town's name was amended recently to emphasize its position at the head of a pretty harbor, graced with its flotilla of sailboats. On one side of the town square is First Parish Church, built in 1807, with a clock face on each side of its distinctive steeple. Visitors come in summer, not just to walk along the waterfront, but also to spend the day on Singing Beach, where the wind "sings" as it whistles along the sand.

▶ *Continue on **Route 127** for 3 miles (5km), then bear right for Magnolia. Continue for 2 miles (3km) through the town center and up the hill on Norman Avenue to Hammond Castle.*

6 Hammond Castle Museum

Whenever you use a remote control button to switch television channels or open the garage from your car, the man to thank is Dr. John Hammond (1888–1965). This genius thought up over 800 inventions and was granted 400 patents, mainly to do with electronics. His quirky mind is reflected in the clifftop mansion he built in 1926, which incorporates bits of European buildings: there is an archway built with lava rock from Mount Vesuvius, and a Roman bath. There are even secret passages and a laboratory. His vast 8,200-pipe organ stands in an impressive hall where concerts are given at weekends. Hammond is buried on the grounds with two of his cats and, as requested, poison ivy grows over his grave.

▶ *Return to **Route 127** and continue for 2 miles (3km) to Gloucester.*

7 Gloucester

The first landmark in town to meet your eye is *The Man at the Wheel*, the statue of a ship's pilot staring out towards the mouth of the harbor. The statue was set in place in 1923 to commemorate Gloucester's 300th birthday, and as a reminder that the town continues to be a working port, America's oldest.

The loss of the *Andrea Gail* in the early 1990s was the inspiration for the book *The Perfect Storm*. Now, visitors come to see where the film (2000) was shot, as well as for whale-watching

FOR CHILDREN

A great way to take children sightseeing in Gloucester is on a Moby Duck tour. Amphibious vehicles transport you around land-based attractions then plunge straight into the water to explore the maritime sights of this famous seafaring town. Children will also enjoy a tour of the schooner *Adventure*, moored in the harbor. A national historic landmark, it was the town's last fishing schooner.

excursions and the annual Schooner Festival in early September. The Cape Ann Historical Museum is a tribute to artist Fitz Hugh Lane, who lived out his life here and specialized in seascapes.

i *Stage Fort Park Information Center, Hough Avenue (seasonal) and 33 Commercial Street (year-round)*

SPECIAL TO...

There really was a Cap'n Birdseye. As early as 1912, Clarence Birdseye of Gloucester was intrigued to see how the Inuit people of Labrador preserved their food by freezing it. By 1924, he had perfected the bulk deep-freezing technique that is taken for granted today. The Freezing Company concentrated on fruit and vegetables in the early days, but as demand for his products grew, Birdseye needed to speed up the process, so he invented the multiple plate freezer, which is still used. In the 1950s, the company developed fish sticks, or fish fingers, a great favorite with children.

The pier at Gloucester
Inset: *The Man at the Wheel*

WHALE WATCHING...

Up and down the coast of New England, boats still set off to hunt for whales. Unlike the 19th century, however, the purpose is not to shoot the majestic mammals with harpoons, but with cameras. Tours depart regularly from Boston, but they also leave from Salem and Gloucester on the North Shore, from Portsmouth, New Hampshire and from Cape Cod towns such as Provincetown. The favorite places for spotting whales are the Stellwagen Bank and Jeffreys Ledge, both popular feeding grounds. Harbor porpoises and Atlantic white-sided dolphins, relatives of the whales, are also abundant, and have teeth rather than the baleen plates of the whales.

RIGHT WHALES

Named by Yankee whalers, because they were the "right" whales to catch, this is the most endangered species in the world. The whales are easily recognized by the callosities, crusty growths, on their backs. Reaching up to 50 feet and 60 tons (16m and 61,000kg), they can be spotted offshore from April to January.

HUMPBACK WHALES

The name comes from their habit of arching their backs before diving. They are also known to "breach," leaping clear out of the water, a particularly impressive sight, since humpbacks grow up to 50 feet (16m) long and 30 tons (30,500kg) in weight. They are resident off New England from spring to fall.

FIN WHALES

The largest whales in New England waters are also the most common. Reaching 70 feet (21m) in length and 50 tons (51,000kg), fin whales can be identified by their dorsal fin, as well as the white chevron on their backs. Like the humpbacks, they are resident from spring to fall.

SPECIAL TO...

May 22 is Motif No. 1 Day in Rockport. It celebrates an old fishing shack, dating from the mid-1800s, that stands at the end of Bradley Wharf in Rockport Harbor. Local lore has it that, back in the 1920s, art teacher Lester Hornby was confronted by yet another student's sketch of this dark red hut, festooned with lobster traps and colorful lobster floats. "What? Motif number one again!" he exclaimed despairingly to the pupil. Would-be photographers and painters should walk to the end of the wharf to compose their own version of this picturesque icon.

▶ Follow **Route 127** for 1 mile (1.5km), then bear right onto East Main Street for Rocky Neck.

8 Rocky Neck and Beauport

Rocky Neck is a small settlement of working artists. The oldest such colony in the country, it has survived here since 1916. Some 30 people live on the tiny peninsula, with their studios in wood-shingled shacks. The roads are all one-way, narrow, and busy on weekends.

Further towards Eastern Point lighthouse is Beauport. From the turn of the century, big spenders such as R. T. Vanderbilt and J. D. Rockefeller, as well as such stars as Joan Crawford, came out here to consult Henry Davis Sleeper (1878–1934), *the* interior decora-

Rockport's harbor epitomizes coastal New England

tor of his day. In Beauport, his own summer home, he gave each of the 40 rooms a design theme, from the Lord Byron and Paul Revere Rooms to the China Trade and India Rooms. The house is now a museum, full of his collection of antiques and art.

▶ Return to Gloucester and follow signs for **Alternate Route 127A** to Rockport.

9 Rockport

As its name implies, Rockport's early fame was founded on rock, in particular the granite quarried for many of America's 19th-century monuments, bridges, and civic buildings. For the past century, however, Rockport has been better known for its artists' colony and the town is full of galleries and craft shops exhibiting their work, principally the Rockport Art Association's galleries on Main Street.

The heart of the action in this

popular resort is Bearskin Neck, where old fishing lofts have been turned into studios and galleries, restaurants and shops.

Despite this bohemian air, Rockport is "dry," so no liquor may be sold. Years before Prohibition, Hannah Jumper led 200 women of Rockport in the Hatchet Gang Raid of 1856. These militant teetotallers imposed their own ban on booze by smashing every cask, bottle, and flask they could find, and the men of Rockport haven't had the courage to ask for a drop ever since. Visitors need not despair: drinks may be enjoyed with a seafood meal – as long as diners bring their own bottles.

ⅈ *Upper Main Street (seasonal) and 22 Broadway (year-round)*

▶ Leave town, rejoining **Route 127**, and follow signs for Pigeon Cove (2 miles/3km).

10 Pigeon Cove

Just off Route 127, this small community boasts an unusual building. At No. 52 Pigeon Hill Street stands the Paper House, built between 1922 and 1942 by Elis Stenman and his family. It took two decades and both the house and the furniture have been constructed out of 100,000 old newspapers. The walls are 215 sheets thick, the desk is made from the Christian Science Monitor, and a bookshelf uses only foreign papers!

▶ *Continue on **Route 127** and after 1 mile (1.6km) is the turning for Halibut Point State Park. **Route 127** continues past rocky points of land and art galleries to the rotary (round-about) at **Route 128**. Go west on **Route 128**, then turn right onto **Route 133** west for Essex.*

⓫ Essex

The 40 or so antique shops that line Main Street in this small, sleepy-looking town draw deal-ers and amateurs from all over America for the quality and excellent value of their wares. The small Shipbuilding Museum, also on Main Street, recalls the town's heyday in the days of sail.

SPECIAL TO...

Woodmans of Essex is credited with inventing fried clams back in 1916, and is still one of the best-known clam shacks in New England. "Woodie's" is known for serv-ing fresh, delicious fried clams, clam cakes, and New England clam chowder made with milk, butter, lots of potatoes, and clams.

▶ *Continue to Ipswich. **Route 133** north joins **Route 1A**.*

⓬ Ipswich

Ipswich has several fine houses, particularly the 1640 John Whipple House, one of the oldest Puritan homes still stand-ing, and the John Heard House. This Federal-style mansion retains its period furnishings and has collections of art, toys, carriages and sleighs.

Out of town, some 6 miles (10km) along Argilla Road, is the home of Chicago industrialist Richard T. Crane, on the crest of Castle Hill. This 59-room Great

House recalls the stately homes of England, with its 63-foot (18.9m) long gallery and 16-foot (4.8m) high ceilings. It is open for tours, and there are also concerts and an antique auto show on the grounds each summer. Down below, the 5-mile (8km) long beach is one of the most beautiful north of Cape Cod. Beware of the three weeks at the end of July and early August when the voracious, biting "greenhead" flies take over the strand.

▶ *Continue north on **Route 133** and **Route 1A** for 11 miles (18km) to Hanover Street. Turn right for Plum Island and the Parker Refuge.*

BACK TO NATURE

Located 1 mile (1.5km) north of the turn-off to Crane's Beach on Route 133, Wolf Hollow is home to nine North American wolves. After listen-ing to a presentation about this nearly extinct animal, visi-tors can watch the wolves as they respond to commands from their trainers. Fear not, for although they are at close range, a strong fence separates observers from the observed.

⓭ Plum Island and the Parker River National Wildlife Refuge

With its vast expanse of salt marsh, this is a major stopping point for birds migrating north and south each year. Early spring and late fall are the ideal times to see some of the 300 species. Stand on the observa-tion platform built along the roads to observe cranes, herons and Canada geese.

Plum Island, first visited by Samuel de Champlain in 1601, is a 6-mile (10km) long beach that acts as a breakwater to the coastal towns. Stop on the access road and follow the boardwalks across the dunes, but remember that swimming is dangerous here because of the cold water and the strong undertows.

▶ *Return to **Route 1A** and continue into Newburyport.*

⓮ Newburyport

As in so many New England towns, the charming wooden houses of Colonial times were destroyed by fire and have been rebuilt in brick. A renovation program in the 1970s and 1980s tidied up the rundown sea front and restored the line-up of fine Federal and Greek Revival architecture. Now this ship-building town at the mouth of the Merrimack River is an attractive, if busy, place to spend time. The Custom House on Water Street is given over to a museum of all things maritime, including a re-creation of a ship's bridge.

Two centuries ago, the town commissioned Charles Bulfinch, the architect of the State House in Boston, to design the Courthouse on High Street. This street is often called "sea captain row," with mansions such as the three-story Cushing House, built in 1808 by John Cushing. His son, Caleb, was the first emissary sent by the United States to China, and his collection of fine porcelain, paintings, and cabinetware from China fills the 21 rooms.

ⓘ *Merrimac Street*

▶ *Leave on High Street (**Route 113**) and follow signs to I–95 south and **Route 128**. (Do not take **Route 1**.) Take I–95 south, then west. After about 30 miles (48km), turn south onto I–93 for Boston.*

RECOMMENDED WALKS

Halibut Point State Park is a delightful place to stop and stretch your legs, with well-maintained nature and walking trails. The point is not named for fish; it was originally called "Haul About Point" because sailing ships had to "come about" here and tack to sail around Cape Ann.

Cape Cod

2 DAYS • 241 MILES • 387KM

This 62-mile (100km) long peninsula is one of the country's eminent vacation playgrounds. Route 6A, the Old King's Highway, passes through 300-year-old communities where every other house seems to be a craft shop, antique store or bed and breakfast.

ITINERARY	
BOSTON	▶ **Cape Cod Canal** (52m-84km)
CAPE COD CANAL	▶ **Sandwich** (4m-6km)
SANDWICH	▶ **Barnstable** (12m-20km)
BARNSTABLE	▶ **Yarmouth Port** (4m-6km)
YARMOUTH PORT	▶ **Dennis and East Dennis** (4½m-7km)
DENNIS AND EAST DENNIS	▶ **Brewster** (7m-11km)
BREWSTER	▶ **Orleans** (4½m-7km)
ORLEANS	▶ **Eastham** (4m-6km)
EASTHAM	▶ **Wellfleet** (10m-16km)
WELLFLEET	▶ **Truro** (5m-8km)
TRURO	▶ **Provincetown** (10m-16km)
PROVINCETOWN	▶ **Chatham** (32m-52km)
CHATHAM	▶ **Boston** (92m-148km)

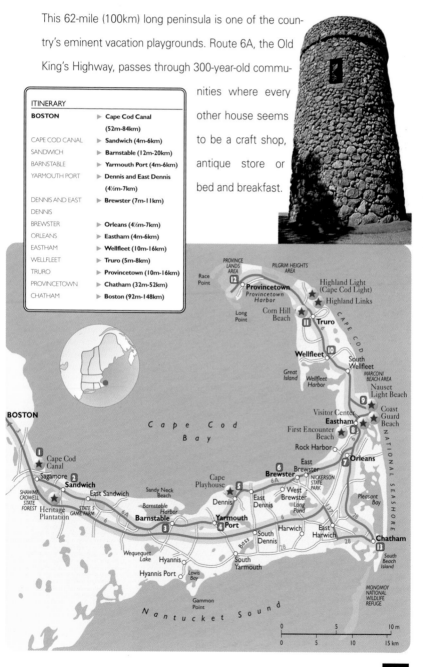

DRIVING TIP

With only two main routes in to and out of Cape Cod, traffic can be slow, so try to avoid the following: Route 28; weekends; driving on to the Cape on Friday afternoon or leaving the Cape on Sunday afternoon. Reservations for hotels are essential, with many inns insisting on a minimum of a two-night stay. A midweek visit might be the best option for a multitude of reasons.

Fine example of Sandwich's famous glass, highly valued by collectors
Page 23: Scargo Hill Observatory

ℹ️ *Cape Cod Chamber of Commerce, Hyannis*

▶ *Leave Boston on **Route 93**; take **Route 3** south to the Sagamore Bridge, crossing the Cape Cod Canal.*

1 Cape Cod Canal

Sailing from Boston around the outside of Cape Cod has always been dangerous. Indeed, even just a century ago, some 25 ships a year foundered on the 135-mile (216km) journey. Traders welcomed the opening of the canal in 1914, 300 years after Myles Standish of the Plymouth Colony first proposed the idea. Running 17 miles (28km) from Cape Cod Bay to Buzzard's Bay, the Canal is 160 yards (150m) wide. Nowadays, recreational yachtsmen take the short cut, watched by fishermen and cyclists on the Cape Cod Canal Bikepath.

ℹ️ *70 Main Street, Buzzards Bay*

▶ *Now on **Route 6A**, continue to Sandwich (4miles/6km).*

2 Sandwich

Sandwich reeks of old-world charm, due to its fine collection of 18th- and 19th-century houses, the Wren-like spire on the First Church of Christ, and tree-lined streets. Overlooking Shawme Pond is shingled Dexter Grist Mill, still in working order, and one of the oldest houses on the Cape, the 1654 Hoxie House. In classic "salt box" style, with diamond window panes, it contains 17th-century furniture, tools, and tableware inside. The Eldred House, next door, is now a museum dedicated to the children's author Thornton W. Burgess, best remembered for his *Peter Cottontail* stories. Despite its 300 years of history, however, Sandwich is no living museum: its lobster boats are

SPECIAL TO...

When Deming Jarves opened his Boston and Sandwich Glass Works in 1825, he banked on a plentiful supply of wood and sand to make his mass-produced household pressed glass. Unfortunately, the local sand was not satisfactory, so he had to import the raw material. The factory closed in 1888 after a dispute with the workforce, but the highly collectible glass may be seen in the Sandwich Glass Museum.

FOR CHILDREN

Josiah K. Lilley's mania for collecting provides an insight into "how they lived back then" at Heritage Plantation, outside Sandwich. Here, the art museum is packed with old tools and folk art, the military museum has antique firearms and battle dioramas, and a replica of a Shaker round barn houses a collection of old cars from the beginning of the century. Children will love riding the wooden horses on the 1912 carousel. The gardens are ablaze with azaleas and rhododendrons in late May and June. Visit the Green Brier Nature Center and Jam Kitchen. In this rustic, pondside setting, preserves have been made, tasted and sold since 1903.

actually working vessels, handled by real fishermen.

▶ *Continue on **Route 6A** to Barnstable (12½ miles/20km).*

3 Barnstable

Off the road to the left, 4 miles (6km) before Barnstable, Sandy Neck is a rich nature reserve where the dunes were trampled by U.S. soldiers training for the North African Desert campaign during World War II. When a north wind blows, watch for windsurfers skimming across Barnstable Harbor.

In town, drop into the Sturgis Library to see the original home of the Reverend John Lothrop, one of the first residents of the 1639 settlement. The library's genealogical records are useful for those searching out family roots, especially if they are descended from the Lothrops, who occupy much of the cemetery. The main industries in the 19th century were growing cranberries, and making bricks, some of which are now collector's items.

▶ *Continue on **Route 6A** to Yarmouth Port.*

❹ Yarmouth Port

The Captain Bangs Hallet House reflects the affluence and sophistication of a successful sea captain's life in the 19th century. Situated near the Yarmouth Port Post Office, its handsome Greek Revival façade hides the original 1740 structure. It is now the headquarters of the local historical society, and the starting point for pleasant walks through a nature preserve along the Botanic Trails of Yarmouth.

The 1680 Thatcher House and the 1780 Winslow-Crocker House next door, now run by the Society for the Preservation of New England Antiquities, are filled with high-quality furniture and household objects made in Colonial and Federal times by New England craftsmen.

i Yarmouth Area Chamber of Commerce, 657 Route 28, West Yarmouth

▶ Continue on **Route 6A** to Dennis and East Dennis.

❺ Dennis and East Dennis

Few men can match Josiah Dennis' claim of having five villages named for him. This 17th-century Congregational minister is immortalized in East, West and South Dennis, as well as Dennisport and Dennis. In his home, the Josiah Dennis Manse, visitors can see his portable pulpit, watch weavers at work and browse round the small maritime museum. There is a 200-year-old schoolhouse on the grounds.

Not quite as ancient, but still the oldest summer theater in the U.S., is the Cape Playhouse, where Bette Davis worked as an usherette. Gregory Peck and Henry Fonda also started their acting careers here. Don't miss the Cape Museum of Fine Arts in the grounds, or the church-like building nearby which is actually an art deco cinema, complete with leather seats and a mural by 20th-century American artist Rockwell Kent.

Take time to see the lie of the land from the Scargo Tower where, on a good day, you can see Provincetown, 20 miles (32km) to the north.

i Dennis Chamber of Commerce, Junction Routes 134 and 28, West Dennis

▶ Continue on **Route 6A** to Brewster (7 miles/11km).

❻ Brewster

On and behind Route 6A, which doubles as Main Street in Brewster, stand the elegant clapboard houses of 19th-century sea captains. At the height of New England's trading with China, as many as 100 lived here, and many are buried in the graveyard next to the "Captains' Church," the First Parish Church. Memories and records of that era are in the Brewster Historical Society Museum at Spruce Hill, East Brewster.

Other museums worth a visit include the New England Fire and History Museum, which has a unique 1929 Mercedes-Benz fire engine, and reconstructions

You can watch the process of corn being ground at Brewster

FOR CHILDREN

The Cape Cod Museum of Natural History at Brewster is popular for its aquarium and lively exhibitions, lectures and tours explaining the Cape's bird and animal life. As well as two short trails in the wildlife sanctuary, the longer John Wing Trail is a fine walk to the unspoiled beach. Remember, though, to check times of tides before setting out. The museum also organizes nature trips by boat to the Monomoy Islands, a wildlife refuge off Chatham.

of a blacksmith's and an apothecary's. More souvenirs of yesteryear include the old Post Office and Barbershop at the 200-year-old windmill at West Brewster.

i Brewster Chamber of Commerce, 74 Locust Lane

BACK TO NATURE

The alewife, a type of herring, spawns in fresh water every three or four years. In spring, these silvery fish swim up the narrow Stony Brook creek, using the fish ladder to bypass the water-powered Grist Mill on Stony Brook Road, just north of Brewster, off Route 6A, and return to the ponds where they were conceived.

▶ *Continue on **Route 6A** to the Orleans roundabout.*

7 Orleans

The name rhymes with "beans," even though it commemorates the French Duke of Orléans, who fled here from the French Revolution in 1797. This busy town has been the "hub of the Outer Cape" for two centuries. Back then fish, and salt for preserving the catch, were shipped direct to Boston from tiny Rock Harbor on Cape Cod Bay.

▶ *Continue north for 4 miles (6km) on what is now **Route 6** to Eastham. Just before the town, the road to Fort Hill, on the right, provides panoramic views above the cupola-crowned Victorian house of whaling captain Edward Penniman.*

8 Eastham

The windmill opposite the Town Hall in Eastham, pronounced East-Ham, was built in Plymouth in 1688, rebuilt in Truro, then moved to its present site in 1808. The oldest windmill on the Cape, it is celebrated on Windmill Weekend in September. Samoset Road leads to Cape Cod Bay. Here, First Encounter Beach is the legendary site of the first meeting between the Pilgrims and the Native Americans. A metal plaque explains how arrows and musket fire were exchanged when the newcomers encountered the Indians, who remembered the slave trader kidnapping some of their people six years before. Don't expect to find any arrowheads, though; the Pilgrims gathered up the arrows and sent them back to England as curiosities.

From here to Provincetown, the Cape is a landscape of steep dunes tufted with grass. On the Atlantic side, breakers pound the flat beaches while lighthouses emphasize the sense of solitude.

At the Salt Pond Visitor Center, beyond Eastham, displays and films explain the ecology and wildlife of the 43,600-acre (17,650-hectare) Cape Cod National Seashore, a stretch of unspoiled coastline some 40 miles long (64km). A road leads to Coast Guard Beach where, in 1929, Henry Beston spent a year writing his classic nature journal, *The Outermost House*. The book is evocative, and perhaps more readable than Henry Thoreau's *Walden*. The beach is superb.

Eye-catching façade on Cape Cod

The Nauset Light serves as a reminder of the region's seafaring heritage

i Eastham Information Center, Route 6

▶ Detour east to Coast Guard Beach, on Doane Road, then turn left on Ocean View Drive to Nauset Light Beach.

SPECIAL TO...

The local Indians taught the Pilgrims how to cook shellfish and New Englanders still use the same method for a clambake on the beach. Dig a shallow pit into the sand, line it with stones and build a wood fire. When the wood has burned down, cover the hot stones with layers of damp seaweed, clean clams, more seaweed, corn on the cob and bluefish. Seal with a tarpaulin. Leave for an hour to steam, then uncover and eat.

🟘 Nauset Light Beach

As you drive through the typical scrub oak and pine that is the natural vegetation of Cape Cod, you will catch glimpses of the ocean to the right. You can venture down to a stretch of seemingly unending sandy beach, where the Atlantic waves thunder in, and you can get away from other people simply by taking a walk.

SCENIC ROUTES

The Cape Cod Central Railroad, complete with commentary, runs by cranberry bogs and marshes between Hyannis and the Cape Cod Canal. This should not be confused with the Cape Cod Rail Trail, where there is no longer a train. The Rail Trail follows the former Boston to Provincetown railroad route between South Dennis and Wellfleet. Here, the bed has been replaced by a smooth, 25-mile (40km) path. Its flatness makes it ideal for joggers, hikers, and cyclists.

▶ Loop back to **Route 6** via Cable Road and Nauset Road to Wellfleet (7 miles/11km).

🟙 Wellfleet

Famous for its oysters since Samuel de Champlain's Gallic taste-buds were tickled in 1606, this charming town, complete with picturesque harbor and photogenic old houses, now attracts artists, whose number is so great that their works fill its 22 art galleries. Fishing still goes

2 DAYS • 181½ MILES • 292KM

The Berkshire
Hills

The Berkshires were once the exclusive playground of the rich. Now these forested slopes are a vacation destination for everyone, particularly music lovers who are drawn to the numerous summer festivals.

ITINERARY		
SPRINGFIELD	▶	**Monterey (32m-51km)**
MONTEREY	▶	**Gt Barrington (9m-15km)**
GREAT BARRINGTON	▶	**Sheffield (7½m-12km)**
SHEFFIELD	▶	**Stockbridge (20m-32km)**
STOCKBRIDGE	▶	**Lenox (7m-11km)**
LENOX	▶	**Pittsfield (6m-10km)**
PITTSFIELD	▶	**Williamstown (22m-35km)**
WILLIAMSTOWN	▶	**North Adams (3m-5km)**
NORTH ADAMS	▶	**Shelburne Falls (29m-46km)**
SHELBURNE FALLS	▶	**Deerfield (11m-18km)**
DEERFIELD	▶	**Northampton**
		(16m-26km)
NORTHAMPTON	▶	**Springfield (19m-31km)**

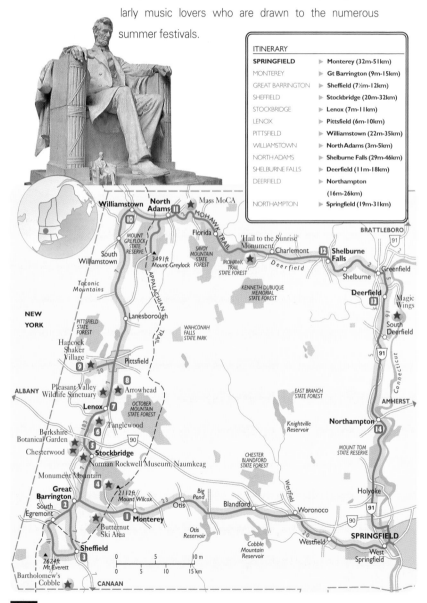

ⓘ *1441 Main Street, Springfield; Riverfront Park Information Center, West Columbus Avenue*

▶ *From Springfield, take **Route 20** west across the Connecticut River, through West Springfield, passing the Exposition grounds, site of the huge "Big E," New England's largest fair, held every September. Bear left on **Route 23** west at Woronoco. Drive through Blandford and Otis to Monterey.*

❶ Monterey
The Mexican name of this town honors General Zachary Taylor, a hero in the Mexican-American War (1846–8). So popular was "Old Rough and Ready" Taylor after his victories at Monterey and Buena Vista, that one Kentuckian predicted (correctly) that the general would win the 1848 presidential election "by spontaneous combustion." Born in Virginia, Taylor had no known connections with the village.

▶ *Continue on **Route 23**, past the Butternut Ski Area.*

❷ Great Barrington
Local inventor William Stanley assured that this small town would have its place in the history books. He first demonstrated the potential of using alternating current here in 1886 by lighting up 24 shops on the main street. Stanley's system, more efficient than Edison's cumbersome direct current lighting, led to more widespread use of electricity. A lamp and plaque in the small park at the corner of Main and Cottage streets tell the story.

On five Saturdays in summer, St. James Church hosts the Aston Magna Festival. It is the oldest festival in America devoted to baroque, classical and early romantic music, all played on period instruments.

▶ *Leave town on **Route 7** and head south for 7½ miles (12km) to Sheffield.*

❸ Sheffield
Back in the 18th century, two minor events helped shape

Monterey's One Room School
Opposite: Abraham Lincoln's statue, Chesterwood Studio

Williamstown's Gothic cathedral
Inset: Hancock Shaker Village

her own rigid specifications. She spent her happiest years here (1902–11), writing such novels as *Ethan Frome* in bed each morning. She delighted in looking east over the "outdoor rooms," the splendid gardens, and the pond that she designed.

Shakespeare & Co., the popular theater group, have moved to their own premises on Kemble Street.

ⓘ *Chamber of Commerce, 75 Main Street*

▶ *Continue north on Route 7A/7 toward Pittsfield. On the right, just before the town, are signs for Arrowhead.*

⑧ Arrowhead

Author Herman Melville (1819–91) was inspired by the Berkshires. Between 1850 and 1863, he lived on this farm where the views reminded him of his seafaring days: "I look out of my window in the morning when I rise as I would out of the porthole of a ship in the Atlantic." He could see the humpbacked, whale-like shape of Mount Greylock, a constant influence as he wrote *Moby Dick*. The novel did not sell, so

Melville was forced to leave Arrowhead and take a job as a customs officer in New York. He died a poor man.

ⓘ *Berkshire Common Level Plaza, Pittsfield; Park Square, Pittsfield*

▶ *Continue north for 2 miles (3km) to Pittsfield, turn left on Route 20 and drive 3 miles (5km) to Hancock Shaker Village.*

⑨ Hancock Shaker Village

The Shakers, a socialist Christian sect, are remembered for their use of dance in religious services, and their exquisitely simple but practical furniture and architecture. The last of the Shakers left Hancock in 1960, after 170 years, but their homes, workshops, herb gardens, and farm have been restored and revived.

Typical is the three-story round barn, built in 1826, where one man standing in the center can feed 54 cows with ease. Shaker food is served on Saturday nights in summer. The tranquility of the 1,200 acres (480 hectares) of meadows and woodlands clearly reinforces Hancock's original Shaker name: the City of Peace.

▶ *Return to Pittsfield and Route 7. Continue north for 22 miles (35km) to Williamstown on Route 7.*

⑩ Williamstown

Revolutionary soldier Colonel Ephraim Williams' gift of money ensured that both the town and college would bear his name. With that, he outdid earlier educational benefactors such as John Harvard and Nicholas Brown, who only saw schools named for them. Today, Williams College is one of the country's most distinguished small colleges, and the town is one of the most attractive in New England.

There is plenty here for culture addicts. First on anyone's list should be the Sterling and Francine Clark Art

Institute, housed in a stunning white, marble, temple-like building. The art collection was created by the Singer sewing machine heir and his French wife and features works by European and American painters. Included are *At the Concert*, one of 30 paintings by Pierre Auguste Renoir; a study of Rouen Cathedral by Claude Monet; and *Rockets and Blue Lights* by J. M. W. Turner.

Next is the college's own Museum of Art, which concentrates on non-Western and ancient art. Contemporary works, such as Andy Warhol's yellow and black self-portrait are on display. For more than 40 years, the Williamstown Theater Festival has attracted such star names as Ben Affleck and Gwyneth Paltrow to participate in the summer season.

ⓘ *Routes 2 and 7*

▶ *Drive east on Route 2 for 4 miles (6.5km) to North Adams.*

⑪ North Adams

The term Museum of Contemporary Art will never be the same after you have been to the innovative new Massachusetts Museum of Contemporary Art (MASS MoCA). Contemporary in every sense of the word, the museum embraces a new approach to putting visual, performing and media arts on show. The whole process of creativity is explored here, and the center not only stages exhibitions and performances by renowned artists, but

> ### BACK TO NATURE
>
> Halfway between Lenox and Pittsfield is the Pleasant Valley Wildlife Sanctuary. With its hummingbirds and beavers, this is a delightful place for a stroll. Some 7 miles (11km) of marked trails meander through the 1,400 acres (560 hectares) of meadow and forest.

also shows work in progress in its art fabrication shops, production studios, performance rehearsals and the use of multimedia technologies. The museum is housed in a converted mill complex consisting of some 27 buildings, linked by covered bridges and elevated walkways.

▶ *Continue east on* **Route 2**.

12 Shelburne Falls
Hamlets dot this rugged road as it passes through forests and along the edges of gorges. Although little seems to have changed in Shelburne Falls since the gushing water drove

---

SPECIAL TO...

Three hundred years ago, Native Americans crossed the Berkshire Hills by walking a trail cut through the forest. Later, pioneer settlers broadened the route on their way through to what is now New York State. Opened in 1914 as one of America's first "scenic highways," the Mohawk Trail is a popular drive these days, especially in the fall (see pages 102–3). The Mohawk tribe is remembered with *Hail to the Sunrise*, the statue of a serene Indian brave, his arms raised to the east.

---

the mills, members of the local horticultural society did have the ingenuity to disguise a 400-foot (120m) long trolley bridge with a hanging flower garden, the Bridge of Flowers.

▶ *Continue to Greenfield and turn south on* **Route 5** *to historic Deerfield.*

13 Deerfield
Called simply "The Street," Deerfield's main thoroughfare is lined with the most impressive

The Hail to the Sunrise *memorial at the entrance to the Mohawk Trail State Forest*

collection of original Colonial houses in New England. The surrounding fields and absence of advertising completes the film-set effect. A dozen of the 65 18th- and 19th-century houses are open to the public, revealing a potted history of early American interior decorating, from furniture to textiles and silverware.

For those in a hurry, the Memorial Hall Museum explains much of the town's rich, if violent, history. In 1675, Indians massacred farmers as they paused to eat grapes, giving a nearby stream its present name of Bloody Brook. In 1704, the French and Indians ravaged the town in the depths of winter, carrying off 112 prisoners to Canada.

The Indian House Door, with its gaping hole hacked by a tomahawk, is preserved in the Memorial Hall. The hall was once used by students at the 200-year-old Deerfield Academy, a well-known boarding school.

By contrast, the colors and restoration work in the Wells-Thorn House recall happier days. In 1774, residents raised a liberty pole, and declared their independence nine days before the historic Fourth of July, 1776.

ⓘ Routes 5 and 10, South Deerfield

FOR CHILDREN

Butterflies never fail to delight children, and they are sure to be captivated by Magic Wings Butterfly Conservatory and Garden, which opened in the spring of 2000. Lush conservatory gardens house a variety of colorful, free-flying tropical butterflies and moths, and outdoor gardens have been planted specially to attract indigenous species.

▶ You can either continue south for 16 miles (26km) on **Route 5** to Northampton or use the faster route, **I–91**.

🔟 Northampton

With its mixture of industrial and educational heritage, Northampton is a pleasant, balanced sort of town. Little evidence remains that it was first settled in 1654. In the 1980s, a vigorous program of downtown renewal sprouted restaurants and boutiques. It is the home of one of America's first women's colleges, founded in 1875 by Sophia Smith, and Smith College is still one of the nation's most prestigious schools.

ⓘ 99 Pleasant Street

▶ Return to **I–91** south and drive to Springfield.

Dwight House is a delightful example of early 18th-century architecture in Deerfield

FOR HISTORY BUFFS

"This is my letter to the world, that never wrote to me ..." penned the poet and recluse Emily Dickinson (1830–86) who lived in Amherst, northeast of Northampton, on Route 9. Of her 1,700 poems, only 11 had been published by the time she died. Hundreds were later found in her bedroom. Dickinson rarely left the house, but was a favorite with local children, lowering baskets of her home-baked gingerbread to them from her window. Most of her papers and belongings are kept at Harvard University and Amherst College, but her white dress hangs in her house. The garden at Amherst is a delight.

SPECIAL TO...

Sylvester Graham of Northampton was a health food fanatic who gave his name to Graham flour, a type of wholewheat flour which is more familiar when made into Graham Crackers.

BOSTON

With its unique blend of history and modern development, its "walkable" downtown and efficient public transport system, Boston is a delight for the visitor. Words like "sophisticated" and "civilized" are often used to describe this city that feels European but is the birthplace of American liberty. Balancing all this is a lively student population of more than 250,000, from around 60 colleges and universities.

The city owes its foundation to the sea. When the Puritans settled here in 1630, they found poor soil, but a fine harbor. By 1700, only the ports of London and Bristol outranked Boston. Until 1755, Boston was the largest city in North America. Its place on the American stage, however, was guaranteed less by wealth and more by its independent thinkers, who had been in the forefront of the Independence movement (see pages 8–9).

Boston's great strength is that it has moved with the times. Soon after Independence, the rich merchants moved to the elegant estate developed on Beacon Hill where families such as the Cabots, Lodges, and Lowells established an almost European aristocracy in the land of democracy. These "Boston Brahmins," as historian Oliver Wendell Holmes dubbed them, considered themselves the "hub of the solar system," and the term "Hub" is one of many nicknames for the city.

When the city's vitality faded in the 1960s, a bold plan of urban renewal revitalized the downtown area. Faneuil Hall Market, once a decaying group of waterside warehouses, became a throbbing tourist attraction, with shops and restaurants.

The USS *Constitution*

As well as theater, music, and art galleries, sport plays a major part in the life of the city. The professional teams boast proud histories in the nation's four favorite sports: baseball (the Red Sox), ice hockey (the Bruins), basketball (the Celtics) and football (the New England Patriots). As for getting around, that is easy. "The T," as locals call the MBTA (Massachusetts Bay Transport Authority), was the country's first such subway system, opened in 1897.

Tour 5

The Boston Freedom Trail is a "must" for anyone interested in American history. A red line on the pavement leads visitors along the world's first self-guided walking tour of its kind. Along the route are buildings that played an important role in the uprising against British Colonial rule over 200 years ago. This is no dry re-run of history, however.

There is also tantalizing trivia, from America's oldest restaurant to the nation's oldest commissioned vessel. Plaques and cemeteries, sculpture and bullet marks are also pointed out to give an fascinating insight into the history of the city, known as the "Cradle of the American Revolution."

Tour 6

There is more to Boston than Revolutionary history. This walk shows off the contrasts in Boston, starting down by the water and the modern aquarium and ending at Copley Square, where the Boston Marathon ends. In between are the cobbled streets and Georgian front doors on Beacon Hill, the chic shops of Newbury Street, and the open-air elegance of the Public Garden. Always a city that has welcomed strangers, there are also moving tributes to Afro-Americans and victims of the Holocaust.

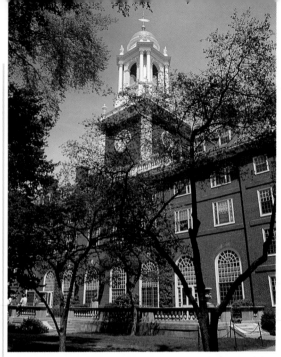

Tour 7

Harvard University is one of the world's great educational institutions. Its libraries and museums boast some of the finest collections in the world, housed in magnificent examples of architecture from the 17th century to the present day. At the same time, the student body, which now includes the women of Radcliffe College, adds zest to Cambridge, where coffee shops and boutiques, bookstores and

Harvard University is one of the pre-eminent Ivy League establishments in the country

art galleries are a pleasure for students and visitors alike. With huge mature trees along the Charles River, and New England clapboard houses, Cambridge retains its own character, totally distinct from Boston, just a bridge or two away.

Boston's impressive skyline at night

The Boston
Freedom Trail

A local journalist, William Schofield, came up with the simple but effective idea of linking Boston's historically important sites with a walking trail. That was back in 1951. Since then, millions have taken the route, marked sometimes by a painted red line, at other times by red bricks.

HALF A DAY

Allow half a day, longer if you want to explore the Charlestown Navy Yard, located near the end of the trail, home of the USS *Constitution*. Remember that in summer long lines build up to see this historic ship.

▶ *Start at the information booth on the Tremont Street side of Boston Common, near the Park Street MBTA stop.*

❶ Boston Common

Often called America's first public park, this common land in the very heart of Boston was set aside in 1634 for "the feeding of Cattell" and as a "trayning field" for militia. Once the cattle left around 1830, the Common was used for recreation and oration. In 1851, Amelia Bloomer, wearing her manly "bloomers," campaigned for women's rights.

In the coming century, charismatic speakers such as Martin Luther King, Jr. and Pope John Paul II have also addressed large crowds here. Today it is an area of lawns, trees, and even baseball diamonds.

▶ *Follow the red line to the State House.*

❷ State House

Built in 1795, this "new" seat of state government replaced the Old State House of 1713. The original red-brick structure was designed by Charles Bulfinch, the most able and sought-after architect of his day. His original dome of wood was replaced first with a copper one, then gilded with 23-carat gold leaf in 1861.

▶ *Just across Beacon Street is a large monument.*

❸ Shaw/54th Regiment Memorial

The lively bronze bas-relief by Augustus Saint-Gaudens pays tribute to the local black soldiers who volunteered to fight for the North in the American Civil War. Prejudice confined blacks to the ranks, but wealthy white Bostonian Robert Gould Shaw led what became the 54th Massachusetts Regiment. He was killed, along with 32 of his soldiers, in the assault on Fort Wagner, South Carolina. Their heroism inspired the 1989 film *Glory*, which won three Academy Awards.

The Robert Gould Shaw/54th Regiment Memorial

▶ *Walk through the Common to Park Street Church.*

❹ Park Street Church

Founded in 1809, this is where anti-slavery campaigner William Lloyd Garrison made his first speech in 1829. Two years later, the hymn *America* was first sung on the steps, and it remains part of the church's Fourth of July tradition. It is ironic that the melody is the same as the British national anthem.

▶ *Adjacent to Park Street Church, facing Tremont Street, is the Granary Burying Ground.*

❺ Granary Burying Ground

Buried here are some of the best-known leaders of the patriot cause: John Hancock, Samuel Adams, John Otis, and Paul Revere (see page 11). One of the most popular graves, however, is that of Mary Goose, also called Elizabeth Vergoose, and supposedly the original Mother Goose. The mother and step-mother of a total of 20 children, she was buried here in 1757. Her son-in-law was

---

SPECIAL TO...

The Omni Parker House, a hotel since 1855, overlooks King's Chapel and the Burying Ground. Parker House rolls became widely known and served, perhaps because they were considered the "patrician accompaniment to formal dining." Ironically, these popular rolls were served to customers by two of the 20th century's most radical figures who both worked here as waiters: Ho Chi Minh, later leader of North Vietnam, and Malcolm X, the 1960s militant black leader.

---

supposed to have published *Mother Goose's Melodies* (*Songs for the Nursery*).

▶ *Turn left on Tremont Street. Cross to King's Chapel, on the corner of School Street.*

❻ King's Chapel

Dating from 1749, King's Chapel was seen as a symbol of British rule in North America. The colony's governors worshipped in a special canopied pew. George Washington also used it in 1789; perhaps one reason that it has survived. Today's congregation follows a curious mixture of Church of England and Unitarian liturgy.

▶ *Walk down School Street. Behind the chapel is the graveyard.*

7 Burying Ground

This cemetery contains the graves of several historic figures, including Mary Chilton, the first of the *Mayflower* pilgrims to reach Plymouth Rock, and John Winthrop, first governor of the colony. Others buried here include William Dawes, who joined Paul Revere in his "midnight ride," as well as Elizabeth Pain, who provided the inspiration for Hester Prynne in Nathaniel Hawthorne's *The Scarlet Letter*. The oldest gravestone in Boston remembers William Paddy, who died in 1658.

▶ *Continue on School Street, passing Old City Hall.*

8 Old Corner Bookstore

This famous bookstore, in one of Boston's oldest buildings, is now home to the Boston Globe Store. What started out as an apothecary shop in 1712 became famous in the mid-19th century as the publishers Ticknor and Fields. Their best-selling authors included Nathaniel Hawthorne, Henry Wadsworth Longfellow, Henry David Thoreau, and Julia Ward Howe, who penned *The Battle Hymn of the Republic*, the anthem of the North during the Civil War.

▶ *Turn right on Washington Street.*

9 Old South Meeting House

Standing in the quiet simplicity of this 1729 Congregational church, it is hard to imagine the fiery debates that inflamed political passions and led to the Revolution. Back then, "Old

South" was the largest space available for public assemblies. After the Boston Massacre in 1770, protesters marched from here to confront the lieutenant-governor.

More than three years later came the meeting that triggered the Boston Tea Party (see page 8). Today, the second-oldest church in Boston is a museum recording those tumultuous days.

i Boston National Park Visitors Center, 15 State Street

▶ *Turn back and follow Washington Street past the Globe Corner Bookstore. Just before the Old State House, a walkway to the right leads to the Old State House.*

10 Old State House

The lion and unicorn symbolize the connection with the Mother Country, a link which James Otis demanded be cut as early as 1761. Five years later, the hated Stamp Act was debated here and, on July 18, 1776, Colonel Thomas Crafts stepped on to the balcony to read the Declaration of Independence. Two hundred years later, Queen Elizabeth II stood on the same spot and spoke in celebration of the American bicentennial. Note

the ring of cobblestones outside the seat of the Massachusetts Assembly, recording the Boston Massacre of 1770, when five Bostonians were shot by British soldiers (see page 8).

▶ *Cross Congress Street diagonally.*

11 Faneuil Hall

In Boston, Faneuil rhymes with Daniel, and the name recalls the French merchant who funded the construction of Boston's marketplace in 1742. In the meeting hall above, freedom of speech was a prerogative. Locals congregated in 1764 to object to the Sugar Act. In the following years, their topics of protest were taxation and English troop movements. Samuel Adams' rebellious speech in 1772, stirring up anti-British feelings, was particularly provocative. But debate did not stop with Independence.

Over the centuries, Bostonians have spoken their minds here on issues such as slavery, alcohol, the Vietnam War, and women's rights. Like the Old State House, there is a reminder of England: the grasshopper that tops the building is thought to be a copy of the weathervane on the Royal Exchange in London.

Union Oyster House where Daniel Webster used to dine

Boston's oldest public building, the 1713 Old State House

▶ *Turn right into Haymarket.*

14 Haymarket

Stall-holders still set out their produce here on Fridays and Saturdays as countless others have done for 300 years. Massive road building and the construction of a tunnel under the city is disrupting much of the downtown area, so Mags Harries' clever sculpture, usually set flat in the street, has been removed temporarily. Called *Asaroton*, the Greek for rubbish, it is a bronze version of market-day leftovers.

▶ *Follow the red line through the construction to Hanover Street. Turn right on Richmond Street, then left on North Street to North Square.*

15 Paul Revere's House

Revere's talent as a silversmith, bell-maker, engraver, and even false teeth-maker fade away in the light of his fame as messenger. He rode to Lexington on the night of April 18, 1775 to warn that "the British are coming!" (see page 11).

His tiny wooden home, at No. 19, is the oldest in Boston (1680) and is as plain and simple inside as Revere left it.

▶ *Leave North Square on Prince Street, turn right on Hanover*

▶ *Follow the red line across North Street to Union Street. (For the Holocaust Memorial, see page 46.)*

12 Union Oyster House

Dating back to 1826, this place enjoys the title of the "oldest continuously operated restaurant in America." It started life as a shop, but became a place to eat in 1826. Lawyer Daniel Webster used to sit at the bar, consuming up to six glasses of brandy and three dozen oysters at a sitting.

▶ *Turn onto Marshall Street for the Boston Stone.*

13 Boston Stone

Myth insists that this millstone marked the true center of Boston, and that all distances were measured from here. This is a tribute to the public relations skills of a tavern owner who set the stone up as a publicity stunt back in 1737. The stone itself was used originally for grinding pigment by Thomas Child, a painter from London.

FOR HISTORY BUFFS

Among the pages of history devoted to the men of the Massachusetts Bay Colony, Ann Hutchinson is only a footnote. Yet this woman dared to discuss her own views of what was, then, the "official" religion.

The punishment for such a challenge to the Puritan hierarchy was exile. In 1638, she left home and, with her followers, moved south. They founded the second settlement in New England in what is now the state of Rhode Island.

Paul Revere's House, restored to its original appearance, now operates as a small museum

Street, then left on Paul Revere Mall to the Old North Church.

16 Old North Church

Sexton Robert Newman had to flash lanterns ("One if by land, and two if by sea") to fellow patriots across the Charles River to warn them of British troop movements. He hung up two from the 191-foot (58m) steeple that is still visible in many parts of the city. Supposedly, one John Childs *flew* from the steeple in 1757, though contemporary reports do not explain how. Officially named Christ Church, it is the oldest in Boston (1723), and remains a place of worship. On the "Behind the Scenes" tour, you can go up into the steeple tower and down into the crypt. Here is the tomb of British Major John Pitcairn (see page 11).

▶ *Go uphill on Hull Street.*

17 Copp's Hill Burying Ground

This is not a resting place of famous historic figures, though Sexton Newman is buried here,

---

SPECIAL TO...

One of the most bizarre accidents in Boston's history took place on Copp's Hill Terrace. In 1919, 21 people were killed by a tidal wave of molasses when a giant tank burst open releasing 2.5 million gallons (11 million liters) of the sticky liquid.

---

as is early black community leader Prince Hall. Nonetheless, the old headstones are worth a look, particularly that of Daniel Malcolm. Used for target practice by the British soldiers who camped here, the scars are still clear to see.

▶ *Continue downhill on Hull Street; turn left on Commercial Street, then right across Charlestown Bridge on the right-hand sidewalk. At the north end of the bridge, follow the red line down the steps and along Water Street.*

18 USS *Constitution*

Like HMS *Victory* in England, this is still a commissioned ship and an icon for the navy. A magnificent example of a

---

wooden warship, her greatest glory came in the war of 1812 against the British, who were then masters of the sea. She destroyed four enemy frigates and sloops and earned the nickname, "Old Ironsides," when, as cannonballs bounced off her hull, a seaman shouted "Huzzah! Her sides are made of iron!" In fact, the ship is made of live oak, a particularly tough wood from southeastern U.S.A.

▶ *From the Navy Yard follow the trail to the Bunker Hill Monument.*

19 Bunker Hill Monument

A 221-foot (67m) obelisk commemorates the first major battle of the Revolutionary War, which was fought on this hill on June 17, 1775. Facing a mighty British force, the ill-equipped Colonists stood their ground, mindful of the now legendary order, "Don't fire until you see the whites of their eyes!" Though the Colonists were eventually routed, they reduced the British army's numbers considerably and the battle was significant in their ultimate victory. There is an exhibition on the site, and musket firing takes place in summer.

FULL DAY

Boston
Old & New

Boston's development started by the water, then moved inland to Beacon Hill where the wealthy lived. Later, it included Back Bay, which was reclaimed land. Allow a full day for this tour, which traces highlights of that growth, from narrow streets to grand boulevards, with Georgian houses and modern skyscrapers.

ℹ️ *147 Tremont Street; 15 State Street*

▶ *Start at the Aquarium MBTA stop. Walk to the New England Aquarium on Central Wharf.*

❶ New England Aquarium

By 1960, Boston's waterfront was an area of vacant warehouses and unused wharves. The decay was reversed in the 1970s by a renewal program that reestablished and emphasized the city's age-old role as a port. One of the first projects was the New England Aquarium, at the end of Central Wharf (1817). At low tide, the smell of the sea and the tidal flats permeates the outdoor plaza in front of the aquarium, where seals swim in the open-air pool and the *Discovery*, an auxiliary boat, hosts shows by trained sea lions.

Indoors, the centerpiece of the aquarium is a huge three-story-high glass salt-water tank (187,000 gallons/41,555 liters), one of the largest in the world, where sharks and eels prowl up and down past Myrtle, a 500-pound (227kg) green sea turtle who likes to have her back scratched by the aquarium's divers.

Whale-watching cruises leave daily from Long Wharf (April to October).

▶ *Return to the Aquarium MBTA Stop. Cross under the expressway to State Street. At the corner of India Street is the Custom House.*

❷ Custom House

This massive 1847 granite building was described as "one of the noblest pieces of commercial architecture in the world" by 19th-century poet Walt Whitman. Certainly it is one of the biggest Greek Revival structures in the country and took ten years to build, with 3,000 pilings each weighing more than 40 tons (36,363kg) being driven into the soggy soil.

In 1915, the 495-foot (148.5m) high tower was added. This shattered the city's height limit and won it the title of the "tallest building in New England." The four clock faces are notorious for showing different times.

▶ *Turn right on Commercial Street and continue into Quincy Market.*

❸ Faneuil Hall/Quincy Market

The well-traveled visitor may see nothing remarkable about this array of shops and restaurants in restored 19th-century buildings. Yet this 1976 urban redevelopment was the first of its kind, and its success has been copied all over the world ever since.

In Colonial days, when sailing ships tied up at Long Wharf, the Marketplace was used by vendors of fruits, vegetables, and other commodities. By 1825, Faneuil Hall was too small, so Mayor Josiah Quincy authorized the construction of the Quincy Market and its two offspring, the North and South markets. Today, restaurants, pubs, and fast-food counters satisfy the hunger of over 14 million visitors a year. (See also page 42.)

▶ *Go through the Market, then cross North Street to Congress Street. Turn right and continue to the Holocaust Memorial.*

Quincy Market, a lively collection of eating places and shops

❹ New England Holocaust Memorial

This memorial, both dramatic and intimate, is located on a busy traffic island between City Hall Plaza and the 18th-century Blackstone Block. The six glass towers are lit from within at night. Each is six stories high and etched with six million random numbers, symbolizing the victims of the concentration camps. On the base of each tower are quotes from survivors, which tell of love, hope, and despair. One, from Gerda Weissman Klein, recalls a 13-year-old's gift to her best friend in the camp: "Imagine a world in which your entire possession is one raspberry, and you gave it to your friend."

▶ *Cross Congress Street and continue up the steps to the City Hall Plaza.*

❺ Boston City Hall Plaza

The area around City Hall was once the red-light district, with its attendant slums, burlesque theaters, and boarded-up shops. Known officially as Scollay Square, it once deserved its "Combat Zone" nickname. In the 1960s, the run-down buildings were demolished and replaced by the John F. Kennedy federal office buildings and a new City Hall, a pyramid standing on its head, designed by I. M. Pei. In winter the plaza

looks barren, but in summer it becomes a lively meeting-place, with pushcart vendors, office workers, and free evening concerts on the stage behind City Hall.

▶ *Continue through the Plaza to Cambridge Street; turn right.*

6 Harrison Gray Otis House

Beacon Hill, with some of the most elegant homes in Boston, dates back to just after the Revolution, when Harrison Gray Otis started to build houses here. This lawyer, mayor of Boston, and U.S. senator was also a property developer, so he could afford to have Charles Bulfinch, the noted architect of the day, design his home at 141 Cambridge Street. Often called the First Otis House, its perfectly proportioned, if rather dull, brick exterior hides a sophisticated and surprisingly colorful interior. At the top of a handsome staircase, the grand drawing-room looks much as it did 200 years ago. Today this is the headquarters of the SPNEA, the Society for the Preservation of New England Antiquities, who look after historic properties throughout New England.

▶ *Cross Cambridge Street and go up Joy Street.*

7 The Black Heritage Trail

At this point the itinerary and Boston's Black Heritage Trail meet. Celebrating the history of the city's Afro-American community, the Trail encompasses 14 significant sites. Two are on this route and are part of the Museum of Afro-American History, which traces the civil rights movement.. The Abiel Smith School in Joy Street has recently reopened after extensive renovation, and contains displays relating to the long struggle for equal education for African American children in the city, which started in 1787 and ended when segregation was finally abolished in 1855. Established with an endowment from white businessman Abiel Smith, the school eductaed black children for some 20 years of that interim period.

Just off Joy Street, in Smith Court, is the African Meeting House, which is the ending point of the Trail. It was built by black Americans in 1805 as a place where they could worship without being relegated to the gallery, as was the case in white churches. The meeting house became the home of the New England Anti-Slavery Society – such a force in the Abolitionist Movement that the building became known as the Black Faneuil Hall.

▶ *Continue up Joy Street and turn right on Mount Vernon Street. At No. 55 is Nichols House.*

8 Nichols House Museum

Red-brick houses line Mount Vernon Street, one of the loveliest streets in Boston. The museum is a time-warp, where nothing has been changed since the owner, Rose Standish Nichols, died in 1960. Her will ensured that "people from around the world without a letter of introduction could see the inside of a fine house." From a wealthy Boston family,

she is remembered as a landscape gardener and a fervent worker for international peace. Her needlework and paintings lend a personal touch to the 1804 mansion, which also has bronzes by her uncle, the sculptor Augustus Saint-Gaudens.

▶ *Continue west along Mount Vernon Street to Louisburg Square.*

9 Louisburg Square

The name of this square recalls the struggle between France and Britain for supremacy in North America. Even though local troops had fought successfully for the Crown against the French at Fort Louisburg, Nova Scotia, back in 1745, this elegant square, named after their victory, was built a century later. Much like a London square, the grassy quadrangle is a private park for owners of the surrounding smart homes. Residents included celebrities such as writer Louisa May Alcott (No. 10), who spent her last two years here. Opera singer Jenny Lind, the "Swedish Nightingale," was married at No. 20.

▶ *Retrace your steps on Mount Vernon Street and turn right on Willow Street, then zigzag right onto Acorn Street, go left on West Cedar Street, then right on Chestnut Street and, finally, left on Charles Street. Across Beacon Street is the Public Garden.*

⑩ Public Garden

Boston can thank a group of public-spirited green thumbs for America's first botanical garden. From 1837 until their success over 20 years later, they battled to protect the city's green heart from developers. Today, their triumph provides a retreat for locals and visitors alike. In spring and summer, flowers bloom by the paths, while the swish of fountains masks the noise of the traffic. Children plead for rides on the slow, stately, foot-pedaled swan boats, introduced

in 1877, and peer at the fountain sculpture of Bagheera, the panther immortalized in Kipling's *Jungle Books*. A home-grown favorite is the sculpture of Mrs. Mallard and her eight ducklings, at the corner of Charles and Beacon streets. Robert McCloskey's *Make Way for Ducklings* is a much-loved children's tale of a mother duck stopping Boston traffic as she shepherds her brood from the Charles River to the pond in the Boston Public Garden. A children's parade each spring retraces the route of the ducklings.

▶ *Cross the Garden using the suspension bridge and exit through the Arlington Street gate onto Commonwealth Avenue. Walk one block, then*

turn left on Berkeley Street, then right on Newbury Street.

⑪ Newbury Street

Water covered this area of Boston until the second half of the 19th century when Back Bay was filled in and transformed into a residential district. The back-bone is Commonwealth Avenue, a Parisian-style boulevard, lined with fine trees and grand statues of long-forgotten worthies. Running parallel to "Comm Ave" is Newbury Street, known for its upscale and trendy art galleries, boutiques and cafés. Yet, the apartments on and around the street create a neighborhood atmosphere. Old buildings have new uses: What was built as a Temple for the Working Union of Progressive Spiritualists is now a major book-store. Boston's former Museum of Natural History is full of expensive menswear; and the severe face of the New England

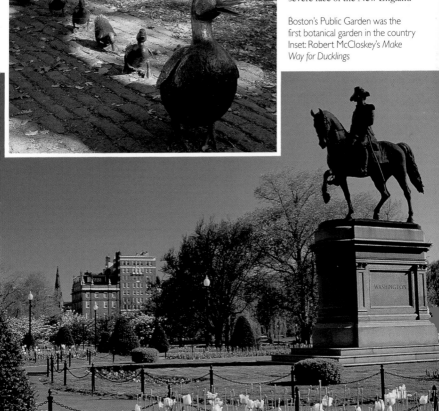

Boston's Public Garden was the first botanical garden in the country
Inset: Robert McCloskey's *Make Way for Ducklings*

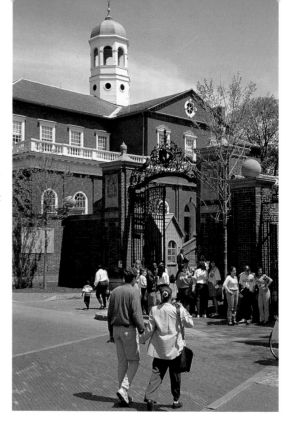

ⓘ *Cambridge Visitor Information Booth, Harvard Square*

▶ *Start at the Harvard Square MBTA stop.*

❶ Harvard Square

All around the traffic island is the bustle and noise of "the square." Here you can buy international newspapers at the kiosk, eat international cuisine at the numerous restaurants, then buy all-American sportswear at the Harvard Cooperative, the large department store, known as "the Coop" (rhymes with hoop).

▶ *Walk up Massachusetts Avenue and turn right through Johnston Gate, the entrance to Old Harvard Yard.*

❷ Old Harvard Yard

Harvard is not only the oldest university in America, but also one of the most influential. From its earliest days, it has symbolized the independent attitude of the Colonists and, significantly, America's first printing press was set up here in 1640. Harvard Yard, the center of the campus for more than 350 years, is really two vast, open quadrangles, totalling 22 acres (8.8 hectares). The first yard is

FOR HISTORY BUFFS

America's oldest university is also one of its most prestigious. One of the seven so-called Ivy League schools (so old that ivy grows on their hallowed walls), Harvard emphasizes academic excellence, shunning the sports scholarships and razzmatazz of the country's younger universities. The 7,000 undergraduates now include the women of Radcliffe (see page 55), but there is also an impressive graduate program ranging from the prestigious Harvard Law and Medical Schools, to newer disciplines, such as Business Administration and Government.

the home of the Freshmen (first-year students) who live in the red-brick dormitories. On the right is Massachusetts Hall, the university's oldest surviving building. Established as a laboratory and dormitory in 1720, it housed American troops at the start of the Revolution.

ⓘ *Harvard Information Center, Holyoke Center*

❸ John Harvard Statue

Directly across the yard, in front of the granite University Hall (1815), this seated statue is labeled "John Harvard, founder 1638." The sculpture is wittily referred to as the "Statue of the Three Lies." Harvard was a benefactor rather than a founder, the foundation year was 1636, and the statue is actually of Sherman Hoar, a Harvard student who modelled for 19th-century sculptor Daniel Chester French.

▶ *Continue past University Hall and enter New Yard.*

Johnston Gate, the main entrance to Old Harvard Yard

❹ New Yard

The second, larger portion of the Yard is also called Tercentenary Theater because it was here that the 300th graduation ceremonies were held in 1936. Criss-crossed by walking paths, a figurative bridge links the spiritual and intellectual centers of the university. To the left is Memorial Church, "Mem Church." It was completed in 1932 as a tribute by Harvard alumni to classmates killed in World War I, and has been updated for victims of World War II and, later, the Korean and Vietnam conflicts.

▶ *To the right is the Widener Library, the world's largest university library.*

❺ Widener Library

In this temple to the written word, information spans the centuries, from a first folio of Shakespeare and a Gutenberg

Bible, to microfilm files and computer screens. Built between 1913 and 1915, the library was given in memory of Harry Elkins Widener, a wealthy graduate who drowned on the *Titanic*. The library is not open to the public.

▶ *Straight ahead is Quincy Street.*

⑥ Carpenter Center for the Visual Arts

This glass and concrete block at No. 24 Quincy Street is the only example in America of a building by the 20th-century Swiss architect Le Corbusier. Its film archives are famous for their variety and depth. Film shows of unusual or historic movies are often held here.

⑦ Fogg and Busch-Reisinger Art Museums

Many institutions of higher learning have their own museums. Harvard has eight on campus, of which the Fogg, Busch-Reisinger and the Arthur M. Sackler have world-class reputations.

The Fogg, which opened in 1895, is the oldest of the three. Behind the neo-Georgian façade on Quincy Street is a courtyard modeled after a 15th-century Italian palazzo. The collection concentrates on European art from the Middle Ages to the present, with a strong line-up of Italian Renaissance paintings, as well as a self-portrait by Van Gogh, and *Red Boats* by Claude Monet.

Directly behind the Fogg is the Busch-Reisinger Museum, in the Otto Werner Hall. Here, the main focus is works by the Expressionists, Europeans such as Franz Marc, Paul Klee, Wassily Kandinsky, and Emile Nolde.

▶ *Go north on Quincy Street, cross Broadway, and the Arthur M. Sackler Museum is on the right.*

⑧ Arthur M. Sackler Museum

This is the university's third art museum, in British architect James Sterling's strikingly

contemporary building, opened in 1985. Famous for its exquisite collection of Chinese ceramics, bronzes, and jades, it specializes in Ancient Greek, Islamic, and Asian art, from Indian miniatures to Japanese prints. On the fourth floor, among the Greek art, are several large ceramic vases dating from about 340 BC. There are also jade dragons, bronze ritual bells, and a large bronze wine container, more than 3,000 years old, from China.

▶ *Continue along Quincy Street, crossing Cambridge Street. Memorial Hall is on the left.*

⑨ Memorial Hall

Memorial Hall reopened after a major restoration in 1996. Built in 1878 to honor the Harvard men who died in the Civil War, it epitomizes the Gothic Revival style, with a Great Hall soaring up to a jig-saw puzzle roof of

Well-displayed period furnishings complement the Fogg's paintings and sculptures carved beams and timbers. Here, Winston Churchill was given an honorary degree in 1943. The stained-glass windows portray stories and heroes from the Bible, American history, and Greek mythology. In a controversial move, "Mem Hall" has been made into a dining room. Where nervous undergraduates once took exams, first-year students gossip at mealtimes under the chandeliers. To one side is Sanders Theater, an intimate auditorium finished in dark wood. It was the setting for Harvard graduations up until 1911, but is now used for the performing arts.

▶ At the end of Quincy Street bear left across Kirkland Street, then turn right onto Oxford Street.

10 Museums of Natural History

Don't be put off by the fusty-sounding names of the four museums: there is plenty to fascinate adults and children alike in this brick building. Highlights include the 22-pound (10kg) meteor which fell from the sky in 1992, and landed on a car in Peekskill, New York, and the life-size skeleton of a 42-foot long (12.5m) *Kronosaurus*. This gigantic crocodile lived 135 million years ago.

Best known of all is the unique Ware Collection of Glass Flowers, 3,000 scientifically accurate, life-size models of flowers and plants made out of blown glass.

▶ From Oxford Street, go into Harvard Law School. Pass under the arch to the right of Pierce Hall, and bear left on the path along Langdell Hall.

11 Harvard Law School

The Law School was started in 1817, with six students. Today, each new class of 540 students has been selected from over 7,000 applicants. Langdell Hall, on the right, has the largest law library in the world, and a public reading room on the fourth floor that stretches the length of two football fields.

Next is Austin Hall, a small brownstone building completed in 1881 by Henry Hobson Richardson. Each spring in the Ames Courtroom, on the second floor, finalists in the third-year competition argue their cases before a Justice of the U.S. Supreme Court. The sessions are open to the public, but seating is by ticket only.

▶ Bear right upon leaving Austin Hall and follow the path between Hemenway Gymnasium and Gannett House. Cross Massachusetts Avenue at the traffic light and walk across Cambridge Common.

Longfellow House: this clapboard building was abandoned by its Loyalist owner in 1774

12 Cambridge Common

This small green park is all that remains of the fields and pastures where the American army assembled after the 1775 battles of Lexington and Concord (April) and Bunker Hill (June). On July 3, George Washington took command of the American army here, and a plaque marks the location of the Washington Elm beneath which this event took place. At least, that is the story ...

▶ On the far side of the Common, turn right on Garden Street, then left on Mason Street. Turn right on Brattle Street and continue to No. 101.

13 Brattle Street

All along Brattle Street are fine houses, built before the American Revolution. Since most were then occupied by supporters of the Crown, it was called "Tory Row." The owners left hastily, and all that remains are their names, recorded on blue plaques. Hastings House, No. 101, is a fine example, as are Nos. 113 and 115, which belonged to the daughters of Henry Wadsworth Longfellow, who lived at No. 105.

Built in 1685, the Hooper-Lee Nichols House at No. 159 is

now the headquarters of the Cambridge Historical Society, who also organize guided walks.

14 Longfellow House

The Tory, or British sympathizer, John Vassall lived in this yellow clapboard mansion. He built it in 1759, in anticipation of his marriage to Elizabeth, the sister of the last Royal Lieutenant Governor. In 1775, he was thrown out by the patriots, who moved in with the wounded from the Battle of Bunker Hill. Next, the hospital became George Washington's headquarters for nine months. Washington enlarged it to make room for guests.

In the following century, the celebrated American poet Henry Wadsworth Longfellow rented a room here. Later, he received the house as a wedding present and lived here from 1837 to 1882. During that period he wrote *Hiawatha* (1855) and *The Village Blacksmith* (1839) here, and completed his translation of Dante, among other works. Here, also, he entertained Dickens, Emerson, Hawthorne, Twain, and Wilde. Longfellow was particularly fond of the view across the Charles River, and it remains unspoiled, thanks to his children, who gave the land to the City of Cambridge in 1913.

After extensive restoration, the Longfellow House reopened in 2002. Visits are by guided tour only and there six each day.

▶ *Retrace your steps on Brattle Street and turn left into Radcliffe College.*

15 Radcliffe Yard

Radcliffe College started out in 1879 with just 27 women students in a small two-story house. It was named in honor of Londoner Lady Anne Radcliffe, who gave £100 to Harvard back in the 17th century. Admissions to Radcliffe have always been highly competitive, and many "Cliffies" have become well known, including Helen Keller,

whose life was portrayed in the film *The Miracle Worker*. Nearly a century after its founding, Radcliffe merged with Harvard. The name, however, lives on thanks to the Radcliffe Institute for Advanced Study, founded in 1999. In Radcliffe Yard, the Federal-style Fay House was built in 1807 and was the first building acquired by the college. Today it is an administration building.

▶ *After crossing the Yard, exit onto Garden Street, and bear right to Christ Church.*

16 Christ Church and the Old Burying Ground

In the foyer, just inside the outer door of Christ Church, a plaque on the right marks a bullet hole made, so the story goes, when the British were marching to

Christ Church, designed by Peter Hamson, the architect of King's Chapel in Boston

Lexington in April, 1775. Later that year, George and Martha Washington attended services here, using the pew directly below the pulpit, on the left. Between the Christ Church and the First Church is Cambridge's oldest cemetery, God's Acre. The earliest grave is that of Anne Erinton, an early settler who passed away on December 24, 1635. Eight presidents of Harvard are also buried here.

▶ *Continue down Garden Street to Massachusetts Avenue and bear right to Harvard Square and the MBTA stop.*

SPECIAL TO...

Close by the sidewalk is a stone milestone, carved in 1734. Look carefully at the words: "Boston 8 miles." Today that distance is covered in 8 minutes on the MBTA.

CULTURAL CRADLE

America's culture, as well as its sense of history, started in New England. The 19th century, in particular, saw the development not just of American themes but of a distinctive American "voice" and viewpoint. What binds the most talented artists and writers together is their sense of New England, in print and on canvas, set to music or presented on stage. Names such as Robert Frost (poet), Nathaniel Hawthorne (novelist), Winslow Homer (painter), Norman Rockwell (illustrator), and Eugene O'Neill (playwright) conjure up bleak landscapes and clapboard houses, glistening seas and "salt-of-the-earth" families, while Charles Ives' music interprets the moods of the countryside.

Literature

The first New England writer to make an international name for himself was Henry Wadsworth Longfellow (1807–82), a poet who was also a professor at Harvard. Hugely popular, his narrative poems told home-grown tales, from *The Song of Hiawatha*, a story of Native Americans, to *The Midnight Ride of Paul Revere*, which encapsulates the start of the American Revolution. Nathaniel Hawthorne (1804–64) also took inspiration from New England history, though he explored the psychological effects of Puritanism in novels such as *The Scarlet Letter* and *The House of the Seven Gables*. His friend Herman Melville (1819–91) received little critical acclaim in his lifetime. A New Yorker who wrote at Arrowhead in Western Massachusetts, Melville's most famous novel was *Moby Dick*, an allegory of good and evil which drew on his experiences aboard a New England whaler as a young man.

While Hawthorne and Melville relied on the realism of history, two authors, Emerson and Thoreau, took a more spiritual path. Transcendentalism was a movement led by Ralph Waldo Emerson (1803–82), a charismatic speaker and writer whose philosophy is best summed up by his often quoted saying: "who so would be a man must be a non-conformist." He appealed to Americans to throw off the yoke of European tradition and to look at their individual experiences. His friend, Henry David Thoreau (1817–62), did just that, going "back to nature." The result of his simple life by Walden Pond, on the edge of Concord, was the idealistic book *Walden: Or Life in the Woods* (1854).

Both men spent time in Concord, where Louisa May Alcott (1832–88) also lived and wrote *Little Women*, a huge best-seller, based on family life. Another woman writer, Harriet Beecher Stowe (1811–96), brought the issue of slavery to thousands of homes with *Uncle Tom's Cabin*. The book, which was originally published as a weekly serial, sold 300,000 copies. While Stowe wrote to further a cause, Emily Dickinson (1830–86) wrote for herself. A recluse whose poems were only discovered after her death, she lived her entire life not just in Amherst in Western Massachusetts, but also in the same brick Federal house where she had been born.

New England also attracted writers from elsewhere in the States. Samuel Longhorne Clemens, better known as Mark Twain (1835–1910), was born in

Left: Henry Wadsworth Longfellow
Below: Topsy, from Harriet Beecher Stowe's *Uncle Tom's Cabin*

(Mrs Keeley as Topsy, "I's dreffel wicked")

"SLAVE LIFE" OR "UNCLE TOM'S CABIN."

Missouri, but many of his best-loved stories, such as the antics of Huckleberry Finn and Tom Sawyer, were written in his Hartford home. His tales of the American West, written with humor and an easy style, brought him a wide audience. By contrast, high society was the subject of novelist Edith Wharton (1862–1937). The author of *The Age of Innocence* did much of her writing at The Mount, her retreat in Lenox, Massachusetts.

The quintessential New England poet was Robert Frost (1874–1963), who spent most of his life in New Hampshire and Vermont. So great was his stature that he was the first poet to participate in a presidential inauguration. In 1961, he read his poem *The Gift Outright* at President John F. Kennedy's swearing-in. His descriptions of a Vermont snowstorm and swinging on birch trees are easily remembered; his forthright expression of universal truths have a darker side.

Theater

New York was always the cradle of American theater, but America's first major playwright, Eugene O'Neill (1888–1953), learned his craft in New England. The New Yorker studied at the 47 Workshop of George Pierce Baker in Harvard before making an impact with the Provincetown Players on Cape Cod. Ten of his plays were produced from 1916 to 1920. A Nobel and Pulitzer prize winner, O'Neill is remembered at the theater bearing his name near New London, Connecticut. The cottage where he spent his boyhood summers was the setting for *Long Day's Journey into Night*.

Music

While Puritan influences restricted early New Englanders to music in churches, the region has been a powerhouse of classical music in the 20th century. The best known composer is the avant-garde Charles Ives (1874–1954), born in Danbury, Connecticut, the son of a bandmaster. Fiercely proud and inde-

The Boston Symphony Orchestra performs at Symphony Hall from the beginning of October to the end of April

pendent, Ives bucked European tradition to draw on traditional American folk songs, hymns, and marches. The result was his *New England Symphony, Three Places in New England,* and *Sonata No. 2* for piano and flute. The last was nicknamed *Concord, Mass 1840–1860,* perhaps because of its dedication to the town's literary circle of Emerson, Thoreau, Hawthorne, and the Alcotts.

New Englander Colonel Henry Higginson enjoyed the Austrian attitude to music so much that he set up the legendary Boston Pops in 1885, based on the romance and fun of Viennese orchestras. In 1929, the Pops went outdoors to perform, as they still do to this day. The Boston Symphony, now one of the world's great orchestras, has extended its popularity and fame thanks to the summer season in Tanglewood, in western Massachusetts.

CONNECTICUT

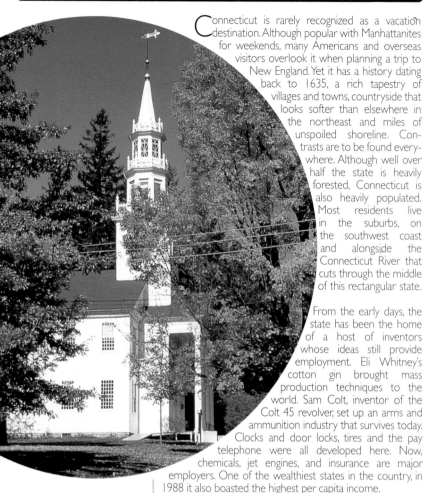

Connecticut is rarely recognized as a vacation destination. Although popular with Manhattanites for weekends, many Americans and overseas visitors overlook it when planning a trip to New England. Yet it has a history dating back to 1635, a rich tapestry of villages and towns, countryside that looks softer than elsewhere in the northeast and miles of unspoiled shoreline. Contrasts are to be found everywhere. Although well over half the state is heavily forested, Connecticut is also heavily populated. Most residents live in the suburbs, on the southwest coast and alongside the Connecticut River that cuts through the middle of this rectangular state.

From the early days, the state has been the home of a host of inventors whose ideas still provide employment. Eli Whitney's cotton gin brought mass production techniques to the world. Sam Colt, inventor of the Colt 45 revolver, set up an arms and ammunition industry that survives today. Clocks and door locks, tires and the pay telephone were all developed here. Now, chemicals, jet engines, and insurance are major employers. One of the wealthiest states in the country, in 1988 it also boasted the highest per capita income.

Norfolk is one of the best preserved villages in the northeast

The affluent southwestern corner of Connecticut is virtually a suburb of New York City. Further north, the Litchfield Hills, idyllic for artists and craftsmen, are also a retreat for show business celebrities. Two hundred years ago, the same wooded hills were stripped to fuel the furnaces and forges that processed iron for the guns used during the Revolution.

The coast, especially the eastern strip, is the most popular with visitors. Mystic is an admirable re-creation of an early 19th-century seafaring village complete with sailing ships.

There is a rich cultural heritage, because of the influence of Yale University and writers such as Mark Twain, Harriet Beecher Stowe, and dictionary-writer Noah Webster. Painters and actors have also made their homes here, and antique shops and art galleries abound.

Tour 8

Hartford is known as the "Insurance Capital of America." The business began in 1794. It is also a city of "firsts" and "oldests." It claims the first municipal rose garden and development of the first American dictionary; the oldest newspaper, the *Hartford Courant*, and oldest state house. Two of America's most revered writers also lived here: Mark Twain and Harriet Beecher Stowe, who was Twain's neighbor. Twain's Victorian house is one of the most intriguing you'll see, deliberately designed to be unusual.

Tour 9

When it comes to universities, Yale and Harvard go together like Oxford and Cambridge, in England. Just as Harvard and Cambridge are in attractive towns, so Yale and Oxford are in industrial cities. Yale, with its ivy-covered buildings, is one of the finest academic institutions in the country, with impressive museums and art galleries. Countering all this culture, the Frisbee was supposedly invented here, along with two of America's most popular fast foods: the hamburger and the pizza.

Tour 10

Western Connecticut has bumpy, wooded hills dotted with villages that don't seem to have kept up with the 20th century. Although New York City is within commuting distance, urban frenzy is banned here. This is the countryside the way urban folk prefer it, with waterfalls and covered bridges, pleasant shops and small art galleries. As for history, Litchfield boasts the first American law school, which was set up in a tiny house over 200 years ago. The innocent-looking town of Lakeville turned out tons of arms to fuel the battle against Britain, winning itself the nickname of the "Arsenal of the Revolution."

Tour 11

Connecticut's coast was settled in the early 17th century by British emigrants who named the small towns after their homes: New London, Guilford, Essex and Old Lyme. The oldest stone house in New England, complete with fortifications, was built back in 1640. Later, locals turned their hand to building ships and submarines. The finest maritime museum in the States is at Mystic, where boats and docks re-create the romance, if not the reality, of life aboard the sailing ships of the 18th and 19th centuries.

Later, the seaside attracted artists and writers, while the Eugene O'Neill Theater Center outside New London gave actors such as Al Pacino and Meryl Streep their early opportunities. Despite the popularity of the bigger towns, there are still sleepy corners where visitors can sit and munch a sandwich in peace, overlooking tranquil Long Island Sound.

Mystic Seaport is a re-creation of a 19th-century seaport

Hartford

One of the oldest cities in the country, Hartford was founded in 1636 by a native of Hertford, England. There is an English flavor to the narrow streets and parks of Hartford, downtown is easily navigable, and skyscrapers rise high above the Connecticut River with its renovated riverfront. In this state capital are well-preserved historic places, the nation's oldest public art museum, a world-famous rose garden, and the homes of two of America's best-known and best-loved writers, Harriet Beecher Stowe and Mark Twain.

HALF A DAY

The Senate Chamber of the Old State House – the first state house in a newly independent United States

☐ *1 Civic Center Plaza*

▶ *Park your car in the Civic Center garage, entrance on Asylum Street.*

❶ Civic Center
Under a circular dome in the heart of downtown Hartford, the Civic Center is a shopping center, restaurant and professional sports arena, all in one. Since the Hartford Whalers ice-hockey team left, a little of the glamor has gone, but the outstanding University of Connecticut basketball squad fills the arena, while the Hartford Wolf Pack, an affiliate of the New York Rangers ice-hockey team, now faces off here.

▶ *Leave the Civic Center and walk east on Asylum Street to Main Street. Cross and enter the Old State House.*

❷ Old State House
Painstaking restorations have revived the oldest state house, designed in 1792 and completed in 1796 by New England's star architect Charles Bulfinch. It stands on Meeting House Square, where the Colony was founded in 1636. There is no mistaking the daily opening time at 10am; it is preceded by the ceremonial firing of a cannon by uniformed "Continental troops." Guides in full period dress give the facts and relate anecdotes about rooms, such as the Council and restored Senate Chambers. The highlight in these high-style, Victorian masterpieces is the original version of Gilbert Stuart's famous portrait of the first president of the U.S., George Washington. Also in the Old State House is Mr. Steward's Museum of Natural and Other Curiosities, plus an interactive center of state history. The Museum Store specializes in state products, crafts and foods. Outside, a farmers' market follows the Colonial tradition

of setting up stalls by the meeting house.

▶ *Walk south one block to Travelers Tower, on the corner of Gold Street.*

SPECIAL TO...

The Connecticut Freedom Trail was established in 1995 to honor the history of the state's African American community, and covers a series of buildings and sites that represent the concept of freedom. Hartford's Old State House features in the trail for the part it played in the famous Amistad trials, a two-year legal battle that ultimately set free and repatriated to Sierra Leone a group of Africans who, in 1839, had taken control of the Spanish vessel carrying them to a life of slavery in Cuba. Reenactments of the trial feature in the Old State House's program of events.

3 Travelers Tower

Soaring 527 feet (160m) above street level, the "free Renaissance"-style, pink-granite Travelers Tower is capped by a prominent beacon light. From the observation deck atop the tower, visitors are rewarded with a breathtaking view of downtown Hartford, the Connecticut River and the entire Connecticut Valley from Mount Tom to Meriden Mountain in the south.

▶ *Across the street, on the corner of Main and Gold streets, is the Wadsworth Atheneum.*

4 Wadsworth Atheneum

One of New England's leading "must-see" museums, "the Wad" was founded in 1842, so it takes the title "the nation's oldest public art museum." Housed in an impressive neo-Gothic building, it boasts masterpieces from the 16th through the 20th centuries, including classics by Picasso (*Harlequin*) and Van Gogh (*Self Portrait*). The most intriguing painting is *House Fronting New Milford Green* by Ralph Earl, painted in 1796. The house still stands. Other home-grown talent includes members of the Hudson River School, the 19th-

The Gothic Revival Wadsworth Atheneum. Inset: statue of Nathan Hale, local schoolmaster and patriot

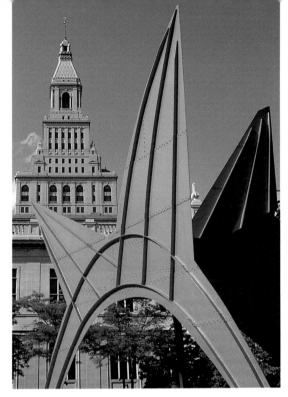

show dates of birth from the 1590s to the early 1600s, in Hertford, England.

▶ Continue walking down Gold Street to Bushnell Park. Turn right along the border, Jewell Street. Opposite Ann Street, across from the YMCA, the Bushnell Park Carousel is in the park.

7 Bushnell Park Carousel
The carousel is a Stein and Goldstein, hand-carved merry-go-round built in 1914, with 48 prancing horses and chariots rollicking to the tunes of a 1925 Wurlitzer band organ. At only 50 cents a ride, it is one of New England's bargains. Hot dogs and other snacks are available when the park is open.

▶ Walk a few steps west to Trinity Street. Look right to the Sailors and Soldiers Memorial Arch, built in 1886 to honor the 4,000 Hartford citizens who served in the Civil War. Turn left and proceed up the hill half a block to the State Capitol. A statue of the French General Lafayette, ally of George Washington, sits on horseback in the middle of the street at the driveway entrance.

8 State Capitol
Another refurbished landmark (built 1789), the Capitol is the home of the House of Representatives and Senate, Connecticut's legislature. Against a backdrop of white Connecticut marble are Gothic spires, a gleaming gold dome, statues, medallions, and bas-reliefs commemorating important people and events in state history. Gaudy to the point of being brash, architect Frank Lloyd Wright called it "The most ridiculous building I know of." Open to the public, the assemblies are in session from February to May in even years and January through June in odd years. More statues and historical relics decorate the interior.

Travelers Tower was once the tallest building in New England

5 Stone Field Sculpture
"$250,000 for a pile of rocks? That's ridiculous!" That was the reaction of many locals when the Hartford City Council voted to fund the sculpture created by Carl Andre in 1977. His work of art consists of 36 large stones laid out in rows to form an isosceles triangle. A similar furor erupted in England when London's Tate Gallery bought "a pile of bricks," a total of 120 bricks in two layers which the American sculptor entitled *Equivalent VIII.*

6 Ancient Burying Ground
Center Church, built in 1632, is Hartford's oldest church. Behind it, the Ancient Burying Ground is one of the city's few surviving historic sites from the 17th century. In the small, green, fenced-in graveyard, more than 400 brownstone markers stand at attention, marking the final resting places of Hartford's founding families. Epitaphs record lives that were only occasionally lengthy, more often short. Many

century group of landscape painters who achieved a definite American style. There is also a fine collection of African-American art, decorative arts, costumes and textiles.

▶ Cross the street diagonally to the north side of Gold Street and proceed down Gold Street, stopping at the Stone Field Sculpture and the adjacent Ancient Burying Ground.

New Haven &
Yale University

Founded in 1638 by a group of settlers, the town first depended on seafaring. In the 19th century, thanks to inventors such as Eli Whitney, assembly lines turned out clocks, carriages, and guns by the thousand. More recently, New Haven has had to face the urban problems of unattractive development and crime, though efforts to renew and restore civic pride are paying off. At the heart of the city is Yale, one of America's leading universities, adding an enviable cultural dimension to the city.

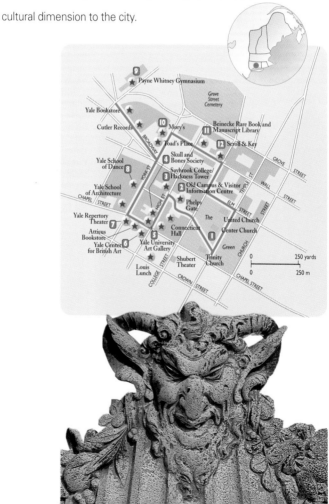

i 59 Elm Street; Yale
University, 149 Elm Street

▶ Start on The Green on the
corner of Temple and Elm
streets.

❶ The Green

New Haven has been called
"the first planned city in the
U.S.A." because of its original
(1638) grid-like street design,
visible from the 16-acre (6.4-
hectare) Green. Here, residents
came to gossip, to debate, and to
pray at the trio of handsome
churches, each with its different
architecture, but all built in the
early 1800s.

The United Church, often
compared with London's St.
Martin-in-the-Fields, has long
held public meetings and
debates on topics ranging from
slavery in the 1800s to Civil
Rights in the 1970s. It is also
sometimes referred to as the
North Church.

In the middle of The Green
is Center Church, and ever since
the mid-1600s, a meeting house
or church has stood on this site.
Cool and elegant within, handsome Tiffany stained glass fills
the arched window above the
altar. Trinity Church, the third,
was the first Gothic Revival
church in the country, and was
constructed with materials

Neo-Gothic Harkness Tower,
a New Haven landmark

SPECIAL TO...

Ever wondered who invented
the hamburger? One of the
strongest claims comes from
Louis Lassen of New Haven
who served them here at
Louis Lunch. That was back in
1895, and the simple brick
house with a communal table
and two booths probably
looks much now as it did then.
It stands in the middle of a
parking lot at 263 Crown
Street. The hamburgers, however, come as a surprise.
Forget the griddle and the
buns, these beef patties are
cooked in front of diners on a
vertical gas grill and served on
toast.

---

allowed to pass through the
British blockade of New Haven
harbor during the War of 1812.
Compared with the white cupola
and steeple of its neighbors, the
tower seems heavy and ponder-
ous. Two impressive buildings,
City Hall and the Post Office,
overlook the Green.

▶ Walk diagonally north across
the Green toward the impos-
ing battlements and towers of
Yale University and enter the
Old Campus through the
Phelps Gate.

Litchfield, a classic example of the perfect New England town

ⁱ **Hartford Civic Center**

▶ *Leave Hartford on **Route 44** west. After 16 miles (26km), **Route 202** branches off to Torrington. Continue through Torrington and drive 6 miles (10km) to Litchfield.*

❶ Litchfield

Rather as a judge surveys his court, so Litchfield dominates the local landscape. Appropriately, the Tapping Reeve House on South Street was owned by Judge Tapping Reeve, who had America's first law school built in the grounds. Opened in 1773, it produced judges by the score, as well as three justices of the U.S. Supreme Court, 28 senators, and two vice-presidents. Exhibits here relate the importance of the school and its students to the new nation. During that era, Litchfield was also famous for its leather goods, mills, and factories. Townspeople have deliberately redesigned their homes and the common to re-create the

The Housatonic River valley

classic New England village seen today. The First Congregational Church, with its white columns, has a stately position at the head of the Green with North, South, East and West streets reaching out in their appropriate compass headings. North Street, often labeled one of the country's most beautiful, boasts textbook examples of late 1700s Georgian and Federal architecture, such as the Sheldon Tavern. The red-brick building

Grill is known for its celebrity customers, from politicians to movie stars.

i *Information booth, The Green*

▶ *Drive west for 11 miles (18km) on* **Route 202**.

2 New Preston

The road climbs abruptly to New Preston, alongside the tumbling waterfalls of the Aspetuck River, which give a clue to the town's industrial background. In the early 1800s, no less than 21 water-driven mills operated between New Preston and Marble Dale, barely a mile (1.5km) away. The mills did not survive the transition to steam power, but New Preston thrives on a new economy centered on its chic antique shops.

▶ *Continue through New Preston for ½ mile (1km) to Lake Waramaug.*

3 Lake Waramaug

To the Indians, Lake Waramaug was the "place of good fishing." Today, most visitors just come to catch the view, and to visit the Hopkins Vineyard, where the red-painted Yankee barn houses the winery and shop.

SPECIAL TO...

Skitch Henderson, Broadway veteran and director of the New York Pops Orchestra, lives in a typical New England country home called The Silo, located halfway between New Preston and New Milford. It is also home to a school of cookery, an art gallery, and a gourmet store of limitless variety, and attracts friends of the Hendersons and neighboring celebrities such as Bill Blass, Whoopi Goldberg, and Tom Brokaw.

▶ *Return to New Preston and take* **Route 202** *south for 8 miles (19km) to New Milford.*

4 New Milford

The Town Hall on The Green stands on the site of Roger Sherman's birthplace. He is the only native of Connecticut whose signature appears on all the significant documents concerning America's independence. Near the bandstand is a tank whose small scale and Victorian styling make it an unusually decorative armed forces memorial.

▶ *Drive through New Milford on* **Routes 202** *and* **67** *southwest, cross the Housatonic River bridge, turn right at the traffic lights onto* **Route 7** *north and continue through peaceful countryside to Bull's Bridge.*

5 Bull's Bridge

Bull's Bridge, one of just two covered bridges in the state which still see daily use, is barely longer than a large car. Beneath, the Housatonic River rushes through a particularly rugged gorge. Raging waters and winter ice jams destroyed four successive bridges until the present one, which has lasted since 1842. Back in 1781, a horse in George Washington's party fell into this gorge while making the crossing. Washington's own financial accounts record "getting a horse out of Bull's Bridge falls, $215.00." The high price suggests that the horse was probably the general's.

▶ *Continue on* **Route 7** *to Kent.*

SCENIC ROUTES

From New Milford north to Canaan is one of Connecticut's prettiest drives. Running parallel to the Housatonic River the entire way, Route 7 is bordered by the Litchfield Hills to the east and the Taconic Mountains to the west. Housatonic is an Indian word meaning "place beyond the mountains," and it offers tempting photo opportunities.

SPECIAL TO...

White Flower Farm, 3½ miles (5.6km) out of Litchfield via South Street, is an emporium of flower gardening. Its *Garden Book*, a weighty catalog published twice a year, offers a wealth of horticultural information. Visitors from mid-June through August are treated to the technicolor extravaganza of the begonia displays, a high point in the season.

at the corner of North and West streets was the Litchfield County Jail. Built in 1812, it was in use until the 1990s.

Also on North Street is a red saltbox house. On this site lived two 19th-century personalities: the charismatic preacher Rev. Henry Beecher and his sister and author, Harriet Beecher Stowe. The Litchfield History Museum on The Green has a fine collection of early paintings, decorative arts, and furniture, and The Green is lined with trendy shops, galleries, and restaurants. The West Street

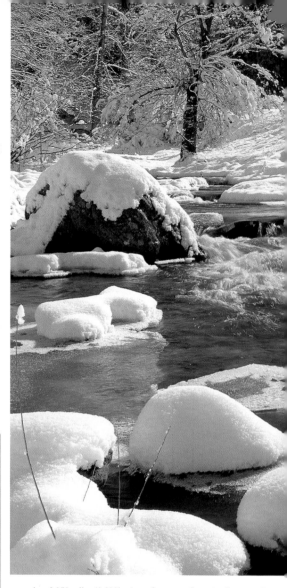

6 Kent

Just as Litchfield was once industrial, so Kent was known for its iron foundries. Where pig iron was smelted in the early 1800s, the Sloane-Stanley Museum and Kent Furnace now stands. A dedicated historian and fine artist, Sloane chronicled all aspects of early American life, from the building of barns to his favorite subject, the making and using of tools. The museum, housed in a big barn, includes a dog-powered butter churn, an authentic frontier cabin, and a re-creation of his art studio, right down to his paint-splattered telephone. Ruins of the furnace stand on the grounds, recalling a vanished local industry. Next door is the Connecticut Antique Machinery Association Museum, with its large collection of steam engines and tractors, and a working narrow-gauge railroad.

▶ Stay on **Route 7** north for 5 miles (8km) to Kent Falls State Park. Continue to Cornwall Bridge.

RECOMMENDED WALKS

Kent Falls State Park is one of a dozen or so state parks and forests in this corner of Connecticut. All are popular spots for picnics and hiking. Here, the special attraction is a broad view over Connecticut's wild terrain.
For a grand view, climb the steep 200-foot (60m) path beside the falls, which are often used for advertisements and feature in the TV soap opera *The Guiding Light*.

---

7 Cornwall Bridge

From here north, the valley narrows and the hills steepen. Hardly more than an intersection and the bridge, the hub of this little community is Baird's General Store, a well-known stopping point for Appalachian Trail hikers. The "world's longest continuous footpath"

stretches 2,050 miles (3,280km) from Georgia to northeast Maine. It crosses Route 7 only a few steps from the front porch where weary walkers stack their backpacks.

SPECIAL TO...

You can visit the workshop of the Cornwall Bridge Pottery, south of Cornwall Bridge, to see the craftspeople at work and view the huge wood-fired kiln in which their stylish pots are fired. Seconds are on sale here; the main shop is in West Cornwall.

▶ Cross the Housatonic again; bear right after the bridge and continue north to West Cornwall on **Route 7**.

SPECIAL TO...

The only covered bridges for cars in the state are here: at West Cornwall and Bulls Bridge, Kent

Water tumbles down a 200-foot (60m) flight of natural steps in Kent Falls State Park

8 Cornwall Bridge to West Cornwall

This is one of the prettiest stretches of the Housatonic, known as a fly-fisherman's paradise. Throughout the summer, anglers practice the elegant art of casting and placing the fly delicately on the water.

Somewhat rougher are the sports of white-water canoeing and kayaking. Paddlers meet at Clarke's Outdoors, a log cabin on the left. Although U.S. Olympic teams may make this their home base, Clarke's also outfits day trips for recreational paddlers and provides a shuttle service to and from the entry/exit points. The favorite "playground" for the kayakers is beneath the covered bridge at West Cornwall, built in 1837.

▶ *Stay on* **Route 7** *north for 4½ miles (7km), bearing left on* **Route 112** *for ¾ mile (1km) to Lime Rock Park.*

9 Lime Rock Park

Deep in the rural idyll, the self-styled "Road Racing Center of the East" comes as a surprise. The deceptively simple 1½-mile (2.4km) track has tested the best from every category of motor-sport. Drivers from Formula 1 to NASCAR and sports car racing have all taken the wheel here. Among celebrity competitors often seen here are the actors Paul Newman and Tom Cruise.

▶ *Continue west for 3¾ miles (6km) on* **Route 112**. *Climbing out of the Housatonic Valley, grand views open up of magnificent farms. To the north and west, the Berkshire Hills continue and blend into the Catskill Mountains of New York and the Green Mountains of Vermont. Turn north onto* **Route 41** *and drive for 1½ miles (2.4km) to Lakeville.*

10 Lakeville

Two fascinating museums lie opposite each other at the heart of the Lakeville Historic District. The first is Holley-Williams House Museum, where costumed guides portray the everyday life of a late 19th-century family and the social issues of the times. You can see an early vacuum cleaner, view a seven-holer outhouse and learn about topics as diverse as pre-electric refrigeration and women's suffrage. Across the street, the Salisbury Cannon Museum is where weapons were made during the Revolutionary War. Children especially enjoy the hands-on experience, learning about important figures during the Revolution, and Salisbury's ironmaking history.

▶ *Continue north on* **Routes 41** *and* **44** *for 2 miles (3km) to Salisbury.*

11 Salisbury

Salisbury has unofficially become the "Tea Capital" of Connecticut thanks to Chaiwalla, a specialty tea room, and Harney & Sons, master tea blenders and manufacturers found on Main Street. Nearby is the venerable Salisbury Ski Jump, where the annual winter festival in February brings competitors from as far as Norway and Finland.

i *Chamber of Commerce, Main Street*

▶ *Follow* **Route 44** *for 7 miles (11km) to Canaan and on for another 7 miles (11km) to Norfolk.*

12 Norfolk

Connecticut's highest town, tucked away in the northwestern corner, has an elevation of 1,770 feet (540m). Here, the Battell Chapel, with its Tiffany glass windows, faces the central Green which sits atop the hill. Each summer, the Norfolk Chamber Music Festival, with the Yale Summer School of Music, attracts music fans as it has for almost a century. Rachmaninov, Caruso, and Paderewski are among the legends who have performed during the season. Many of the street signs, painted by hand, have been brightened up with pictures of animals.

▶ *From The Green take the tranquil country drive back to Torrington on* **Route 272**. *This is a peaceful stretch of hilly evergreen and oak forest, dotted with lovely homes and farms. Return to Hartford.*

❻ Essex

In a 1996 book called *The 100 Best Small Towns in America*, Essex came out number one. Founded in 1648, it became quite wealthy due to the skill of its carpenters and shipwrights. The splendid Colonial, Georgian, and Federal homes on Main Street were built by their bosses, the shipbuilders and sea captains. The town's social hub is the 200-year-old Griswold Inn. Here, collections of marine art and 19th-century firearms add to the atmosphere of "the 'Gris,'" a busy, though jolly, hotel-restaurant. At the end of the street, in an old warehouse on Steamboat Landing, is the Connecticut River Museum. This tells the story of Essex and of the Connecticut River, from its source in northeastern New Hampshire to the mouth. Star attraction is the reproduction of

Cruising on the Connecticut River near East Haddam

David Bushnell's remarkable underwater craft, *American Turtle*. A stone's-throw away, the keel was laid for the *Oliver Cromwell*, the colony's first custom-built warship, back in 1776. From then on, Essex was an important ship-building center. The tradition continues nearby at the Brewers Dauntless Shipyard, which produces sleek modern yachts. The 1732 Pratt House is well preserved in the style of 1800, with a herb garden.

▶ *Return to Route 154 and drive north to Route 82 east. Turn right and cross the Connecticut River on the turntable bridge to East Haddam.*

SCENIC ROUTES

The Essex Steam Train and Riverboat Ride is organized by the Valley Railroad Company, whose volunteers restore, maintain, and operate old steam engines and cars. They puff through the countryside for the hour-long trip up to Chester and then stop at Deep River to connect with a river boat for an hour-and-a-half-long cruise.

SPECIAL TO...

No prizes for guessing how Ivoryton, 2 miles (3km) west of Essex, got its name. In the old days, ivory from Africa was unloaded in Essex and driven here in horse-drawn carts. It was then cut and polished into piano keys, buttons and combs. Although a factory nearby is now the world's largest producer of piano and organ keyboards, ivory is no longer used. The hamlet itself is tranquil, with huge beech trees on its main street, a general store, and a summer theater.

7 East Haddam

Just at the end of the bridge, high above the river, stands the Goodspeed Opera House. This six-story, white "wedding cake" is a grand reminder of the late 19th century, when East Haddam was a resort town, used by Mr. William Goodspeed's very own steam ships. Restored in the 1960s, the house's specialty is musical comedies. It hosted pre-Broadway runs for brand-new shows such as *Man of La Mancha*, in 1966, and *Annie*, in 1977. Now, new musicals are presented in a second theater in Chester, while this house concentrates on revivals. Land for East Haddam's original 17th-century settlement was sold to the English by local Indians in exchange for 30 coats. The one-room schoolhouse, where hero Nathan Hale once taught, is preserved next to the church.

▶ Continue on **Route 82** south to Gillette Castle.

8 Gillette Castle

At the turn of the century, actor William Gillette (1853–1937) had superstar status, drawing huge audiences to see his 1,300 performances portraying Sherlock Holmes. By 1919, he had poured a million dollars into this extraordinary fake medieval stone castle. An amateur inventor with an odd sense of humor, he made many of the "puzzle locks" on its doors and designed a system of mirrors to be able to see who was visiting. After a major renovation, which included a new visitor center, the castle reopened in 2002. The 184-acre (74-hectare) grounds make a fine picnic spot, high on the bank overlooking the Connecticut River.

▶ Continue on **Route 82** for 5 miles (8km) to **Route 156** south. Drive to Old Lyme.

9 Old Lyme

Old Lyme, one of America's first art colonies, is the unofficial home of American Impressionism, thanks to Florence Griswold. At the turn of the century, "Miss Florence" decided to take in boarders; first one, then more artists moved into her fine, Greek Revival home, drawn by the light and the serenity of the surrounding beaches and marshes. Instead of signing the visitors book, guests such as Willard Metcalf, Childe Hassam, and William Chadwick painted scenes on their landlady's doors and wall panels. The dining room is profusely decorated. This 1817 house, in the heart of the Old Lyme Historic District, is now a

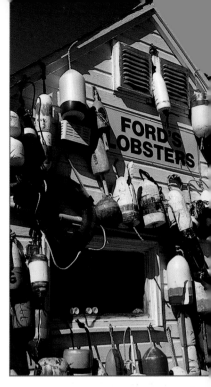

Lobster shop in Noank

museum with a fine collection of the *plein air* movement. Next door, the Lyme Academy of Fine Arts is one of America's leading art schools.

▶ Leave town and follow **Route 156** east, crossing Niantic Bay, with a view of the Millstone Energy Center, a nuclear power plant. After 16 miles (26km), arrive in New London.

SPECIAL TO...

Called the "Fresh River" by Dutch explorer Adriaen Block and the "Great River" by English settlers, the waterway for which the state of Connecticut is named was always the Quinnetukut to the Indians. The name means "the long river whose waters are driven by wind and tide." It starts in the three Connecticut lakes, way up in the northeastern corner of New Hampshire, near the Canadian border.

---

⑩ New London

Although New London is slowly renewing its image, it still remains a working town, just as it has been for 300 years. While not as attractive as smaller, more gentrified places in New England, the history here is just as impressive. The deep harbor made this an important port in the early 18th century, and the Hempsted Houses offer an insight into the lives of seafarers' families in Colonial times.

During the American Revolution, New London was the headquarters of the patriots' naval resistance, which made it a target for the British Army. Later, the port became one of the world's biggest and busiest whaling ports, with as many as 80 ships in its fleet. Whale Oil Row has four splendid 1832 mansions, grandiose Greek Revival temples of affluence.

The town's nautical history was boosted further in 1876 when the U.S. Coast Guard Academy opened. Its 60-year-old German barque, the *Eagle*, was confiscated from Germany by the U.S. Navy after World War II. Now, this 295-foot (109m) long sail training ship welcomes visitors on Sundays when in port.

Near the Coast Guard Academy is the Lyman-Allyn Art Museum which offers something for everyone: toys and a dolls' house, Indian artifacts and paintings by Connecticut artists.

Playwright Eugene O'Neill spent unhappy boyhood summers at Monte Cristo Cottage, to the south on Pequot Avenue. Bleak family events there a century ago are recalled in three O'Neill plays, including *Long Day's Journey into Night*. On Route 213, 6 miles (10km) south, is the Eugene O'Neill Theater Center, known for presenting staged readings of new productions.

▷ *Follow signs to I–95 east and cross the Thames river. Exit 86 leads north on Route 12 to the Nautilus Memorial.*

⑪ USS *Nautilus*

The USS *Nautilus*, dating from 1954, is the world's first nuclear-powered sub and the first to venture under the ice cap at the North Pole. Now open for visitors, it shows just how crowded conditions are when living underwater in a "sub."

▷ *Return on Route 12 and take Route 1 east. Turn right on Route 215 for Noank.*

⑫ Noank

Noank is as salty and undiscovered a town as there is on the Connecticut shoreline. A fishing and shipbuilding community in the past, it now looks as if every house might have a retired lobsterman or sea captain sitting out on the front porch. Pearl Street is the main thoroughfare and provides all the high points, from the Deacon Robert Palmer House with its whimsical gingerbread architecture and wild colors to Abbott's Lobster-in-the-Rough. This is a lobster house of the sort found in Maine – informal, with picnic-style eating.

FOR CHILDREN

The Science Center of East Connecticut, in the Connecticut College Arboretum at New London, offers educational fun with its puzzle parlor, science theater, marine touch tanks and other hands-on exhibits. For letting off steam, take them to Ocean Beach Park, where swimming pools, waterslides, mini-golf and a playground are among the attractions.

FOR HISTORY BUFFS

Benedict Arnold was a brilliant but vain American general who switched sides in the middle of the war. In 1781, he attacked New London with 1,700 British troops. Having grown up nearby, at Norwich, Arnold knew the area and the communication codes of the local militia. He caught the defenders off guard and burned New London to the ground. This was the final engagement of the war in New England. Discover more at Fort Griswold State Park, Croton.

Monte Cristo Cottage, named after O'Neill's actor-father's greatest role

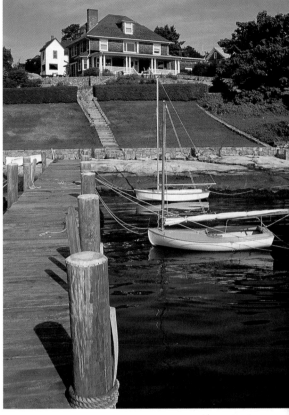

▶ Continue on **Route 215**, then **Route 1** to Mystic.

🔢 Mystic

The town itself is attractive, but often overlooked by the visitors who swarm to Mystic Seaport, the re-creation of a 19th-century fishing village. A mixture of real and replica, this is much more than a conventional open-air museum, with the largest and most complete maritime collection in the country. Taking full advantage of its waterside location, it has sailing vessels and models of every description and size on display. The 1841 *Charles W. Morgan*, the last wooden whaling vessel ever to be built, and the *L. A. Dunton*, a sleek 123-foot (45.5m) Gloucester fishing schooner which looks more like an America's Cup race competitor, can be seen.

Every possible craft and trade associated with seafaring life can be found and studied somewhere on the 40-acre (16.6-hectare) site. Active craftsmen re-create the workaday world of an early 19th-century fishing village. Nautical terms such as "sandbaggers," "smacks," "chandlers," "coopers," and "cordage" are all explained, while the latest attraction is the replica construction of the *Amistad*, used in Steven Spielberg's 1997 movie about slavery. You can even board a steam-boat for a trip out onto the river. Also in town is the Mystic Aquarium, its centerpiece a coral reef stocked with sharks, sting-rays and reef fish. You can learn about alligators and other swamp life, then watch Beluga whales in the Alaskan Coast exhibit. Undersea exploration, such as finding the *Titanic*, is the theme of Challenge of the Deep.

▶ Take **Route 1** toward Stonington. After 3 miles (5km), turn onto **Route 1A** for the village.

🔢 Stonington

Stonington Borough, a peninsula covered in old houses, remains peaceful and untouristy. The docks of this working fishing

The sleepy little town of Noank,

port, which has Connecticut's largest commercial fleet, provide an atmospheric place to stroll and watch the dragger fleet and lobster boats come in each afternoon. At the end of the long narrow main street is the Land Battery, with two of the cannons which helped repulse a British naval attack in the War of 1812. A few steps further is the Old Lighthouse Museum (1823), the first Government-operated lighthouse in Connecticut with gear for whaling and "ice harvesting" displayed in the "pocket-sized" lighthouse.

Guided tours are available at the home of Captain Nathaniel B. Palmer, who discovered Antarctica. Exhibits in the house cover his career and his family life.

▶ Return to **Route 1**, then join **I-95** west and return to New Haven.

THE MARITIME TRADITION

The Atlantic Ocean has had a profound affect on the development of New England. Five of the six states in the region are adjacent to the coastline, and the Europeans who first arrived all had to cross the stormy North Atlantic. Once they arrived, ships maintained the umbilical cord linking them with the Mother Countries, and permanent communities grew up around safe harbors. The abundance of fish offshore made fishing an easy and reliable means of finding food, and it became so vital to the early settlers that fishermen were exempt from military service.

Once the Colonies were established, shipping became an important part of the economy, though strict laws from London insisted that all manufactured goods had to be imported from England, alone. Enforcement was another matter, and not only were "illegal" cargoes landed, customs duties were, on occasion, evaded.

Ships were a necessity for England, and the navy increasingly relied on timber from Maine. Soon, the boats themselves were being constructed in the Colonies, since shipbuilding costs were from 20 to 50 percent less than in the Mother Country. Shipbuilding thrived and by 1760, one-third of the total British merchant tonnage was produced in the American Colonies.

By this time, the patterns of triangular trade routes were established. Merchant ships sailed from New England with grain, timber, and fish for the West Indies. These were traded for fruit, sugar, and molasses, which were taken on to England. There, the holds were loaded up with manufactured goods to be transported back home. Similar routes connected New England with Africa and the Mediterranean.

After years of lax enforcement, Britain decided to toughen up its policing of the trade laws in order to raise more revenue from the Colonies. Not only did this

hurt the New England economy, but it fostered anti-London feelings. The major ports of Boston and Portland, along with New York to the south, were targets before and during the Revolution.

Shipping again became a contentious issue during the Napoleonic Wars in Europe. Although the U.S. remained neutral, Britain interfered with American shipping, hoping to deprive the French of supplies. In addition, seamen were taken off captured ships and forced to sail for Britain. Eventually, these grievances led to the War of 1812.

From their early days, Colonists learned from the Indians how to catch whales when the mammals swam near shore, and towns such as New London and Mystic in Connecticut, and New Bedford and Provincetown in Massachusetts thrived at the expense of the whale. In 1774, 360 whaling ships sailed from Nantucket. Rhode Island developed a huge candle-making industry based on whale products. The oil was used to light streets and homes in Europe, while bones and baleen were used to make anything from umbrella spokes to corset stays. Only the discovery of oil (made into kerosene) in Pennsylvania, in 1859, ended the bloody trade. The business of whaling was epitomized in Herman Melville's novel, *Moby Dick*, based on his own experiences

Above: humpback whales can reach 40 to 50 feet (13 to 16m)

aboard ship. Today, museums such as Nantucket's Whaling Museum, housed in a former whale oil refinery, record the exploits of American sailors who roamed the oceans in the early 19th century.

Apart from their heavy involvement in the slave trade, "Yankee traders" sailed round South America to do business with China and the Pacific islands, bringing back huge wealth to towns such as Boston, Salem, and Portsmouth. Along the Maine coast, at Kennebunkport and Kittery, Bath, Camden, and Belfast, shipbuilders continued traditions begun as early as 1607, when the *Virginia* was the first ship built in the Colonies, near Bath.

Today, New England's nautical traditions concentrate on the pleasure industry, with yachting keeping the shipbuilders and sail-makers of the region at the forefront of technology. For the first half of the 20th century,

Tall ships at Mystic Seaport

Newport rivalled Cowes (in England) as the sailing capital of the world. The rich and famous built ever-larger yachts and raced them. Battles in the wind-swept seas off Newport for the legendary America's Cup were a feature of the town between 1930 and 1983.

In Bristol, Rhode Island, the Herreshoff Marine Museum recalls the Herreshoff Company's contribution to sailing. Between 1893 and 1934, eight consecutive winners in the America's Cup competition were built on the site, as well as the first torpedo boats for the U.S. Navy. In Newport, the Naval War College Museum emphasizes America's rise to power as a world force on the high seas. Out at Fort Adams State Park, at the Museum of Yachting, is the breathtaking *Shamrock V*, Sir Thomas Lighton's 1930 challenger for the America's Cup.

"Windjammers," old sailing ships, are now a popular way of spending a vacation, afloat along the coast. In Maine, Rockland and Camden are the best-known centers, while summer festivals such as Windjammer Days in the Boothbays and the finish of the Great Schooner Race, at the Rockland Breakwater, celebrate the nautical tradition.

Nowhere records New England's tradition better than Mystic Seaport on the Mystic River in Connecticut. An American whaler, the *Charles W. Morgan*, built of wood in 1841, is one of several sailing vessels ready for visitors to explore.

RHODE ISLAND

Rhode Island, "Little Rhody," is the smallest state, yet it also boasts the longest name: officially, it is The State of Rhode Island and Providence Plantations. This densely populated and heavily industrialized state received its title back in 1644, when two colonies were combined. A mere 48 miles by 37 miles (77km by 59km), it is nicknamed the "Ocean State" because of its 400 miles (640km) of shoreline, which includes some 100 beaches with public access. Not all the coast runs along the Atlantic Ocean; it also borders Narragansett Bay, which bites into the southeast corner of the state and stretches 28 miles (45km) inland, to the capital city of Providence.

Although the Vikings may have visited North America in the 11th century, Giovanni da Verrazano, the Italian explorer, is on record for sailing past what is now Block Island in 1524. He named it after the Island of Rhodes in Greece. When Roger Williams and a band of followers fled the intolerance of the Puritan colony in Massachusetts in 1636, they settled in what is now Providence. Two years later, Anne Hutchinson was similarly banished, and led another group to Aquidneck Island, now better known for the town of Newport. Both communities believed in religious freedom, for Christians as well as non-Christians. The first synagogue in the U.S. was built in Newport, while the first Baptist church was founded in Providence.

Rhode Island has been a holiday destination for almost two centuries. In the early 1800s, the seashore attracted wealthy Southerners, keen to escape the summer heat of the plantations. Families such as the Astors and Vanderbilts spent the summer social season in their "cottages," whose magnificence rivaled European palaces. Tennis, then the sport of the rich, made its American debut at the casino in Newport, and the International Tennis Hall of Fame now has its home here.

But it is sailing, rather than tennis, that is most associated with Newport. For some 50 years, the town hosted the America's Cup challenges, until 1983 when Australia broke the home team's winning streak and took the cup "down under." Nevertheless, Newport remains the sailing capital of the East Coast.

Sailboats reflected in Newport's harbor

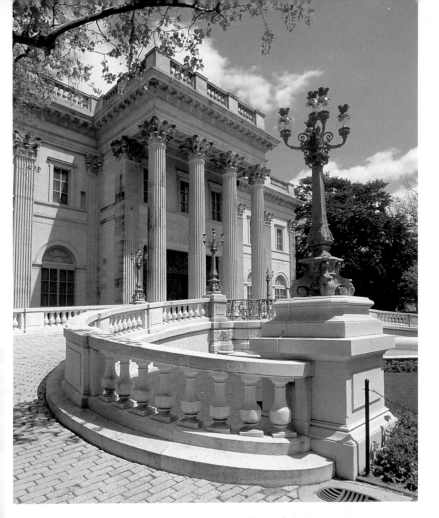

Tour 12

Providence, the capital of Rhode Island, is a gem of a city, all too often overlooked by visitors to New England. The riverfront and downtown area have been successfully restored and revitalized, while the historic district around Benefit Street is full of 18th- and 19th-century houses, now used for offices and museums, classrooms and private homes. Nearby is Brown University, the seventh oldest in the country, founded in 1764, and the Rhode Island School of Design, one of the country's leading art schools. Not surprisingly, this area is known as College Hill. Across the river is Federal Hill, where Little Italy is full of delicatessens and cafés. With its ethnic mix and large student population, Providence is a lively city, with a thriving music scene, art galleries, and numerous restaurants. The *haute cuisine* is a by-product of Johnson and Wales University, which specializes in the culinary arts and hospitality business.

Tour 13

Newport is situated at the southern tip of an island, with a harbor on one side and beaches stretching along the other. This town of contrasts has its share of plain pre-Revolutionary houses as well as opulent summer homes, such as Château-sur-Mer and The Breakers. A century ago, entrance was only for the privileged few; today, visitors are welcome to see the priceless art and grandiose architecture.

Marble House, Newport, was modeled on the Grand and Petit Trianon at Versailles

Sailing has long been popular here, with the most famous race of all, the America's Cup, a long tradition. Even though the cup has been lost to Australians and, most recently, New Zealanders, Narragansett Bay still brings in the sailing crowd. Newport also attracts tennis fans, who visit the Hall of Fame. In summer, you can see one of the few professional tournaments outside the British Isles that is still played on grass. The town also draws music lovers. Since the first Newport Jazz Festival in 1954, the outdoor summer concerts have become important fixtures on the U.S. music calendar.

Providence

Providence, the third largest city in New England, is only now getting the credit and attention it deserves as one of New England's most approachable destinations. Compact and walkable, with fine examples of pre- and post-Revolutionary architecture, it has a lively and artistic student body as well as high-quality restaurants, thanks to the influence of one of America's leading culinary schools.

HALF A DAY

Statue with the State House behind

ⓘ *Convention Center*

▶ *Start at the Convention Center (park the car here, or in one of the public parking lots nearby). Walk to Memorial Boulevard.*

❶ Waterplace Park

This gem of design is the focal point of Providence's extensive riverfront redevelopment. Cobbled walks, brick paths, planted terraces, amphitheaters, gleaming wrought ironwork, and graceful bridges make the Providence River area a model of downtown urban beauty. This is the perfect place to view the State Capitol, sitting imperially on the hill. Built in 1904 of Georgia marble, its dome is the third largest unsupported dome in the world. On top, the gilded statue *Independent Man* symbolizes the free-thinking founders of Rhode Island. Inside hangs one of the most famous paintings in the country: the full-length portrait of George Washington, which appears on dollar bills, painted by Rhode Islander Gilbert Stuart.

▶ *Continue along Memorial Boulevard, cross the Providence River on Steeple Street Bridge; follow Steeple Street up the hill to No. 75 North Main Street.*

❷ First Baptist Meeting House

Although Roger Williams founded the Baptist congregation in 1638, the first church was not built for 50 years. This house of worship dates from 1775. A plan for St. Martin-in-the-Fields in London provided the inspiration for architect Joseph Brown, but the ability of the 185-foot steeple (56m) to withstand storms was due to the carpenters' extensive shipbuilding experience.

▶ *Turn up Thomas Street to Benefit Street. Turn right to No. 224 Benefit Street.*

❸ Rhode Island School of Design Museum of Art

Rhode Island School of Design, always abbreviated to RISD ("Ris-dee") is one of America's leading art schools. The modern entrance to the school's museum is in the Daphne Farago Wing where the focus is *Mantled Figure*, Howard Ben Tre's sculpture in solid cast glass. Works by Monet and Picasso, an Egyptian mummy, and a 9-foot (2.7m) tall Buddha, dating back ten centuries, are among the rich and varied 65,000-piece collection.

▶ *Continue along Benefit Street to No. 251, on the corner of College Street.*

❹ Providence Athenaeum

In the old days, a club for learned men was often called an "athenaeum," in honor of Athena, the goddess of wisdom. This Greek Revival building was finished in 1838, and its stern exterior contrasts with the warm intimacy of the main reading room, with its tiers of books. Here, poet Edgar Allen Poe met and wooed local widow Sarah Whitman, who accepted, then rejected him (she is thought to have inspired his poem *Annabel Lee*). Today, anyone in need of inspiration needs only to look up to busts of the Greek historian Homer, the English authors Milton and Keats, and the American statesman, Daniel Webster. Among the fine bindings and rare editions is an original portfolio of illustrations of American birds by the 19th-century naturalist John James Audubon.

▶ *Walk up College Street. On the left is the List Art Center and the David Winton Bell Gallery.*

Providence has undergone massive renewal and revitalization in recent years

5 David Winton Bell Gallery

A distinctive modernistic building on College Street houses the List Art Center and the David Winton Bell Gallery. The gallery has a permanent collecion of more than 4,000 works, from Rembrandt prints to contemporary pieces, and also stages a varied program of exhibitions.

▶ *Continue to the corner of College and Prospect streets.*

6 Libraries

This could be called "library corner." On the right is "the Rock," the bustling J. D. Rockefeller Library, open only to Brown students. Opposite is the "Hay," the hushed John Hay Library, where the public may explore the vast book collection and the small gallery in the lobby.

John Hay graduated from the university in 1858. A poet and

The famous Brown Bear statue at Brown University

historian, he was also the U.S. Secretary of State at the turn of the century.

▶ *Cross Prospect Street and enter the campus of Brown University.*

FOR HISTORY BUFFS

Roger Williams founded Providence, but the city's success in the late 18th and early 19th centuries followed the fortunes of the four Brown brothers.

John was a merchant. Joseph, the architect, designed the Market House, First Baptist Church, and a mansion for brother John. Moses founded the Providence Bank and financed the mill at Pawtucket, which started the Industrial Revolution in New England. Nicholas gave land and money to Rhode Island College, which was to be later renamed Brown University in 1804.

---

7 Brown University

The Van Wickle Gates, leading to the quadrangle, open just twice a year: to let new students in and graduates out. Founded in 1764, Brown is the seventh-oldest university in the country, and became co-ed in 1971. The main quadrangle boasts a variety of architecture, with the oldest building, University Hall (1771), being used as a barracks by French and American troops during the Revolution. The larger-than-life bronze *Brown Bear* statue rearing up, with its rather kindly expression, supposedly stands on a slate from the rock where Roger Williams first set foot on his arrival from Massachusetts in 1636. At the upper end of the college's grounds is the Carrie Tower, built by Paul Bajnotti of Turin in memory of his wife. It is inscribed: "Love is as strong as death."

▶ *Return down the hill on College Street and turn left on Benefit Street.*

FOR HISTORY BUFFS

Which Civil War general gave his name to a fashion trend? General Ambrose Burnside, whose statue stands in City Hall Park. So well-known were his side whiskers that the style became known as "sideburns." He went on to be governor and senator for Rhode Island, and lived at No. 314 Benefit Street.

---

8 Benefit Street

Originally known as Back Street, because it ran behind the houses facing the main street, Benefit Street was transformed from a path into a proper road in 1758 "for the common benefit of all." Now it is known as the "Mile of History," with its many 18th- and 19th-century houses: note details such as the old-fashioned street lights and boot scrapers.

At No. 43 Benefit Street, on the corner of Hopkins Street, stands the clapboard Governor

Stephen Hopkins House. This delightful example of early 1700s architecture was the home of the ten-time Governor of the state and signatory of the Declaration of Independence.

▶ *Continue along Benefit Street.*

9 First Unitarian Church

John Holden Greene, the architect, rated this 1816 church his finest achievement. High in its steeple hangs the largest ever bell cast by the Paul Revere Foundry. Better known now as the messenger who rode from Boston to Lexington in 1775 to warn the Colonists that the British were approaching, Revere was a silversmith and bell-maker.

▶ *Continue on Benefit to the corner of Power Street.*

10 John Brown House

John Brown was a successful merchant who opened up trade with China after the American Revolution. His brother, Joseph, designed this imposing brick house, whose entrance is at No. 52 Power Street. President John Quincy Adams once called it "the most magnificent and elegant mansion that I have ever seen on this continent." Filled with fine examples of Rhode Island's furniture-making tradi-

tion, it exemplifies the gracious living of the 18th century.

▶ *Continue a few steps further along Benefit Street to No. 357.*

11 Joseph Nightingale House

Supposedly the country's largest wood-frame house, this 200-year-old ochre and cream merchant's home has been restored so completely, it could have been built yesterday.

▶ *Return to Power Street and walk down the hill. Turn right on South Main Street and walk 1 1/2 blocks to No. 86, the Old Stone Bank.*

12 Old Stone Bank

After the geometric simplicity of most of the buildings on this walk, the art nouveau-style gilt and green dome seems extravagant.

▶ *Continue to Westminster Street, then cross the river to The Arcade.*

13 The Arcade

Shopaholics in the early 19th century had their own indoor shopping malls. This was the U.S.A.'s first, built back in 1828. The stores and goods may have

Brown University's first building, University Hall, is now a National Historic Landmark

changed, but it is still popular with visitors as well as locals. The cantilevered stairways and ironwork are remarkable even today. The Greek Revival porticoes give this building the look of a bank or university library. Imagine teams of oxen dragging the 20-foot (6m) long columns from the granite quarry, 5 miles (8km) away in Johnston.

▶ *Continue on Westminster Street to Dorrance Street. Turn right, heading toward the restored Union Station. At Exchange Street, turn left and return to the Convention Center.*

SPECIAL TO...

Quahogs, often pronounced *ko-hogs* in Rhode Island, are the local clams. The shells were once used as *wampum*, or currency, by the Native Americans. Nowadays, big shells are often saved for a dish or ashtray. Baby quahogs, called cherrystones or littlenecks, are eaten raw, on the half shell, while mature quahogs are used in chowder.

▶ *Continue to the building next door.*

❻ Newport Historical Society

The Newport Historical Society, a driving force behind the preservation of Newport's historic buildings, was established in 1853, though it evolved from an even earlier club. The Seventh Day Adventist Meeting House, built in 1729, was moved here in 1887.

▶ *Return to Washington Square and turn left on Clarke Street. Walk halfway down this street of colorfully painted houses to Nos. 23–25, the Armory of the Newport Artillery Company.*

The moon rises over white-steepled Trinity Church

❼ Newport Artillery Company

Uniforms worn by Field Marshall Montgomery, Prince Philip, and President Anwar Sadat of Egypt are among the uniforms, flags, regalia and other artifacts in the museum

contained in this 1836 stone building. The "1741" over the door refers to the date of the artillery's charter, making this the oldest military organization in the country.

▶ *Walk to the corner of Clarke and Mary streets.*

❽ Vernon House

In 1781, General Washington met with French Generals Lafayette and Rochambeau to decide tactics for the next stage of the war. Rochambeau, commander of the French troops quartered in Newport, lived in this house. If you look closely you will see that what appears to be weathered stone block is actually wood.

▶ *Continue up Mary Street, turn right on Spring Street and proceed to Trinity Church.*

❾ Trinity Church

Since 1726, the tall white spire has been a landmark on the hill above the harbor. In the vestibule is the church's original bell, "probably the first bell that rang over a New England church." The church's organ, made by Richard Bridge, came from London in 1733 and may have been played by composer Friedrich Handel himself. On the main floor stand box pews, which are privately owned and can be bought and sold. Note the individually chosen cushions and elaborate needlepoint covers for the kneelers. The inscriptions on Pew 81 commemorate the most famous worshippers, from George Washington to Queen Elizabeth II and Archbishop Desmond Tutu of South Africa. Stained-glass windows by Tiffany stand out against a background of white walls and green-gray woodwork. They were paid for by wealthy summer residents such as Cornelius Vanderbilt.

▶ *The next left is Mill Street. Turn left, and walk up the hill past Touro Park and the mysterious Stone Tower. Legend says that it*

was erected by Vikings in the 11th century. More probably, it was a look-out for Governor Benedict Arnold (grandfather of the Revolutionary traitor) who owned much of the land. Continue up to Bellevue Avenue and cross the street to No. 50.

❿ Redwood Library

A £500 donation in 1746 bought the first books for what is the oldest continuously used library in the country. The benefactor was Abraham Redwood, a rich trader from the West Indies. The building is typical of the pre-Revolutionary era, with wood painted to look like stone. As well as books, there is a sculpture of Benjamin Franklin

by Jean-Antoine Houdin and paintings by Gilbert Stuart.

▶ *Walk next door.*

⓫ Newport Art Museum

Clipped gables, airy verandas, scroll-sawed trim and ornamental timbers, or "sticks," epitomize the "stick style" of 19th-century architecture.

Dating from 1862, this is the first of many buildings in Newport designed by Richard Morris Hunt, but it is vastly different from the extravaganzas that made him the defining architect of the later "Gilded Age."

▶ *Cross Bellevue to Touro Park and walk down Pelham Street to the harbor area. Along the way, you pass the tiny Arnold Burying Ground, where the stones date back to 1677. At the bottom, turn right and return to the Gateway Information Center. The rest of the route is followed by car. Drive up Memorial Boulevard and turn right on Bellevue Avenue and head for No. 194.*

for "little house." The first major commission for Stanford White and the McKim, Mead and White architectural firm, its "shingle" style was another popular Victorian trend. It spreads over almost a full city block; there are shops on the ground floor, with the ever-expanding Tennis Hall of Fame above. Outside are the world's oldest continuously used grass tennis courts, dating from 1881. (The All-England Club is older, but moved to its present Wimbledon site in 1922.) The annual professional tournament here is played each July, immediately after Wimbledon.

On entering the main gate to the Hall of Fame, there is the

players volleying. If you feel so inclined, book time on one of the 13 courts and play where the U.S. Open Tennis Championships were born.

▶ *Drive along Bellevue Avenue. Single and multiple tickets for Preservation Society houses can be bought at all their properties.*

⑬ Kingscote Mansion
In 1841, the Bellevue Avenue area was only starting to develop as a residential neighborhood, and Kingscote Mansion looks positively simple compared to the grandiose designs of the 1890s. Typical of the Gothic Revival style are the elaborate

The Redwood Library, designed to look like a Roman temple

⑫ Newport Casino and the International Tennis Hall of Fame
The Casino, not a gambling casino but a gentlemen's club, was founded in 1880 as a rival to the Newport Reading Room. It takes its name from the Italian

distant roar of cheering tennis fans and the voice of an announcer calling a famous match from the past. The all-encompassing collection of tennis memorabilia ranges from an 1876 tennis racquet-bending machine right up to a Monica Seles' ensemble, while state-of-the-art computer displays provide a net judge's view of two

barge-boards, lancet arch casement window, and sawn cornice trim. Designed by Richard Upjohn and built for George Noble Jones, some say that the expression "Keeping up with the Joneses" originated here.

▶ *Continue on along Bellevue Avenue.*

14 The Elms
When Pennsylvania coal baron
Edward Berwind went to
France, he was so impressed by
the 18th-century Château
d'Asnières, near Paris, that he
made it the model for this house.
The Elms, built in 1901, has
furnishings that span the Louis
XIV and XV styles, while the
formal gardens have spacious
terraces and lawns. At the top of
the house, a hidden third story
contains the servants' quarters.

▶ *Continue on Bellevue Avenue.*
To the left, on Narragansett
Avenue, is Chepstow, an
Italianate mansion built for a
cousin of the Astors, with a
fine collection of 19th-century
American paintings.

15 Château-sur-Mer
In 1857, William Wetmore
invited 2,500 guests to a party in
his five-year-old home. He paid
for those festivities, and for this
lavishly decorated mansion, with
profits from trading with China.
The grounds have some fine old
trees, a Chinese moon gate and a
Colonial Revival pavilion.

▶ *Continue on Bellevue Avenue.*

16 Vernon Court
Most of the mansions that are
open to visitors are historic
monuments; this grandiose
version of a 17th-century French
château is a private home. On
the ground floor is the National
Museum of American
Illustration, a pictorial history
of American society from 1880
to 1950.

▶ *Turn left at Ruggles Avenue*
and follow the signs to The
Breakers.

17 The Breakers
This is the ultimate in extrava-
gance and the most famous
summer "cottage" of all. Two
decades after Richard Morris
Hunt renovated Château-sur-
Mer, he created this mock 16th-
century Italian palace for the
railroad tycoon Cornelius
Vanderbilt II. Hundreds of

SPECIAL TO...

Newport's wealthy loved racing huge yachts. Their money
and patronage stimulated
interest in the America's Cup,
the world's oldest international
sporting challenge. The first
race was held in England,
round the Isle of Wight, in
1851, but from 1920 onward,
Newport was the host. The
American winning streak finally
ended in 1983, when Australia
took the cup. In recent
decades, the port has also act-
ed as the finish line for single-
handed transatlantic races. The
full story is told in the Museum
of Yachting at Fort Adams State
Park, which also has fishing,
sailing, and swimming exhibits.

---

craftsmen were employed, many
brought over from Europe, but
the grand salon was actually
built in France, disassembled,
shipped across the Atlantic, and
reassembled by the same
French craftsmen. In the dining
room, a painted ceiling is two
stories above the life-sized
figures and gigantic marble
columns. Although the kitchen
is the size of an average house, it
looks surprisingly simple and
functional, hung with yard after
yard of copper cooking pots and
pans. The stables house a
display of family items, including historic coaches.

▶ *Return to Bellevue Avenue*
and continue.

18 Rosecliff
The Grand Trianon of Versailles
was the inspiration for the
summer home of Mrs. Hermann
Oerlich. Soft-white tiles cover
the outside; inside, the 80-foot
(24m) long ballroom is all cream
and gold. Elegant and refined,
Rosecliff sits near the ocean and
was used for shooting the 1974
film, *The Great Gatsby* and, more
recently, *True Lies* with Arnold
Schwarzenegger.

▶ *Continue along Bellevue*
Avenue.

---

19 Beechwood
At the end of the 19th century,
Caroline Astor was the reigning
queen of American society. To
be invited to her parties meant
social acceptance. Her famous
list of "The Top 400" people
supposedly reflected the capac-
ity of the ballroom in her New
York City residence. Today,
costumed guides play the parts
of the Astors, their guests and
their servants, bringing to life
the heyday of the country house
party.

▶ *Next door is Marble House.*

20 Marble House
Marble House is another
Richard Morris Hunt creation,
built in 1892 by William
Vanderbilt, the brother of
Cornelius. The overpowering
entrance is covered in Italian
marble, while the dining room
boasts one-of-a-kind bronze
Louis XIV chairs weighing 60
pounds (27kg) each. Most
amazing of all is the ballroom,
where "all that glisters" really is
gold, or gilded. When Alva

Cornelius Vanderbilt's Breakers, Newport's most splendid estate
Inset: the Newport coastline

23 Hammersmith Farm

This shingled 1888 beach house was the location for the wedding reception of Jacqueline Bouvier to John F. Kennedy. From 1961 to 1963 it was also the "Summer White House" for President Kennedy. (No longer open.)

SCENIC ROUTES

The 3½-mile (5.6km) Cliff Walk, starting at Cliff Walk Manor on Memorial Boulevard and ending at Bailey's Beach, is an excellent way to see the splendors of the mansions from a different angle.

Vanderbilt divorced her husband, she took the house, then married Perry Belmont (see below).

▶ Proceed along Bellevue Avenue to Belcourt Castle.

21 Belcourt Castle

Alva Vanderbilt did not move far after she divorced William K. Vanderbilt and married his good friend Perry Belmont. Where Vanderbilt was keen on yachts, Belmont followed horse-racing and helped build the Belmont Track in New York.

▶ Opposite is Rough Point.

22 Rough Point

Peek at the 1889 mansion built for a Vanderbilt, then owned by the Dukes. It remains a time capsule, left just as it was when the heiress, Dorothy Duke, lived here. It is only open via the shuttle from the Visitor's Center.

▶ Ocean Drive starts here and follows a scenic stretch of shoreline, dotted by breathtaking private homes. Bailey's Beach, the first on the left, was the beach favored by the "400." Some 5 miles (8km) farther, also on the left, is Hammersmith Farm.

▶ To return to the Newport Harbor area, follow Harrison, Halidon and Wellington avenues to Thames Street. Turn right, then left on McAllister Street and left on Spring Street to Memorial Boulevard.

VERMONT

Vermont has been called "every American's second state" because of the small farms with red barns, and villages with white churches that make up the traditional image of "old-fashioned America." The most rural of all states, it has only one major town, Burlington, with 40,000 inhabitants. The remainder of the half million or so Vermonters are scattered throughout the rolling hills and valleys stretching north–south between Canada and the Massachusetts border.

Although Lake Champlain lies on its western flank and the Connecticut River forms the eastern border, Vermont is the only New England state with no access to the sea. What it does have is mountains. French explorer Samuel de Champlain first remarked on the *verts monts*, the green mountains, back in the 17th century. While still a colony, Vermonters argued over land ownership with neighboring New York; the Vermonters won. When the colonies threw off the yoke of the English crown, Vermont went its own way; from 1777 to 1791 it was a republic, minting its own coins and printing its own stamps.

Vermont's gentle rolling landscape

The population has always been small. The roller-coaster landscape is difficult to farm, winters are bitter and summers are short. Despite that, Vermont has had its moments of affluence. Early in the 19th century, its wool was in demand world-wide. When that trade was lost, dairy farming took over. Although forests now cover acres of land once cleared for pasture, cattle remain a significant revenue earner. The sharp flavor of Vermont cheddar cheese is rated by gourmets, while a more recent dairy-related success is Ben and Jerry's Ice Cream. Other natural resources such as marble and granite provide a base to the economy, matched by furniture-making, paper production, and computers. Most important of all, however, is tourism.

Each autumn, "leaf peepers" by the thousands invade the state, drawn by the natural phenomenon of the maple leaves turning to brilliant shades of red and gold. Since the first ski tow was set up in Woodstock in 1934, the winter season has attracted both downhill and cross-country skiers.

Tour 14

The southern Vermont town of Bennington rarely rates more than a few lines in the history books, yet it played its part in the Revolution, and a 306-foot (93m) high stone needle commemorates the 1777 battle. Nearby is the grave of one of the country's favorite poets, the 20th-century writer Robert Frost. Bennington's museum displays a fine collection of naive paintings by Grandma Moses. These, along with handsome old houses and business buildings, add up to a town that is worth exploring.

Tour 15

Southern Vermont looks softer than points further north and is known for its photogenic farms and villages. Weston, set on a hilltop, preserves the atmosphere of a typical 19th-century Vermont village. Ludlow offers its own ski mountain; while the center of Grafton, known for its cheese, has been preserved, scrubbed clean, painted white, and seems suspended in time. The only crowded place is Manchester, full of shoppers hunting for bargains at the numerous factory outlet stores.

Tour 16

This part of Vermont is best known for the world-class ski resort of Killington. Apart from that, it is also another peaceful area where artists and crafts-people create minor master-pieces in small villages tucked away in the Green Mountains. Former U.S. President Calvin Coolidge is a local hero, his birth-place and homestead have become minor shrines. A few villages, such as Woodstock, have been deliberately "prettied up," but overall, the natural, unhus-tled pace of life will reward those looking for a relaxed vacation. Take time to bike the back roads.

Tour 17

Compared with the quieter regions to the south, the north-ern section is a bustling part of the state. Celebrities range from Ben and Jerry, whose ice creams have taken the world by storm, to the Von Trapp family of *Sound of Music* fame, who run an inn near Stowe. Teddy bears and Icelandic horses, a house with secret passages, and the Robert Frost Trail are some of the off-beat attractions. The Shelburne Museum is an outstanding collection of American folk art, housed in buildings that were moved here lock, stock and barrel from locations all over New England. The elongated Lake Champlain is fine for a ferry ride, water sports, or for those merely in search of quiet contemplation.

The first pumpkins of the season: they must be picked before the frosts arrive

Bennington

Outside the state, Bennington is best known for Ethan Allen and his Green Mountain Boys. This group of feisty Vermonters not only had a grievance against the British, but also against the land-greedy "Yorkers" (New Yorkers) in the state next door. The historic district and its college make this an attractive small town.

"I paint from the sky down," was Grandma Moses' simple explanation of her style. "Once I tried to do a landscape without people, but it looked so lonely I just had to put some in," she explained. Born Anna Mary Robertson, she was inspired by childhood memories of country life, as well as the popular Currier and Ives 19th-century prints. After the death of her husband, she found some brushes in a barn and began to paint as a hobby. A chemist in Hoosick Falls, New York, hung a few of her works in his window in 1939. Louis Caldor, a wealthy Manhattan collector, saw them and promptly bought up everything of hers. A year later, she had a one-woman show in New York, when a journalist nicknamed her "Grandma Moses." The name stuck.

ℹ️ *Veterans Memorial Drive*

▶ *Park at the Bennington Museum to start the tour.*

1 Bennington Museum

Grandma Moses (1860–1961) was known as much for her longevity as for her "primitive" portrayals of rural life. This farmer's wife only started to paint when she turned 70, recording countryside activities such as haymaking and maple sugaring. Critical acclaim led to an exhibition at New York's Museum of Modern Art. Although she lived just across the state line, in Eagle Bridge, New York, this Vermont museum has the largest collection of her work, with 28 paintings shown in a special gallery. A favorite picture, often used on greetings cards, is *Over the River*, which depicts the trip to Grandmother's house for Thanksgiving. Memorabilia are found in the old schoolhouse where she, her grandchildren, and her great-grandchildren all

studied. The museum also houses the 1777 Battle of Bennington flag, thought to be the oldest "Stars and Stripes" in existence. Watch for the Bennington pottery and glass collection from the 19th century and the Bennington Wasp (1920s), the only automobile ever to be manufactured in Vermont.

▶ *Walk up the hill to the small green in the center of Old Bennington. Look to your left.*

meeting house was replaced in 1805 by this handsome church, whose stylish belfry contrasts with the usual spiked steeple.

Less than a mile (1.5km) along Route 9 is the Bennington Center for the Arts. In three buildings are a museum, with its collection of Native American and Southwestern Art, and the Oldcastle Theater.

▶ *Turn right on Monument Avenue and head towards the obelisk. Just on the right is a statue.*

The grave of Robert Frost, a simple memorial to the poet, lies in Bennington cemetery

2 Old First Church

*"And were an epitaph to be my story
I'd have a short one ready for my own.
I would have written of me on my stone:
I had a lover's quarrel with the world."*

The final line of Robert Frost's 1942 poem, *The Lesson for Today*, is engraved on the plain stone marking his grave in the cemetery. One of the best-loved poets of his time (1874–1963), he captured the essential sights, smells, and character of New England.

Also buried here are five Vermont governors and many patriots who fell in the Battle of Bennington. The original 1763

Robert Frost has succeeded where so many poets have failed. His verse is not only intellectually satisfying, but also accessible by readers of all ages. In the U.S., he is widely read in schools, where poems about swinging on birch trees or trudging through snow relate to the everyday life of children in the country. He was 11 when he moved from San Francisco to Massachusetts with his widowed mother. After a spell in England, he returned to New England and became both prolific and successful. Ironically, he returned to be poet-in-residence at Dartmouth and Harvard, colleges where he had failed to get a degree.

3 Catamount Tavern

Looking ready to pounce on unwary passers-by, this big bronze wild cat commemorates the site of the Catamount Tavern, built in 1767. It was the meeting place of Ethan Allen and the Green Mountain Boys. The catamount, or catamountain, is the state mascot of Vermont. It is also called a puma, cougar, and lynx.

▶ *Walk to the top of Monument Avenue.*

4 Bennington Battle Monument

Confusingly, the Battle of Bennington took place in New York. In 1777, the British were running low on food and arms, so General Burgoyne sent troops to capture the American stores which were stashed in a depot in Bennington. Before the Redcoats could reach the town, they were intercepted and overpowered by the patriots led by General Stark and Colonel Seth Warner. This was a significant victory in a regional campaign that ended with the surrender of Burgoyne at Saratoga a few months later.

The statue of local hero, Colonel Seth Warner, stands before the simple monument on the site of the supply depot. Over a century old, the statue, built of locally quarried lime-

stone, ranks as the tallest man-made structure in Vermont, soaring 306 feet (91.8m). Take the elevator to the observation levels for spectacular views of three states – New York, Massachusetts and Vermont. Each year, the victory is celebrated in style on Bennington Battle Day Weekend, in mid-August.

▶ *Return down Monument Avenue, noting the fine examples of Federal and Georgian houses on either side. Turn left on West Main Street and head down the hill into town. On the left is a service station.*

5 Hemming's Sunoco Station

You could be forgiven for thinking this is a museum of classic vehicles. Although it is a functioning Sunoco station, the owners are the Hemmings family, the publishers of *Motor*

The observation platform on top of Bennington's Battle Monument gives excellent views over the city

News. The store is full of car books, models, toys and artwork, as well as Vermont products. Unusual models of restored tractors, wreckers, steamrollers, and panel trucks from the 1920s to the 1940s are often on display outside.

▶ *Walk on for a block, then turn left on Depot Street. Continue to the junction with River Street.*

6 Historic Bennington Railroad Station

The Bennington and Rutland Railroad was successful a century ago, when this temple of limestone and blue marble was built. However, passenger trains have not stopped here since 1933, although freight trundled through up to the 1950s. The handsome building survives as Bennington Station Restaurant, with evocative photographs of old steam engines on the walls.

▶ *Turn left on River Street, then right onto Benmont Avenue.*

▟ Holden Leonard Mill

Back in the 19th century, Bennington was a manufacturing town, using the river to power grist and paper mills such as the Holden Leonard Mill. This massive building, with a central tower rising four stories high, has been converted to offices, but stands as a legacy to the industrial past.

▶ *Turn right on County Street. At the corner of North Street is the Hawkins House with its contemporary crafts. Cross North Street and continue to No. 324 County Street.*

▟ Potters' Yard

In the 19th century, the town was known for its pottery, as the 4,000-piece collection in the museum shows. Today, around 40 potters still work in what was an old grist mill on County Street. This arts and crafts center, with small shops and a restaurant, was founded by David Gil, whose colorful splatterware has been popular since 1948. Although he died in 2002, the Bennington Potters continue to produce the jugs, pitchers, and vases, and his dinner services are in great demand, both in restaurants and homes.

▶ *Return to North Street and turn left. This becomes South Street after the intersection with Main Street.*

▟ Pennysaver Building

The houses and churches of 19th-century New England are familiar from postcards and calendars, but the commercial architecture can be just as fascinating. The former Putnam Hotel block curving round from South to Main and the Pennysaver Building at 107 South Street are typical. The

Pennysaver, a free newspaper, still occupies the premises. The huge, globular lights outside were originally gaslit.

▶ *Return to Main Street and turn back west, returning to the car. Drive to the main intersection and go north on Route 7A, then left on to Northside Drive (which becomes Route 67A). After 3 miles (5km) reach Bennington College.*

▟ Bennington College

Founded in 1925 to offer further education to women, Bennington College is now co-ed. It was once the most expensive private college in America, and former students include Broadway actress Carol Channing and film star Alan Arkin, as well as a host of artists. Known for its programs of fine arts, the campus is an attractive blend of mock Colonial and modern buildings in a rural setting.

▶ *Continue on Route 67A to North Bennington (2 miles/3km). Three covered bridges cross the river on the left: the Silk Road, Papermill Village, and the Bert Henry Bridge on Murphy Road. On the right, entering the town, is a fine complex of water-driven mills on Paran Creek. This is a convenient place to park. Cross Main Street and bear left up West Street. At the corner of Park Street is the Park-McCullough House.*

⑪ Park-McCullough House

With its handsome curving veranda, this early example of an American Second Empire-style mansion (1875) gives an idea of how the wealthy lived in the latter half of the 19th century. The name combines that of lawyer Trenor Park, who built the house, and his son-in-law, John McCullough, one of the two Vermont governors who lived here. The 35-room house has a collection of early photographs by Carlton Watkins, who recorded life in the Wild West. Out in the stables are old sleighs and carriages. Open to the public, there is a small replica of the mansion on the front lawn.

▶ *Return to Main Street and turn left up the hill, past the imposing Greek columns of Powers Market. It is no more than a country store inside, but at the top of the hill is the station.*

⑫ Old Train Station

This delightful Victorian railroad station, decorated in shades of green and barn-red trim, dates back to 1880. Today, it is a popular dining venue.

▶ *Return to the car at the bottom of the hill.*

Taking a quiet moment in Bennington, once a center of Revolutionary action

THE FALL

While most of the world experiences a dull, even sad end to the year, New England's landscape goes out in a blaze of glory. Due to a combination of soil and trees, sun and rain, the hillsides change from green to a tapestry of scarlet and gold, purple and orange. This is the "foliage season." Rudyard Kipling, who lived for a while in Vermont, felt almost powerless to depict the transformation. "No pen can describe the turning of the leaves – the insurrection of the tree people against the waning year. A little maple began it, flaming blood-red of a sudden where he stood against the dark green of a pine-belt. Next morning there was an answering signal from the swamp where the sumacs grow. Three days later, the hill-sides as far as the eye could range were afire, and the roads paved with crimson and gold." (*Leaves from a Winter Notebook*, 1900.)

in Vermont and New Hampshire. The Columbus Day holiday (second weekend of October) is the most crowded of the year in those tiny states. Hotels and inns tend to have "foliage season rates" that start in mid-September and carry on through mid-October. Of course, there is no promise from Mother Nature that she'll get her paint-brushes out at this time: a dry summer and the leaves could change earlier; a wet summer and the "foliage" could be delayed. To avoid the inevitable

Photographs cannot prepare you for your first sight of New England in September and October. Millions of visitors, "leaf peepers," visit the region every year, with cameras at the ready. Most go by car or on bus tours, but hot-air balloons and river cruise boats also provide a spectacular experience.

Science

Scientists have a clinical explana-tion for the changes. They say that sunny days, allied with chilly nights, stop the production of chlorophyll, the chemical that turns leaves green. This, in turn, allows other pigments such as anthocyanin (red) or carotenoids (orange, yellow) to show through in the leaves. The Native American explanation is far more entertaining: the Great Bear (in the sky) was killed in a hunt, and its blood dripped down onto the leaves. As for the yellow, that was attributed to the fat of the bear splashing out of the cooking pot.

The time

The leaves change color in a tide that sweeps down from north to south, usually starting in late September in Maine, northern Vermont and New Hampshire and reaching Connecticut in the south, around the middle of October. The most intense period is, by tradition, the first two weeks in October, especially

The dazzling colors of fall

crowds, a few visitors gamble and go north to Maine, where the weather might not be so gentle, but the roads are almost certainly quiet. Otherwise, the trick is stay off the main roads, and drift along the twisting country lanes which often have poor or even no signs at all. Take warm clothing; leaf watching is warm in the sun, but can turn chilly by the end of the day.

The trees
The dark green is usually provided by fir and spruce. Scarlet and crimson: dogwood, red (or swamp) maple, sassafras and red oak.
Gold and yellow: poplar, elm, birch and gingko.
Orange: hickory, mountain maple and mountain ash.
Brown: oak.
Purple: sumac.

Hotlines
As well as information on the web, the New England states have special telephone numbers with up-to-date information on the progression of the color, and where to find it. It is also an indicator as to where the most "leaf peepers" are likely to be!

Connecticut (tel: 800/282-6863)
Maine (tel: 800/777-0317)
Massachusetts (tel: 800/227-6277)
New Hampshire (tel: 800/258-3608)
Rhode Island (tel: 401/222-2601)
Vermont (tel: 802/828–3239).

Mountain Inn with memorable views across to Quebec, New York, New Hampshire, and Massachusetts. Cars are warned to have good "brakes, radiators and transmissions" before attempting the drive. Cyclists and sports-car racers frequently test themselves on "hill climbs." The record ascent is just over eight minutes by racing car.

SPECIAL TO...

Roadside stands and stores all sell maple syrup, a product synonymous with Vermont, even though the sticky, sweet liquid from the maple tree is made all over New England. Today, the traditional buckets and wooden sugar-houses of yesteryear have been replaced by plastic tubes inserted directly into the trees. Once the warm sun and cold nights of late winter/early spring cause the colorless liquid to rise, the sap is siphoned off. A good tree produces about 8 gallons (36 liters) per season. The sap is then boiled down to make the caramel-colored sweetener. Anything from 30 to 50 gallons (135 to 225 liters) of sap is needed to make one gallon (4.5 liters) of syrup. Grade A, the most delicately colored and flavored, costs the most, while Grade D would do for baking.

▶ *Continue on Route 7A to Hildene.*

3 Hildene

Robert Todd Lincoln was the son of President Abraham Lincoln. As a child, he visited the Equinox Hotel with his mother, just before his father was assassinated, but only returned to the area many years later. Hildene, Lincoln's summer home, was built in 1904, and it was here that he died in 1926. Lincoln descendants lived here until 1975; the house is filled with authentic memorabilia of the Civil War leader, including Abe's "stovepipe" hat. The stately 24-room Georgian Revival home boasts a huge pipe organ and magnificent grounds. Polo matches are played on summer Sundays and, in winter, the former carriage house is a base for visitors who cross-country ski the 13 miles (21km) of trails. Candlelight tours of the interior are particularly evocative.

▶ *Continue for 2 miles (3km) to Manchester Village.*

4 Manchester Village

There are three Manchesters: Center, Depot, and the oldest and highest, the Village. This is where the rich and powerful summered, either in their own luxury mansions, or at the legendary resort hotel, the Equinox. Dating back to 1769, this splendid Victorian hotel has been expanded and renovated over the years and today has 183 rooms and the renowned par-71 Gleneagles golf course.

▶ *Drive half a mile (800m) into Manchester Center.*

5 Manchester Center

Amid this rural bliss, outlet shopping comes as a shock to some visitors. Despite the out-of-place presence of Armani, Burberry, and Calvin Klein, some small-town charm remains. Down-home favorites such as the Quality Restaurant have served up genuine Vermont cooking for years.

▶ *Drive 2 miles (3km) and turn onto Route 11 east.*

6 Bromley Mountain

The road climbs steadily to Bromley ski area, a pioneer among ski resorts since 1937. Visitors come in summer to try out the alpine slide, the longest of its kind in the U.S.

▶ *Continue on Route 11 east, then turn off to Peru.*

7 Peru

Peru, one of the state's little-known hamlets, was featured in the 1987 film *Baby Boom*, with Diane Keaton. A small woodworking shop shares the street with a church, an antique shop and several lovely homes.

▶ *Return to Route 11, east, and drive to Londonderry. Turn left onto Route 100, north for Weston.*

8 Weston

Weston is well known, not only for its prettiness, but also for the two rival stores across the street from one another. The Vermont Country Store and the Weston Village Store both do everything

The Old Tavern Inn, in the pristine village of Grafton

pleasant shops, and a narrow green. An important business since 1912, the National Survey is a map-making company and shop which has everything to do with cartography.

Chester Depot, the site of the old railway station, is now home to the *Green Mountain Flyer*, a summer tourist train with nice old carriages. The *Flyer* runs up to Bellows Falls through the Brockway Mills Gorge.

[i] *The Green (seasonal)*

▶ Take **Route 35** south for 7 miles (11km) to Grafton.

11 Grafton

In a state of many lovely villages, Grafton is probably the most photogenic of them all. It was once an affluent town on the Boston to Albany post road, with soapstone quarries and a thriving woolen industry, but after the Civil War, its economy collapsed. There was a revival in 1801, when the handsome Old Tavern was built with a California gold miner's money, but by the middle of the century, the village had all but died yet again. Help was at hand, however. In her will, Pauline Fisk instructed her nephews to use her fortune for a good cause of their choice. They came up with the idea of reviving Grafton.

In 1963, the Windham Foundation began the restoration of Grafton's historic charm that draws admiring visitors. For some, the houses are almost too pretty, too perfect for such a rural setting. The village has also revived a former industry: a nutty cheddar-style cheese, made by the Grafton Village Cheese Company. The tiny Village Store also has locally made preserves and hand-knits, and there is a working blacksmith's shop. Two covered bridges complete the scene. On Sunday evenings in summer, the cornet band plays on the green, a tradition dating back to 1867.

but bottle the nostalgia, and both offer an incredible variety of "country" and "Vermont" items that will bring visitors and their wallets to their knees. The circular town green, with its bandstand, inn, and brick church on the hill above, is extremely photogenic. The Weston Playhouse is one of New England's oldest and most popular summer theaters.

Just north of the village is the Benedictine monks' religious community of Weston Priory, a tranquil place where visitors are welcome to join in services and walk in the grounds.

▶ Continue to Ludlow.

9 Ludlow

Where Weston is picture-perfect, Ludlow is full of character, though recent years have brought some gentrification to this former mill town on the banks of the Black River. Here, wool was recycled into inexpensive cloth called "shoddy," which has become a pejorative description for anything cheap.

The mill on Main Street is now a condo and the area has been revitalized. The successful Okemo Mountain resort is widely acknowledged as having the best snow-making and grooming facilities in Vermont.

[i] *Clocktower, Okemo Marketplace, Route 100/103*

▶ Take **Route 103** south for 13 miles (21km) to Chester.

10 Chester

Hidden away in the woods on the way to Chester was the home of Russian Nobel Prize-winner Alexander Solzhenitsyn. He lived here in isolation during his exile from the Soviet Union. The Stone Village on North Street, has, unusually for Vermont, some 30 cottages built of local stone. Dating from before the Civil War, these had hiding places for slaves escaping from the southern states on the so-called Underground Railroad to Canada.

The heart of Chester is the broad main street, with its inns,

▶ *Leave Grafton on **Route 35**
south, which turns briefly into a
dirt road after 6 miles (10km).
At Townsend, take **Route 30**
south for 5 miles (8km) to
Newfane.*

12 Newfane

In summer, Newfane shows off
its classic white Courthouse,
church, and inns, all of which
have gleaming Greek Revival
columns. The long-established
air of the place is deceptive. Two
hundred years ago, the buildings
stood 2 miles (3km) away, on
Newfane Hill. In 1825, the residents moved the town, using the
slippery snow and ice of winter
to slide the beams and boards to
today's site. Jail accommodations
were so comfortable and the
food so palatable that paying
guests were allowed in to enjoy
"good pies and oyster soup"
along with the inmates.
Excellent fare is still a tradition,
with both of the town's inns
renowned for their cuisine.
During the summer, everyone
turns out for the free concerts
on the green. Also popular are
the flea markets held on
Sundays; just outside the village
on Route 30, this is one of
Vermont's biggest and best.

The local museum is easy to
spot, with its early 19th-century
bell standing outside. Inside are
simple memorabilia from the
area – Victorian dresses, old
maps, and a variety of household
items.

Beyond town, Route 30 runs
parallel to the West River, where
rafters and paddlers take up the
challenge of high water in
spring. In summer, the river is
low, but fine for cooling off or
"tubing," floating downstream
in an inner tube.

▶ *Continue on **Route 30** to
Brattleboro.*

13 Brattleboro

Fort Dummer, the first site in
the state to be settled by
Europeans, has now been
covered by the waters of the
nearby dam. Originally, this was
the western frontier of the Bay

Colony, used in defense against
the French and the Indians.

Brattleboro is situated just
down the road. In recent years,
there has been a clean-up of the
town's industrial infrastructure,
centered about the main thoroughfare, Elliott Street. The
former Union Railroad Station is
now the Museum and Art
Center, with five galleries. The
focus here is on contemporary
art and each year there is a
different theme for the regularly
changing exhibitions.

Just north of the town at
Dummerston, in a house called
Naulakha, author Rudyard

Kipling lived and worked from
1892 to 1896, after marrying a
local girl, Carrie Balestier. Books
such as *Captains Courageous*, the
Jungle Books and the *Just So
Stories* were all written here. One
celebrity who never left town
was the notorious 19th-century
swindler Jubilee Jim Fisk.
"Jubilee Jim," who once
cornered the New York gold
market, is buried in the cemetery, with a monument by local
sculptor Larken Mead. Mead
gained true recognition for his
memorial honoring a more
reputable man: he carved the
statue that graces Abraham

Lincoln's tomb in Springfield, Illinois.

▶ *Take **Route 9** west and start climbing into the hills. Pass Whetstone Valley Farm, known for maple sugaring in early spring, to Marlboro (10 miles/16km).*

🄫 Marlboro

The countryside looks attractive today, but back in 1763 it must have been daunting for the European settlers. Two families

Newfane's County Courthouse offers a touch of grandeur

are credited with founding Marlboro, but neither pioneer family knew the other was nearby for over a year. The focus of town is Marlboro College, with its music school founded by pianist Rudolf Serkin. The four-week-long summer chamber music festival is a well established highlight, due to the long residency and efforts of cellist Pablo Casals in its early years.

▶ *Continue west on **Route 9**. After 15 miles (24km), there is a panoramic view from one of the highest points on the road. Continue to Wilmington.*

🄬 Wilmington and Woodford

The alpine-looking village of Wilmington is at the crossroads with Route 100, the north–south route that winds its way through the villages and ski resorts of the Green Mountains. Haystack Mountain and Mount Snow are just to the north.

Route 9 climbs on into the Green Mountain National Forest, passing through Woodford, Vermont's highest village. Prospect Mountain offers hiking opportunities.

▶ *Return to Bennington.*

Central
Vermont

The central part of the state gets busy in winter, due to the appeal of internationally known ski resorts such as Killington. In summer, attractions range from the Quechee Gorge, a sudden tear in the landscape, to Plymouth, the home of Calvin Coolidge. Rutland is nicknamed the "Marble City," because local quarries have provided floors and walls for many of America's grand civic buildings.

1 DAY • 109 MILES • 175KM

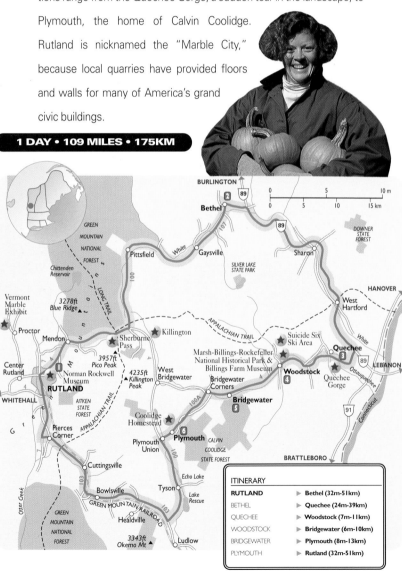

ITINERARY		
RUTLAND	▶	**Bethel (32m-51km)**
BETHEL	▶	**Quechee (24m-39km)**
QUECHEE	▶	**Woodstock (7m-11km)**
WOODSTOCK	▶	**Bridgewater (6m-10km)**
BRIDGEWATER	▶	**Plymouth (8m-13km)**
PLYMOUTH	▶	**Rutland (32m-51km)**

---

i *256 North Main Street*

▶ *Leave Rutland on **Route 4** east. After 2 miles (3km) is the Norman Rockwell Museum on the right.*

❶ Norman Rockwell Museum

Better known collections of the popular illustrator's work can be found in Stockbridge (Massachusetts) and Arlington (Vermont), but you'll find 2,000 reproductions of well-loved covers from magazines such as *Saturday Evening Post*, *Life*, and *Literary Digest* here. There is enough to keep nostalgia hunters interested for an hour or so; some of his illustrations from children's books are also on display. After the museum, the road starts its long climb into the Green Mountains. Just before the Pico/Killington ski area, watch for hikers following the Appalachian Trail and Long Trail which crosses Route 4 but then splits, with the Appalachian Trail heading off to New Hampshire.

▶ *Continue on **Route 4** over the Sherburne Pass, turn onto **Route 100** north, then take **Route 107** to Bethel.*

❷ Bethel

Vermont Castings' popular wood-burning stoves, seemingly essential to any Vermont home, may be seen at Bethel's Brick Store on Main Street. An exhibition at the White River National Fish Hatchery explains an ambitious project to bring back the Atlantic salmon to the Connecticut River. Abundant when the Colonists arrived, the fish have been virtually wiped out by dams, over-fishing, and pollution.

▶ *Follow **Route 107** and turn onto **I–89** south. After 18 miles (29km) take exit 1. **Route 4** leads to Quechee.*

❸ Quechee and Quechee Gorge

Quechee (Kwee-chy) Gorge is 162 feet (49m) deep. Jagged chunks of schist rock protrude from the walls. While the best view of Vermont's "Little Grand Canyon" is from the old railway bridge that spans the ravine, there is also a half-mile (800m) hike to the bottom. The Ottauquechee River that used to drive the woolen mills of Quechee now powers the converted Downer's Mill. It is

Quechee Falls, on the Ottauquechee River

here that Simon Pearce's well-known glass is made. Visitors can watch his craftsmen at work blowing glass. The Irishman opened his studios in 1981 and has since added a restaurant. All around the town are retirement communities.

RECOMMENDED WALKS

Two of the Northeast's most famous hiking trails part company near Pico Peak. The Long Trail runs the length of the state, some 260 miles (416km) from the Massachusetts line to Québec. This "Footpath in the Wilderness," which touches some of the main peaks in the Green Mountains, opened in 1926. The southern part of it overlaps with the even longer Appalachian Trail, which runs from Maine down to Georgia. Be warned! These hikes are only for the hearty. They are administered by the Green Mountain Club, in Waterbury (tel: 802/244–7037) and have simple shelters on the trails.

▶ *Continue on **Route 4** to Woodstock.*

④ Woodstock

This is New England as most people imagine it: a covered bridge, bandstand on the green, shuttered Colonial homes, and an elegant inn. Regularly voted one of America's prettiest towns, Woodstock was one of the first in the state to develop as a two-season resort. In 1934 a Model T Ford car engine, set up at the bottom of a hill, was hooked up to a piece of cable on a wheel and Woodstock had the first ski tow in the U.S.A. The colorfully named Suicide Six Ski Area still tests even the most competent of skiers.

Woodstock has been a cultural center from its early days. One of the most intellectual of all its sons was George Marsh (1801–82), the lawyer, diplomat, and fervent conservationist. His friend, Frederick Billings, promoted modern farming techniques.

The Marsh-Billings-Rockefeller National Historical Park, which opened in 1998, is named in honor of the two, along with Laurence and Mary

Rockefeller, who did so much to shape the landscape we see here today. Tours of the mansion show the countryside in art, with a fine collection of American works, while tours of the surrounding forests interpret the way in which the estate has been managed in order to balance the requirements of woodcrafts, recreation, education and ecology. A splendid new Visitor Center opened in 1999.

The park is in partnership

Everyday exhibits at the Billings Museum, Woodstock
Right: red barns and silos are a common sight in Vermont

with Billings Farm Museum, a working dairy farm where visitors can watch work in progress, including butter churning and ice-cream-making. An excellent introduction to both the park and the farm can be seen in the museum theater, where the Academy Award-nominated film *A Place in the Land* is shown hourly.

Four bells cast by patriotic hero Paul Revere are at the Congregational Church.

▶ *Continue for 6 miles (10km) to Bridgewater.*

⑤ Bridgewater

Bridgewater and its namesakes further upstream, West Bridgewater and Bridgewater Corners, were all mill towns. In Bridgewater itself, one old mill has been turned into an outlet

One of the dozens of Victorian stained-glass windows in Wilson Castle, northwest of Rutland

center for designer clothes, with a crafts center.

The Long Trail Brewing Company has a pub-style visitor center here, where you can sample the brews and have a meal, either inside or on the deck overlooking the river.

▶ *Continue west on **Route 4**. After 2 miles (3km), turn left on **Route 100A** south for Plymouth.*

⑥ Plymouth

Calvin Coolidge (1872–1933), the 30th president of the United States, was born here, the only president born on the Fourth of July. The five-room Coolidge Birthplace, his father's general store next door, the Coolidge Homestead, and the Wilder House, his mother's childhood home, have been kept much as they would have been when Coolidge was a boy. The summer White House, used in 1924 by Coolidge, has been re-created nearby. He and many other Coolidges are buried in Plymouth cemetery. The President's father founded the Plymouth Cheese Company over a century ago; in 1960, a descendant revived the tradition which continues to make cheese on the site.

▶ *Continue on **Route 100A**, then turn left on **Route 100** toward Ludlow, passing the Green Mountain Sugar House. Set on the shore of Echo Lake, the Sugar House is a good place for maple-related products. Turn right on **Route 103** and return to Rutland.*

FOR HISTORY BUFFS

Vermont farms are built to cope with the extremely cold weather. The early settlers soon realized that the less they went outside in winter, the warmer they would stay. The farmhouses were often joined to the barn with a small hallway, an idea developed by the Dutch. In this way, the farmer could tend to his animals without having to go outside.

FOR HISTORY BUFFS

Despite the esteem with which he is held in his native state, Coolidge made his political career in Massachusetts, where he was Governor. Coolidge was visiting his father on the family farm in Plymouth when President Warren Harding died suddenly on August 3, 1923. At 2.47am, Col. John Coolidge took up the old family Bible and, in his role as a justice of the peace, administered the presidential oath to his son. Harding's administration had been tainted by corruption, so Coolidge's frugal New England virtues were welcomed. Famous for his quote that "the business of America is business," Coolidge believed that government should not interfere with industry.

Northern Vermont

In this sparsely populated part of the state, there are a surprising number of attractions.

2 DAYS • 134 MILES • 215KM

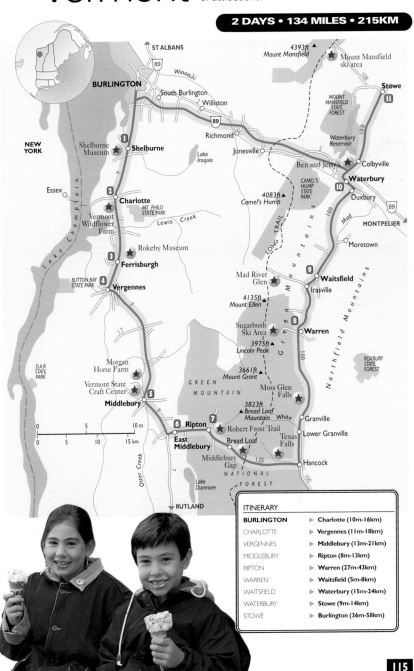

ST ALBANS

4393ft
Mount Mansfield

Mount Mansfield
ski area

NEW YORK

BURLINGTON

Winooski

South Burlington

Williston

89

Stowe

11

MOUNT MANSFIELD STATE FOREST

Richmond

Jonesville

Waterbury Reservoir

Ben and Jerry's

Colbyville

Shelburne Museum

1

Shelburne

Lake Iroqois

Waterbury

10

Essex

Duxbury

89

2

Charlotte

MT PHILO STATE PARK

CAMEL'S HUMP STATE PARK

4083ft
Camel's Hump

MONTPELIER

Vermont Wildflower Farm

Lewis Creek

Moretown

Rokeby Museum

3

Ferrisburgh

Mad River Glen

9

Waitsfield

BUTTON BAY STATE PARK

4

Vergennes

Irasville

4135ft
Mount Ellen

D.A.R STATE PARK

Sugarbush Ski Area

8

Warren

3975ft
Lincoln Peak

ROXBURY STATE FOREST

Morgan Horse Farm

3661ft
Mount Grant

Moss Glen Falls

Vermont State Craft Center

5

GREEN MOUNTAIN

3823ft
Bread Loaf Mountain

White

Granville

Middlebury

6

Ripton

7

Robert Frost Trail

Lower Granville

East Middlebury

Bread Loaf

Texas Falls

Middlebury Gap

Hancock

NATIONAL

Lake Dunmore

FOREST

RUTLAND

0   5   10 m
0   5   10   15 km

ITINERARY

BURLINGTON	▶ **Charlotte** (10m–16km)
CHARLOTTE	▶ **Vergennes** (11m–18km)
VERGENNES	▶ **Middlebury** (13m–21km)
MIDDLEBURY	▶ **Ripton** (8m–13km)
RIPTON	▶ **Warren** (27m–43km)
WARREN	▶ **Waitsfield** (5m–8km)
WAITSFIELD	▶ **Waterbury** (15m–24km)
WATERBURY	▶ **Stowe** (9m–14km)
STOWE	▶ **Burlington** (36m–58km)

ℹ️ *60 Main Street*

▶ *From Burlington, take Route 7 south for 5 miles (8 km) and turn right for Shelburne Farms.*

❶ Shelburne

Most Vermont farms are humble affairs, with red barns, a white silo and a low-slung farmhouse. Shelburne Farms is the opposite, a millionaire's toy built in the 1880s and 1890s on a giant scale and using all the latest technical equipment available. After William Webb married Lila Vanderbilt, daughter of the rail-

Frederick Law Olmsted, the man who landscaped New York's Central Park, to map out their property. Like so many millionaires of the late last century, the Webb's "summer cottage" was extraordinary – a 110-room Queen Anne-style manor house. It is now the Inn at Shelburne Farms. The farm continues to be an experimental and working farm, where visitors can watch cheese-making, bread-baking, and furniture-making. Old-fashioned pleasures such as hay rides will entertain the small children.

When J. Watson Webb, the

Apothecary store, one of the exhibits at Shelburne Museum

road tycoon, they created a European-style estate.

The Webbs called upon

FOR CHILDREN

Children (and lots of adults) always love a boat trip, and there are plenty of opportunities to cruise Lake Champlain. One of the most popular trips is from Burlington Boathouse aboard the *Spirit of Ethan Allen II*, a three-deck cruise ship with narration and on-board meals. Alternatively, you can go your own way. Waterfront Boat Rentals at Shelburne rent canoes, kayaks and motor boats.

SPECIAL TO...

Lake Champlain is shaped like a sausage, 120 miles (192km) long and anything from 400 yards (400m) to 12 miles (19km) wide. Samuel de Champlain, the 17th-century French explorer, recorded seeing a 20-foot-long (6m) serpent with a head like a horse, and visitors have been trying to spot "Champ" ever since. Lake Champlain has four ferry services that cross from Vermont to the New York shores: from Grand Isle to Cumberland Head (12 minutes), from Burlington to Port Kent (an hour), from Charlotte to Essex (20 minutes) and from Larrabee's Point to Ticonderoga (6 minutes).

son of the Webbs of Shelburne Farms, married Electra Havemeyer, they began collecting art objects, large and small, and these now form the remarkable Shelburne Museum. The 37 buildings in which the quilts, paintings, toys, and farm equipment are displayed are themselves collector's items. These buildings, each a historical landmark, have been rescued from all over New England and reassembled. You'll find a schoolhouse, railroad station, general store, barn, jailhouse, and inn, now serving as galleries. Most arresting of all is a boat – the 220-foot (66m) long side-wheel steamer *Ticonderoga*. It was hauled for 2 miles (3km) from Lake Champlain to its final landlocked berth here on the farm. Although the folk art

Church Street market, Burlington

from Burlington to Troy. The old houses in the historic district remain, along with three covered bridges.

Slightly further along Route 7 is the Vermont Wildflower Farm with 6 acres (2.4 hectares) of woodland and flower fields. Self-guided trails explain the folklore of wildflowers and how Native Americans used them for herbal remedies. Visitors can also buy seeds. This stretch of Route 7 has magnificent views across Lake Champlain to the Adirondack Mountains.

▶ *Continue to Ferrisburgh. On a hill to the left is the Rokeby Museum.*

❸ Ferrisburgh
One of the state's underrated museums is the Rokeby, home of the Robinson family for generations. Beautifully furnished, the house is a tribute to their own artistic talents, with portraits and landscapes they have personally painted lining the walls. Rokeby was also one of the last stops on the Underground Railroad, the escape route for black slaves from the American South to Canada. It contains a secret passage and hiding room.

▶ *Continue south to Vergennes.*

❹ Vergennes
Vergennes was named after France's foreign minister, a great supporter of the Americans in the Revolution. It is one of the smallest cities in the country, just one square mile (259 hectares) with 2,500 inhabitants. On Basin Harbor Road, in a 19th-century stone schoolhouse, you'll find Lake Champlain Maritime Museum. During both the Revolution and the War of 1812, American and British warships battled for supremacy on this elongated strip of water. Benedict Arnold (see page 80), later a notorious traitor, delayed the British in 1776 with a series of clever ploys, as explained in

the museum. A full-size replica of his gunboat, the *Philadelphia II*, is the highlight of the visit.

▶ *Continue on **Route 7** south to Middlebury.*

❺ Middlebury
Middlebury is best known for its college, founded in 1800. Visitors who come to admire old buildings such as Painter Hall and the Sheldon Museum use it as a base. For more contemporary culture, the Vermont State Craft Center, in Frog Hollow, on Otter Creek Falls, is a modern showcase for the talents of some 230 artists and craftspeople from all over the state. (There are also branches in Manchester and Burlington.) Across the creek are the old marble works, filled with shops.

Middlebury College claims to be the birthplace of the Frisbee in 1938. Yale students may dispute this (see page 68), but the Vermonters have a handsome statue of a dog leaping to catch a flying disk. It was unveiled in front of Monroe Hall on what they insist was the 50th anniversary of spinning pie dishes at one another.

ℹ️ *2 Court Street*

▶ *Follow **Route 7** south, then turn onto **Route 125** for East Middlebury.*

❻ East Middlebury
Two hundred years ago the hamlet of East Middlebury was

RECOMMENDED WALKS

Split by the Mad River and the Moss Glen Falls, Granville Gulf State Reservation borders the eastern boundary of the Green Mountain National Forest. There is a 6-mile (10km) scenic drive, as well as two hiking trails. The easy 1-mile (1.6km) loop on the east side of the road contrasts with the shorter, but tougher half-mile (800m) hike to the west.

---

collection is justifiably highlighted as one of the finest in the world, the Shelburne art collection is equally impressive. Pieces by American painters Andrew Wyeth and Winslow Homer are on display, as are European artists Rembrandt and Goya. You need a full day here to do justice to the museum.

The town of Shelburne has a more recent industry: the Vermont Teddy Bear Company, which exports its furry friends world-wide. Children can decorate and stuff "new born" bears.

▶ *Continue to Charlotte.*

❷ Charlotte
Pronounced char-LOT, the town's heyday was in the early 19th century, when it was a stage-coach stop on the journey

little more than a spot for stage coaches to Boston to change horses. Then the television cameras arrived to film the hit TV comedy series *Newhart*, starring comedian Bob Newhart, at the Waybury Inn. Rooms in this quaint 1810 inn have been refurbished in period style.

▶ *Continue for 4 miles (6km) to Ripton on **Route 125**, the Robert Frost Memorial Drive.*

7 Ripton

The poet Robert Frost summered in the woods near Ripton for 23 years, and today the mountain to the north is named after him. Just after the

The densely wooded Green Mountains clothed in fall foliage

hamlet of Ripton is a picnic area on the left, and a rough track leading to his cabin. On the other side of the road is the Robert Frost Interpretive Trail, a ¾-mile (1.2km) walk studded with plaques of quotes by the great man.

Seven miles (11km) after leaving Middlebury is the Bread Loaf Campus of Middlebury College. Once a hotel in the shadow of Bread Loaf Mountain, the campus is now well known for its summer writing schools and conferences. In winter it is a base for cross-country skiing.

▶ ***Route 125** climbs steadily, passing Bread Loaf and the Snow Bowl, a local but challenging ski area. Beyond the summit of Middlebury Gap the*

road drops down to Hancock, passing Texas Falls recreation area. At Hancock, turn left on Route 100 north, alongside the White River. After 4 miles (6km) is Granville, and another 10 miles (16km) further turn right to Warren and Mad River Valley.

8 Warren

Despite the popularity of the neighboring Sugarbush Resort ski area, Warren has changed little. The simple exterior of the Warren Store belies a sophisticated little emporium of gourmet foods and fine wines for the city folk who visit. Simpler pleasures survive, such as glider rides from the little airport.

Just north of Warren is the left turn for Sugarbush, the heart of one of Vermont's premier ski destinations. Opened in 1958, this affluent resort has expensive condominiums and a busy restaurant scene. Vermont's third highest peak, Mount Ellen (4,135 feet/1,260m), and Lincoln Peak (3,975 feet/1,211m) are the two mountains that provide the ski thrills. In summer, golfers test themselves on the course designed by Robert Trent Jones, Sr. There are also tennis courts.

▶ *Continue to Waitsfield.*

9 Waitsfield

The Mad River Glen Ski Resort is smaller, older and less formal than the nearby Sugarbush Resort, but it offers more challenging runs for the advanced skier. Mad River Valley also attracts cross-country enthusiasts, thanks to a total of four cross-country touring centers. As for Waitsfield, what was once a lumber and dairy town a long time ago is now a destination both in winter and summer. First there are the shops selling the work of local artists and craftsmen; then there is the photogenic old covered bridge.

Nearby, the Vermont Icelandic Horse Farm is a treat for small children.

▶ *Take Route 100 north to Waterbury (15miles/24km). Ben and Jerry's is 1 mile (1.6km) north of I–89.*

10 Waterbury

Waterbury means just one thing to ice cream aficionados: Ben and Jerry's. Ben Cohen and Jerry Greenfield's rags-to-riches story is the American dream, set deep in the Vermont countryside. In 1977, they started by producing home-made ice cream in Burlington, in a disused and dismantled service station. These days, the factory is in Waterbury, where tours with free tastings are a constant draw. In summer, old-fashioned ice cream machines and real cows, ready for milking, keep children entertained.

Waterbury has expanded to include other tasty attractions: the Lake Champlain Chocolate Co., and the Cold Hollow Cider Mill, with its excellent pure pressed apple juices. The Green Mountain Club, half way to Stowe, administers the Long Trail and other outdoor activities.

▶ *Continue to Stowe, then follow Route 108 to the Mount Mansfield Ski Area.*

11 Stowe

The Stowe ski area on Mount Mansfield is one of New England's premier ski resorts, built on Mount Mansfield, Vermont's highest peak (4,393 feet/1,338m). In summer, a gravel toll road, the Stowe Auto Road, leads to the summit, a 4½-

Low mist over Stowe, the main skiing and recreation center for this popular area

mile (7km) journey. This steep route, with numerous steep, tight curves, is a test of both car and driver. For a more relaxed journey use the Stowe Gondola, a half-hour scenic swing over the forested slopes. With tennis courts, a golf course and In-Line Skate Park, this is a summer destination for the active.

Another attraction is the Trapp Family Lodge in Stowe, built by the real-life family of *The Sound of Music* fame. A new attraction is the Vermont Ski Museum, which traces the century-old history of the sport in the state. Inside the 1818 Old

Town Hall, Vermont's first single chair, double chair, quad chair and gondola hang from the ceiling, like a mobile, above old photos and memorabilia.

ⓘ *Main Street, Stowe*

▶ *Return on* **Route 100** *to* **I–89**; *drive northwest to Burlington.*

RECOMMENDED WALKS

The Stowe Recreation Path is a 5-mile (8km) trail alongside a mountain stream. Undulating gently, and carefully cleared in winter, this trail is used for walking, cross-country skiing and snowshoeing and is a tribute to the generosity of local residents, who have donated the right of way past meadows, woods, and cornfields for visitors to cross their land.

SPECIAL TO...

Justin Morgan was a Vermont teacher who created the country's first horse breed. A hardy colt called Figure was born in 1793, a mixture of Arabian and thoroughbred. The Morgan, as it became known, with its deep chest and powerful hindquarters, stands some 14 to 15 hands (1.42–1.52m) high.

Usually long-lived, mildmannered, and bay in color, this multi-use equine was a boon to the army, who rode it and also used this hardy breed to pull guns and equipment. Now owned by the University of Vermont and open to the public, the Morgan Horse Farm is 2 miles (3km) north of Middlebury. The grounds are immaculate, with a slate-roofed 19th-century barn, lush meadows, and parade grounds, and is home to the 70 stallions, mares, and foals.

FOR CHILDREN

Stowe is a wonderful area for children with an adventurous spirit. They can hurtle 2,300 feet (700m) down Spruce Peak on the Alpine Slide, for instance, or speed around the Launch Zone Skate Park's ramps and street scenes on skates, skateboards or BMX bikes.

There are miles of mountain bike trails in the area, and younger children will love the public playground at the Stowe Elementary School. Local children raised the funds for it, including a donation from "Superman" (actor Christopher Reeve).

NEW HAMPSHIRE

New Hampshire's nickname is the "Granite State." Some say it refers to the rocky scenery, others maintain it describes the implacable nature of the residents. Certainly, the terrain is the very opposite of the English county that lent it its name. New Hampshire has only an 18-mile (29km) strip of Atlantic coastline, and a mere 80 miles (128km) away are the White Mountains, the tallest in New England. Hundreds of lakes, often bearing the Indian names given by earlier residents – Sunapee, Winnipesaukee and Squam – are scattered throughout the thick pine forests. Sixty covered bridges stretch across tumbling streams.

The Kancamagus Highway, in the White Mountains, is famous for its fall foliage

The early settlers were "economic refugees," who had left Europe to make a better life rather than to find religious freedom. The land and climate made the early days a struggle. Later, the Scots-Irish added their resolute character to the New Hampshire persona. Today, car license plates bear the state motto: "Live Free or Die." The rest of this Revolutionary rallying cry is "death is not the worst of evils." The fiery words are attributed to farmer-turned-general, John Stark, one of the New Hampshire men who formed the backbone of the American troops in the early days of the Revolution.

Today, the politics in New Hampshire are notably "grass-roots," with the 221 townships often regarded as "little republics." The state scorns income tax and sales tax, preferring to raise money by taxing liquor and betting. This tax – or lack of tax – structure has attracted businesses to move across the state line from Massachusetts. Shoppers also drive over the border from neighboring states to load up and save money. Since most of the one million inhabitants cluster near the Massachusetts border, the rest of the state seems sparsely populated. While agriculture has long been a mainstay of the economy, it has been the fast-flowing streams driving machinery that have benefited residents most. Towns like Manchester may not manufacture locomotives and fire engines any longer, but plastics, electronics, and paper products have successfully taken their place.

Tour 18

Portsmouth, New Hampshire's port, is wedged between Massachusetts and Maine. Forty years ago it was a rundown city, a place to escape rather than a tourist destination. However, the residents recognized the rich history beneath the dirt – instead of tearing down the old buildings, they started a major restoration project. Now the merchants' houses and warehouses, meeting houses and bankers' offices are the attractive heart of the city and a source of civic pride. Small parks and museums reflect Portsmouth's role as a ship-building center, others are filled with fine antique American furniture. Best known is Strawbery Banke, a collection of houses that show what everyday life was like over a period of four centuries.

Above: Strawbery Banke
Below: The Flume, a giant chasm where a mountain stream tumbles in a series of waterfalls

Tour 19

The White Mountains are a popular destination all year round. The focus is Mount Washington, first climbed by a European 350 years ago. It is now deluged by 250,000 enthusiastic tourists every summer. A cog railroad crawls its way up to the top. Those wanting to avoid the "madding crowds" can explore the numerous well-marked trails throughout the mountains, either for a day hike or a longer trek. In winter, "the Whites" attract both downhill and cross-country skiers. The spectacular scenery on this route includes "the Kanc," the famous Kancamagus Highway, one of America's prettiest drives.

Tour 20

Since 1981, Squam Lake has become a "must see" for fans of the film *On Golden Pond*. Nearby, larger Lake Winnipesaukee has long been a popular destination for summer visitors wishing to escape the heat and humidity of Boston. The western shore has become over-popular and built-up, but for the most part, this is a peaceful drive, with villages, craft shops, and museums en route. Anyone interested in top-quality crafts should plan to spend time in Center Sandwich, while Meredith is best known for its dolls.

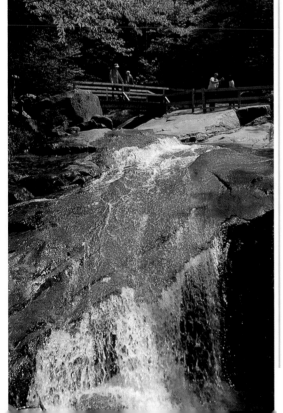

Portsmouth

Portsmouth has one of New England's finest natural harbors and became wealthy on the timber trade, exporting lumber to Britain and the West Indies. Huge fortunes were made and spent on grandiose mansions, many of which still stand. A massive preservation program over recent decades has saved numerous fine buildings, making this a city for anyone interested in the architecture and craftsmanship of 18th- and 19th-century America.

HALF A DAY

i *500 Market Street*

▶ *Start at Market Square, the heart of the city.*

❶ Market Square
The lottery may seem a new idea but it has long been a means of raising money. Back in 1762, the militia's training ground was paved with funds from a public lottery. The Athenaeum, at No. 9, was originally the headquarters of a fire and marine insurance company, but became a private library in 1823. The classic pointed spire of North Church can be seen from anywhere in the downtown area, especially when it is illuminated at night. On the east side of the square stands the impressive wall of Bankers Row, the guardians of civic wealth for

The John Paul Jones House, where the Scots-born navy officer lived

nearly 200 years. No. 24/26 is thought to be the oldest bank in America, and it was extensively rebuilt in 1904.

▶ *Leave Market Square, heading south on Pleasant Street. Turn right on State Street.*

❷ State Street
Contrasting with the elegant white spire of North Church is the squat tower of South Church, at No. 292. This solid-looking granite building dates from 1826 and is still used for worship by the Unitarian Universalists. Nearby was the starting point of the 1813 fire, which blazed toward the waterfront. Some houses survived, only to be lost to a 1950s urban planning project. Still standing is the Abraham Shaw House (1810) at No. 379. A few doors further on is the Rockingham Hotel (No. 401), whose lions

RECOMMENDED TRIP

Just off the coast are nine islands, the Isles of Shoals, partly in Maine, partly in New Hampshire. Take a picnic on the delightful one-hour boat ride. Visit Star, an island used as a church retreat which also has the Vaughan Cottage Memorial and Celia Turner Museum, or Appledore, once an artists' colony.

became the personal emblem of Frank Jones, a flamboyant brewer and entrepreneur whose bust is on the right. He turned the hotel into "the most elegant and superbly furnished establishment ... outside of Boston."

▶ *At the corner of State and Middle streets is Haymarket Square, with its enclave of elegant homes. At No. 43 Middle Street is the John Paul Jones House.*

❸ John Paul Jones House
Scottish-born John Paul Jones is known as the "father of the U.S. Navy." He did not own this handsome clapboard house, but rented rooms from Mrs. Sarah Purcell. The naval hero was in Portsmouth in 1777 to supervise the fitting out of the *Ranger*, and once again in 1781, for the building of the *America*. The house is now the headquarters of the local historical society.

▶ *Turn south on Middle Street. Cross the square to No. 18 Court Street.*

❹ John Peirce Mansion
This is "the best" of the city's 19th-century houses, according to some critics. No expense was spared when Peirce built this home in 1799. It was handed down through the family for generations until 1955, when the Baptist Church bought the property.

▶ *Two blocks further along Middle Street is No. 364.*

5 Rundlet-May House

James Rundlet started out as a farm boy but ended up a wealthy man. With the money he made from importing textiles and wallpaper, he built this mansion in 1807. The garden, pet cemetery, and stables add an extra dimension to the period furniture.

▶ *Retrace your steps to Court Street; bear right and walk two blocks to Pleasant Street. On the corner of Pleasant and Court streets is No. 93 Pleasant Street.*

6 Ann Treadwell Mansion

This house was built to comply with the 1814 law specifying that structures of more than one story had to be made of brick. The previous year, yet another fire had taken its toll, this time along Court Street, with hundreds of houses ruined.

▶ *Retrace your steps. Cross Court Street, then go south on Pleasant Street to No. 143.*

7 Governor Langdon House

John Langdon was one of New Hampshire's founding fathers who made his money in ship-building and buying and selling goods captured from the British.

Langdon became President of the Senate, delegate to the Constitutional Convention of 1787, and finally state governor for three terms. He built this mansion, one of the finest in New England, and the garden to impress, and it still does today. Note the exquisitely carved pale green fireplace in the drawing-room, where Langdon hosted parties. One guest was President George Washington, who commented that, among the town's houses "Col. Langdon's may be esteemed the finest."

▶ *Walk next door to No. 145.*

8 Thomas Thompson House

Portsmouth's importance to the New Hampshire economy is reflected in the state seal and flag, which show shipbuilders at work on a frigate. The first frigate was the *Raleigh*, often called the "first ship in the U.S. Navy." Its owner, Thomas Thompson, erected this house in 1784, and his business partner, John Langdon, put up his mansion next door a year later.

▶ *Continue on Pleasant Street, then bear left on Gates Street.*

Portsmouth lies on the banks of the Piscataqua River

9 Gates Street

James T. Fields (1817–81), the publisher of *The Atlantic Monthly* magazine, gave American writers a boost onto the world literary stage. He was born and lived in the house at 83/85 Gates Street. A few doors down, No. 130 is another fine old place, built as early as 1731 by the Peirce family. This street was one of the first to be saved back in the 1960s rebirth of Portsmouth.

▶ *Turn right on Manning Street, then left at the Children's Museum. Cross Marcy Street to Hunking Street. Turn left on Mechanic Street and walk to No. 50.*

FOR CHILDREN

Portsmouth has a long history of building warships. At Albacore Park, there is a rare chance to explore a submarine, the 205-foot (61m) long USS *Albacore*. The cramped space did not allow room for beds for each of the crew, so, men "hot bunked": when one shift finished, they slept in the bunks of those going on duty. The submarine never fired a shot in anger.

10 Wentworth Gardner House

Tiled fireplaces, fine carving, and paneling make this a "must" for those interested in 18th-century craftsmanship. The owner, Thomas Wentworth, was the younger brother of the last royal governor of New Hampshire.

► Continue on Mechanic Street which bears left; turn right on Marcy Street.

11 Liberty Pole

Colonials showed dissent by putting up a liberty pole on their village or town green. The residents of Portsmouth first did this in 1766, to protest against the infamous Stamp Act. The pole became a permanent reminder of that feisty spirit in 1824. Each season, the gardens in Prescott Park are planted with varieties developed by botanists from the University of New Hampshire.

► Across from the liberty pole is Strawbery Banke.

12 Strawbery Banke

Close to the waterfront, the site of the original 1630 settlement is now one of America's finest outdoor museums. Some 40 buildings, examples of Portsmouth's architecture from 1695 to World War II, stand on this 10-acre (4-hectare) site, once a slum. It all comes colorfully to life, with the blacksmith, potter, and boatbuilder working at their trades. A favorite spot is the 1766 William Pitt Tavern, which

> **SPECIAL TO…**
>
> When English settlers arrived in 1623, the meadows running down to the Piscataqua River were so thick with strawberries they called their new home Strawbery Banke. Thirty years later, with shipbuilding becoming the established industry, they changed the name to the more appropriate Portsmouth.

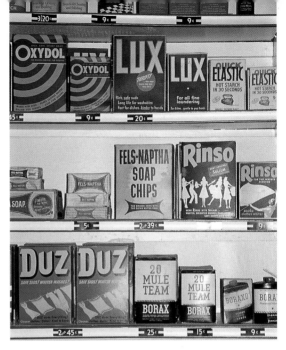

The Old Country Store at Strawbery Banke

shows the role of the pub in everyday life. The newest building is Abbott's Market (1943), complete with products on the shelves from that era.

► Continue on Marcy Street to the end. Turn left, then right across the parking lot to No. 150 Daniel Street.

13 Warner House

The oldest brick house in town was once part of a row of splendid brick mansions built around 1716. The museum-quality furniture behind the 18-inch (45cm) walls was used by the same family for two centuries, while the hall staircase is covered with extensive murals. These murals, possibly the oldest in the country, date from 1720, and include biblical scenes and portraits of two Mohawk Indians. A lightning conductor set into the west wall was supposedly installed by the inventor Benjamin Franklin.

► Turn right on Chapel Street.

14 St. John's Church

Designed by Alexander Parris to replace a church burned in the fire of 1806, St. John's boasts America's oldest working organ,

the Brattle Organ, as well as splendid *trompe-l'oeil* paintings of biblical scenes.

► Continue on Chapel Street to Bow Street. Turn left, then right on Ceres Street. At the end, take the steps to No. 154 Market Street.

15 Moffatt-Ladd House

Little imagination is needed here to visualize the life of a wealthy Portsmouth family. The Moffatts built their home in 1763 directly across from their warehouses. The counting house next door, with its wall safe, was a more recent addition – in 1830. Now a museum, family mementos range from wedding dresses and portraits, to jewelry and silver. Two inventories of household goods in the late 18th century provided the curators with the details to re-create the Moffatt home, where the family lived until 1913. The beautiful gardens are a highlight: the plan is 18th-century but the interpretation is 19th-century.

► Return to Market Square via Market Street.

Seats are limited on the Mount Washington Cog Railway, so advance booking is recommended

Next to the base of the tramway is the New England Ski Museum. Echo Lake, a little further on, is a natural mirror, reflecting Cannon Mountain and Mount Lafayette in its still waters. The energetic can cycle through the Notch on the 8-mile (13km) bike path which passes most of the attractions.

▶ Continue on Franconia Notch State Parkway, which becomes I–93 again. Take exit 38 for Franconia.

8 Franconia

Once a flourishing resort, Franconia has seemingly gone back to sleep. It has been overtaken by the more ambitious towns south of the Notch. Poetry lovers drop by the Robert Frost Place, the 150-year-old, white clapboard hillside farmhouse to which Frost returned in 1915, upon his homecoming from England. Aged 40 and still virtually unknown, he farmed the land, wrote three books of verse and won a Pulitzer prize, all in the next five years. Visitors can see his writing desk, signed first editions and a rare collection of his Christmas card

SCENIC ROUTES

On Route 302, toward Bretton Woods, is the Mount Washington Cog Railway, the most popular way to reach the top of New England's highest peak.

On Mount Washington's western slope is the world's first mountain-climbing railway, a miracle of engineering. Built in 1869 at a cost of $139,500, and powered by a roaring coal-fired steam engine, it is still the second steepest of its kind in the world, and uses a toothed wheel-and-ratchet mechanism designed by Herrick and Walter Aiken and Sylvester March. The round trip takes three hours, grinding along at about 4mph (6km/h), up gradients of 37 percent at their steepest.

5 Gorham

Gorham is a useful stop for those who are keen on wildlife. At dawn and dusk, guides take visitors on a two-hour explanatory Moose Tour in search of these big beasts, which are abundant in the woods.

▶ *Leave town on* **Route 16** *south to Glen House, at the foot of Mount Washington.*

FOR CHILDREN

Six Gun City, well signposted between Routes 115 and 2, is a theme park dedicated to the Wild West. It has a dozen rides, including the Tomahawk Run Waterslide. Youngsters can see the usual cowboy riding stunts, help the sheriff to capture outlaws, and have fun in Fort Splash water play area.

Nearby is Santa's Village, which promotes Christmas in high summer with themed rides, such as the Yule Log Flume and Santa's Express Train, as well as seasonal shows.

poems. In summer, there are readings by a poet in residence and a Festival of Poetry in late July and early August. A half-mile (800m) nature trail, highlighted with plaques along the way, presents 15 of Frost's favorite poems.

Inset: a young moose

ago. Back then, thousands flocked here by train. The air was so clean and clear of pollution that the National Hay Fever Relief Association was started here in the 1920s. Now, apart from its antique shops, Bethlehem is a base for touring and hiking.

▶ *Return to* **I–93** *and drive 6 miles (10km) to exit 40 for Bethlehem. Turn on to* **Route 302** *east.*

4 Bethlehem

The little town of Bethlehem is more Victorian-looking than Colonial, reflecting its heyday as a vacation destination a century

▶ *Stay on* **Route 302** *east for 8 miles (13km) to Twin Mountain. Turn left onto* **Route 3**. *At Carroll, take the* **115** *through Meadows, then join* **Route 2** *and head east to Gorham.*

⑥ Mount Washington

Mount Washington is the tallest mountain in the East, at 6,288 feet (1,916m). A road and railway allow visitors access to the bare granite summit. On the eastern face of the mountain, at Glen House, about 8 miles (13km) south of Gorham, is the start of the 8-mile (13km) toll road to the top and an audio tour, on CD or cassette, gives you an in-car commentary. Built back in 1861, the road is advertised as America's first man-made attraction. Six horses used to pull a wagon full of tourists up the grade, which still averages 12 percent. Today, large vans provide the same service. Bolder folk drive up, a test of their automobiles and their nerves.

The top is surprisingly busy with radio and TV transmitters, an observatory, and the Summit Building, with its glassed-in viewing area. At the peak is the old Tip Top House, a hotel built in 1853. There is also a museum of mountain memorabilia and local wildlife.

the SnowCoach trip up the mountain.

▶ *Continue for 13 miles (21km), then take the left-hand turn on **Route 16A** to detour into the town of Jackson.*

⑦ Jackson

Jackson, a town with a mere 700 inhabitants, offers skiing – downhill and cross-country. The Attitash, Black, Wildcat, and

---

SPECIAL TO...

The Jackson Ski Touring Foundation is dedicated to cross-country skiers. An unusual co-operative effort by the towns of Jackson and Bartlett has produced a network of some 100 miles (160km). The Ellis River Trail (5 miles/8km) is ideally flat for beginners. By contrast, the Wildcat ski area offers 11 miles (18km) of expert cross-country runs.

---

⑧ Glen

As well as being a resort town, Glen has two attractions that come into their own in unfriendly weather. Heritage New Hampshire, a museum/theme park, is a 300-year journey through the state's history, from the first European settlements in 1634, through two revolutions – the American and the industrial. Actors explain their lives and simulated train rides add to the interest. Story Land, a well thought-out theme park, is aimed at a younger audience. There are re-creations of fairy-tales, and rides and flumes.

▶ *Continue to North Conway.*

⑨ North Conway

With no sales tax and an outlet strip mall 3 miles (5km) long, shopping is the number one sport in this popular small town. It's all a far cry from the days when artists would flock to paint Thompson's Falls. The 1874 railway station, North Conway Depot, has survived with much

Summer skiers willing to endure the tough hike can test themselves on the dangerous chutes and headwall of the Tuckerman's Ravine nearby. Skiing on July 4 is a traditional challenge among the hard-core skiers. At the base of the mountain is the Great Glen Trails Outlook Center, with a vast trail system for mountain-biking and hiking. In winter, there is cross-country skiing, snowshoeing and

Fun and fantasy at Story Land

Cranmore mountains offer more than 100 trails, enough to satisfy all levels of ability from mogul masters to modest beginners. Strict controls on building have kept this a picturesque village, with an emphasis on lodging and dining, rather than shopping, motels, and fast food.

▶ *Continue south to Glen.*

of its Victorian ambience, including the wind-up brass clock, the Telegraph Office, and the separate men's and women's waiting rooms. Now the Conway Scenic Railroad, with its Pullman carriages, runs from here for 11 miles (18km) alongside the Saco River to Conway or through spectacular Crawford Notch. A little way north of the village, the Weather Discovery Center, run by the Mount Washington Observatory, is a new attraction. Computer-based interactive displays and audio-visual presentations give a fun insight into the laws of meteorology and how weather affects us.

▶ *Continue south and turn west onto **Route 112**, the 37-mile (59km) long Kancamagus Highway to Lincoln.*

⑩ **Kancamagus Highway**
Following alongside the rushing Swift River, "the Kanc" is New England's only designated National Scenic Byway – there are no private homes, service stations, or other encroachments to spoil the views. The 34.5-mile (55km) stretch of road, from Conway to the Pemigewasset River, climbs to 3,000 feet (900m) on the way, and honors New Hampshire's legendary Indian chief Kancamagus (The Fearless One). He was the grandson of Passaconaway (Child of the Bear) who united and ruled the local tribes from 1627 to 1669. All along the road are Scenic Areas, places to stop. The best known spots include Sabbaday Falls, a short walk from the road, and the Lower Falls and Rocky Gorge, where you can bathe in the pools and sunbathe on the small beaches.

⑪ **Lincoln**
The ski resort of Loon Mountain has transformed Lincoln into a busy year-round resort. The skyride, with its four-passenger gondola, is as attractive in summer as in winter, gliding to the summit with its walking trails and glacial caves. Other popular attractions

include the Whale's Tale Waterpark, with its variety of rides on land and in water, and the less frantic Hobo Railroad, which trundles through the Pemi River Valley for 15 miles (24km).

▶ *Return on **I-93** south, 25 miles (40km) to Plymouth.*

The Kancamagus Highway

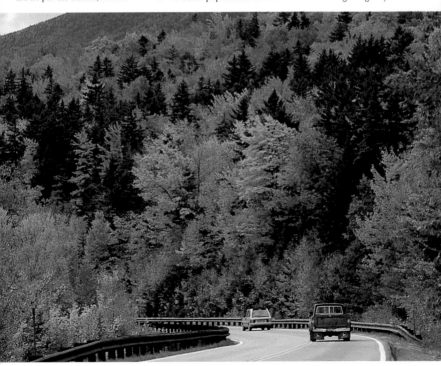

1 DAY • 106 MILES • 169KM

Around Lake
Winnipesaukee

Lake Winnipesaukee is huge, the sixth largest body of water inside the country. The Native American name is "The Smile of the Great Spirit," though some experts prefer the more prosaic translation of "Beautiful Water in a High Place."

North Sandwich

WHITE LAKE STATE PARK

Squam Mountains

Center Sandwich ⑨

Bearcamp Pond

West Ossipee

25

Sandwich

16

Squam Lakes Natural Science Center ★

113

Squam Lake

25

Ossipee Mountains

Ossipee Lake

PLYMOUTH

93

Holderness ②

Moultonborough ④

2975ft ▲ Mount Shaw

Little Squam Lake

East Holderness

Center Harbor

★ Castle in the Clouds

① Ashland

Newfound Lake

25

171

Melvin Village

Lake Waukewan

Meredith ⑧

Mirror Lake

WENTWORTH STATE PARK

Pemigewasset

Weir's Beach ⑦

Lake Winnipesaukee

★ Libby Museum

Paugus Bay

Lake Wentworth

Winnisquam Lake

93

★ Ellacoya State Beach

Wolfeboro ⑤

Wright Museum ★

South Wolfeboro

Smith Point

West Alton

28

Laconia

East Alton

0   5   10 m
0   5   10   15 km

140

Alton Bay ⑥

Merrymeeting Lake

Alton

CONCORD

Gilmanton

ITINERARY		
PLYMOUTH	▶	**Ashland (7m-11km)**
ASHLAND	▶	**Holderness (4m-6km)**
HOLDERNESS	▶	**Center Sandwich (12m-19km)**
CENTER SANDWICH	▶	**Moultonborough (5m-8km)**
MOULTONBOROUGH	▶	**Wolfeboro (17m-27km)**
WOLFEBORO	▶	**Alton Bay (13m-21km)**
ALTON BAY	▶	**Weir's Beach (22m-35km)**
WEIR'S BEACH	▶	**Meredith (8m-13km)**
MEREDITH	▶	**Plymouth (18m-29km)**

_i_ *Lakes Region Association, exit 23, off I-93*

▶ *Start in Plymouth and take I-93 south to exit 24 for Ashland.*

❶ Ashland

The small town of Ashland, once an important stop on the old Boston, Concord and Montreal Railroad line, retains the character of an old mill town. The Ashland Historical Society is based in the former home of Dr. George Whipple, the pathologist who won the Nobel prize for medicine in 1934. Next door, the Pauline Glidden Toy Museum has more than 1,000 early toys. A local resident, the late Milton Graton, was one of New England's experts on the restoration and building of covered bridges. His last was built here in his home town, where his son Arnold continues the tradition.

▶ *Continue on **Route 3** to Holderness.*

❷ Holderness

Holderness sits on Little Squam Lake; to the east is the much larger Squam Lake. The Academy Award-winning 1981 film *On Golden Pond*, starring Katherine Hepburn and Henry Fonda, was filmed here, catapulting Squam Lake to fame, even though the film was supposedly set in Maine. Small boats cruise the peaceful lake and delight in showing visitors where the scenes were shot. It is a favorite nesting place for loons.

▶ *Follow **Route 113** for Center Sandwich (12 miles/19km). Pass Squam Lake.*

❸ Center Sandwich

Sitting between the Squam Mountains and Squam Lake, this is one of several Sandwich villages in the area. New England poet John Greenleaf Whittier (1807–92) spent time in Center Sandwich. This crusading Quaker championed the anti-slavery cause and used poetry in his emotional campaigns:
"What! mothers from their children riven!
What! God's own image bought and sold!
Americans to market driven,
And bartered as the brute for gold!"

Whittier wrote *Sunset* on the Bearcamp, the river which runs through Bearcamp Pond between Center Sandwich and North Sandwich. The Whittier covered bridge crosses the river in West Ossipee.

SPECIAL TO...

Peace and quiet attracted artists to the rural community of Center Sandwich. Sandwich Home Industries, an early collective, opened in 1926 with the aim of helping local craftspeople supplement their incomes. This lead to the founding of the League of New Hampshire Craftsmen, known for its six shops in the state and an annual fair, the oldest in the country, held in August at Mount Sunapee.

BACK TO NATURE

The Squam Lakes Natural Science Center is just to the east of Holderness and enables visitors to observe wild animals such as otters, deer, bears, and various birds of prey. All are unable to live in their natural habitats, due to injury. Follow the ¾-mile (1.2km) nature trail, and try the hands-on puzzles in the children's activity center.

Aerial view of the turreted hilltop Castle in the Clouds

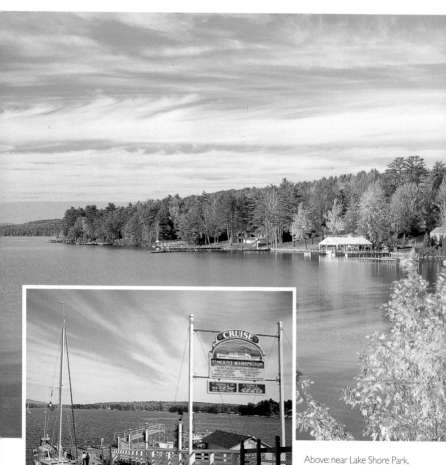

Above: near Lake Shore Park, Lake Winnipesaukee
Inset: Weir's Beach

▶ *Drive south on **Route 109** for 5 miles (8km) to Moultonborough.*

❹ Moultonborough

This typical New England village has the bonus of the lake as a backdrop. Apart from its idyllic setting, the big attraction is "Castle in the Clouds," a reminder of the astonishing wealth garnered a century ago. Set 750 feet (225m) up in the Ossipee Mountains, this mock castle and its extensive estate offers spectacular views. Millionaire Thomas Plant, who made his money from shoes, designed the $7 million house

himself, which explains the variety of architectural styles, from Swiss chalet to Norman castle. A touch of English Tudor is the *coup de grâce*. It was built by hundreds of craftsmen, including Italian stone masons brought over from Europe. Water from a spring on the grounds is bottled commercially. The nearby Loon Center and Markus Wildlife Sanctuary specializes in New Hampshire's ecology.

▶ *Continue south on **Route 109** for 17 miles (27km) to Wolfeboro. The route passes through Melvin Village, known for its antique shops. Continue along the shores of Winnipesaukee, through Mirror Lake.*

❺ Wolfeboro

Just before Wolfeboro, on the edge of Mirror Lake, is the Libby Museum, which explains the story of this hamlet and America's oldest resort. Back in 1768, Massachusetts Governor John Wentworth ordered a summer house here. To reach the house from Portsmouth, he even had the "Governor's Road" built. The retreat burned down in 1820, and is now the site of an archeological dig in Wentworth State Park, 6 miles (10km) east of town.

The Wright Museum, in Wolfeboro, charts the story of America during World War II. As well as its collection of military vehicles, the museum reflects life on the home front, with room settings, costumes and other period items.

▶ Take *Routes 28* and *28A* south for 13 miles (21km) to Alton Bay, right at the foot of Lake Winnipesaukee.

6 Alton Bay

The little town of Alton Bay has much of the appearance it must have enjoyed in its summer heydays. There is a floating bandstand out in the bay, and the railroad station has been spruced up. Scenic lake cruises depart from the docks.

▶ Follow *Route 11* northwest. This side of the lake is much more open, affording great views of the water and to the White Mountains in the north. Weir's Beach is 22 miles (35km) farther on via the Ellacoya State Beach, where you get a sense of how large Lake Winnipesaukee really is. Continue to Weir's Beach.

7 Weir's Beach

Weir's Beach is the Coney Island of the region with amusement parks, crowded boardwalks, beaches, and a weekly fireworks display. One of New England's last drive-in movie theaters is here too. It is especially busy when the annual motorbike races take place for one week in June in nearby Loudon. Weir's Beach has two waterslide parks, but tamer rides are also avail-able, such as the scenic railroad along the lakeshore. Another good way to beat the crowds is to take a cruise on the lake, either for its simple scenic value, or to appreciate the wildlife on a special nature cruise.

▶ Take *Route 3* north to Meredith (8 miles/13km).

8 Meredith

Quieter than Weir's Beach, with pretty docks and landings on the lake, Meredith is the home of the popular felt Annalee Dolls. Annalee Thorndike created these cutesy dolls in 1934 and now the factory is a major local employer. The dolls are bought by fans and collectors from all over the world. There is also a museum dedicated to them, which includes the first doll and some valuable pre-war models.

▶ Return to Plymouth via *Route 3* through Holderness and I-93.

MAINE

The Algonquin Indians called this region the "Land of the Frozen Ground" and the summer season is certainly the shortest here in New England, barely covering June through September. No-one knows how or why Maine received its present name. What is known is that it could swallow up the rest of the New England states. One single county, Aroostook, is bigger than the states of Connecticut and Rhode Island combined. Yet the population is only 1,200,000, mostly in the south and along the coast.

Residents and visitors alike come to Maine to enjoy the unspoiled natural beauty. Geographers estimate that the 230-mile (368km) long coastline would stretch to 3,500 miles (5,600km) if every cove and inlet were measured. Drive down the fingers of land that jut into the sea to find old fishing villages, quiet inlets, and rocky cliffs. Offshore lie around 2,000 islands, some linked to the mainland by ferry, the majority barely habitable, and all surrounded by treacherous rocks and ice-cold water.

View over Camden Harbor

The coast is the biggest draw and some parts, such as Oqunquit and Boothbay Harbor, become quite crowded in season. Getting away from it all, however, is easy since 90 percent of the state is wilderness and forest. Maine attracts hikers and canoeists into its hinterland with 32,000 miles (51,200km) of river and 6,000 ponds and lakes dotted around. There are few people, but thousands of moose.

Although many experts assume that the Vikings could have paid a visit a thousand years ago, it was the French and English who first settled here. In 1677, the territory was assigned to Massachusetts, but in the early 19th century, when that state began to struggle economically, it cut the ties and Maine became a state in its own right.

Maine's nickname, the "Pine Tree State," is appropriate. Not only is the coastline wooded, there are vast forests inland. The tall, strong pines once provided masts for the British Navy; now, they are made into paper and pulp. Shipbuilding started in 1607, in Bath, and continues there today.

Lighthouses stand as symbols of New England's maritime history
Left: L. L. Bean, Freeport

galleries. Much of the handsome brick and granite architecture post-dates the devastating fire of 1866, and some earlier buildings remain. Included among these is the home of the writer Henry Wadsworth Longfellow, dating back to 1785. Do take time to explore the myriad islands of Casco Bay, using the regular ferry or mail boat. Take the morning boat, hop off at Chebeague Island, rent a bike and explore.

Tour 23
Getting away from it all is easy when you head for the lakes and mountains of Maine. This long drive explores the state's remote beauty, while also passing through some charming villages. The famous Shaker religious community lives in a village at Sabbathday Lake. Their pious faith still arouses admiration, even though only a handful of the sect survives. By contrast, the nearby Sunday River ski area is one of the liveliest in Maine. Winter temperatures will test a visitor's fortitude. Rangeley is not only the mid-point of this drive, but the town also boasts being precisely halfway between the North Pole and the equator.

Tour 21
For many, the "real Maine" begins north of Portland. Here, the coastline breaks up into long skeletal fingers of granite, pointing out to form bays dotted with pine-covered islands. The sea has always been the focus of this region and the earliest Europeans who spent time here were transient fisher folk. Seafaring and boat-building are long traditions that have continued with the U.S. Navy in Brunswick, the huge shipyard in Bath, and numerous smaller boat-builders and museums. Although tourism is a major industry, towns such as Camden, Wiscasset, and Damariscotta have been able to retain their charm.

Tour 22
Portland is often rated as one of the best cities in which to live: small enough to feel friendly, but with a lively cultural scene and innovative restaurants. In recent years, it has made a conscious and successful effort to brighten up its downtown and old harbor by recycling historic buildings and employing novel methods of attracting locals to the shops and

cream at the apothecary shop that predated today's store, now called the Wizard of Odds and Ends. That was in 1824, long after Lafayette had helped the Americans during the Revolution.

On High Street is the Musical Wonder House. This is the private collection of Danilo Konvalinka, who calls it "the world's finest museum of restored international antique music boxes and mechanical instruments." The full tour is fascinating, though expensive; but it costs little to wander round the front hall and look at the 19th-century coin-operated music boxes, hurdy gurdies and perforated metal disc players.

At the end of High Street, in a commanding position above the harbor and Sheepscot River, stands Castle Tucker. Built in 1807, it was bought by Captain Tucker in 1858, after he retired from the sea and settled down to married life. From its free-standing switchback staircase to the dramatic southeast façade with

its huge windows, the house is one of a kind, and remains much as Captain Tucker left it. The wallpaper is original, as are the furnishings. A descendant of the captain still lives here.

The Nickels-Sortwell House, on the corner of Route 1 and Federal Street, is another ship-captain's home. Built in the same year as Castle Tucker, it exemplifies the Federal period. Just along Federal Street is Lincoln County Museum and Old Jail. This large and foreboding granite building served as the county jail from 1811 to 1953. Below the tiny barred windows, the cold walls, 41 inches (105cm) thick in places, are covered with graffiti, such as the painstakingly detailed schooner under full sail.

▶ *Continue on **Route 1** northeast to Newcastle and turn right for Damariscotta.*

❹ Damariscotta
This attractive yet unpretentious riverside community has

plenty of old wood-frame and brick homes. The restored 1754 Chapman-Hall House on Main and Church streets is the oldest in the region. In summer, guides in period dress conduct you round the 18th-century kitchen and herb garden.

ⓘ *Damariscotta Region Information Bureau, Main Street*

▶ *Leave town on **Route 130** south for 11 miles (18km). Turn right on Huddle Road at signs for Historic Pemaquid and Pemaquid Point. Service stations are few and far between off the main highways, so be sure to fill up before heading down any of the numerous peninsulas.*

❺ Colonial Pemaquid/Fort William Henry
The re-creation of Fort William Henry stands guard over the water, as did four earlier

Typical wood-frame house, near the township of Damariscotta

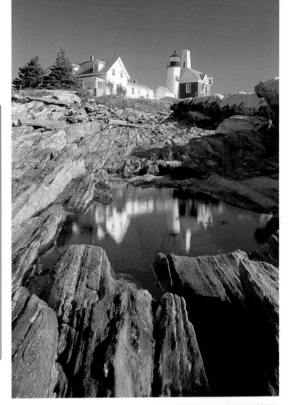

Pemaquid Point Lighthouse juts out on rocky ledges carved by ancient glaciers

FOR HISTORY BUFFS

"Damariscotta" means "the meeting place of alewives." This has nothing to do with women involved in brewing. It refers to a member of the herring family that was popular with Indians. The Indians also relished the local oysters and would congregate for "oyster festivals," leaving heaps of shells behind on the banks of the Damariscotta River. These "middens," an Old English word for rubbish dumps, contain shells as large as plates. Ask at the Damariscotta Region Information Bureau for maps and permission to visit them.

fortresses, and it now houses a museum of artifacts found on the site. Nearby, an on-going archeological dig has uncovered a 17th-century British settlement of houses plus a tavern, jail, burying ground, and customs house. It is thought to have been one of the first European settlements in the New World. Although fishing and trapping were productive in the area, raids by the French and their Indian allies, and long, hard winters took their toll.

▶ *Follow Snowball Hill Road to* **Route 130** *and drive south to Pemaquid Point.*

⬤ Pemaquid Light and Fisherman's Museum

Main is famous for its lighthouses. There are 63 lighthouses in the state, but this is one of the most romantic and most photographed. From sundown to sunrise, the Fourth-Order light flashes its warning every six seconds. From as far as 14 nautical miles away, ships take note and adjust their course accordingly. Although you cannot enter the tower, the memorabilia in the small museum gives an

insight into the fishing industry of yesterday and today. The layers of rock show the geological formation of this distinctive coastline. When climbing upon the rocks near the ocean, be careful. The waters are dangerous; the undertow is strong, too.

▶ *Take* **Route 130** *north, then turn onto* **Route 32** *to New Harbor.*

⬤ New Harbor

New Harbor is a truly picturesque and unspoiled Maine fishing village. A memorial here honors Chief Samoset of the local Pemaquid tribe. The chief learned English from British fishermen, and had traveled south to explore the Massachusetts coast in March, 1621, where he discovered the Pilgrim community. Imagine their surprise when he greeted them with the words "Welcome Englishmen."

▶ *Continue on* **Route 32** *north to Waldoboro (20 miles/ 32km). Turn onto* **Route 1**

FOR HISTORY BUFFS

Just off Route 32 is Round Pond, another fishing harbor. This once supposedly hid the notorious Captain Kidd, who buried treasure under a huge boulder on a nearby island. Some say it was on Devil's Oven, others on Otter Island. The mystery remains.

RECOMMENDED TRIPS

From New Harbor, take a daytrip out to tiny Monhegan Island, only 1½ miles (2.5km) across at its widest, with the highest cliffs on the East Coast. The energetic can hike through a wildlife sanctuary with hundreds of species of wildflowers and birds, while the less energetic can visit the artists' studios. There are also cruises for watching seals and Atlantic puffins, now a protected species.

northeast and drive 12 miles (19km) to Thomaston.

8 Thomaston

This is another ship captain and ship owners' town, although the most imposing house in Thomaston was built by a general, Henry Knox. He was an important figure in the Revolution and the country's first Secretary of War. He retired here in 1795 and built his mansion high on a hill overlooking the town. Still filled with its original furnishings, this building, with its white-painted façade and its two-story bay, looks remarkably like the south front of the White House in Washington D.C., designed in 1792.

Down on the waterfront, the Maine Watercraft Museum preserves a collection of vessels that represents the state's boat-building heritage, including a number of rare examples. Some of the boats can be rented by the hour; others are used for conducted sightseeing trips.

▶ *Continue on **Route 1** to Rockland.*

9 Rockland

The "Lobster Capital of the World" boasts a gem of a museum, the result of a 1935 legacy left by an eccentric 96-year-old. Lucy Farnsworth left money to the city for the upkeep of her family home and to found an art gallery in memory of her father. The William A. Farnsworth Art Museum specializes in American painters from the 18th, 19th, and 20th centuries, and highlights Maine's role in American art.

The Wyeth Centre, which opened in 1998 in a historic church near the museum, houses the collection of Andrew and Betsy Wyeth. The Shore Village Museum has a fine collection of lighthouse equipment.

i *Harbor Park*

▶ *Follow **Route 1** north to Rockport.*

FOR CHILDREN

South of Rockland, in the state park off Route 73, is Owl's Head Light. The 52-step climb is worth it for the view over Penobscot Bay, but vertigo-sufferers should not peer over the 87-foot (26m) sheer cliff. Nearby is the Owl's Head Transportation Museum, a world-class collection of vintage cars, airplanes, motorcycles and carriages in working condition. Demonstrations are held throughout the summer, though the museum is open year round.

SPECIAL TO...

One of the most famous artistic images of Maine is Andrew Wyeth's *Christina's World*, portraying a crippled girl in a meadow looking toward her house. It was just one of his many depictions of members of the Olson family and their house outside Rockland. "I just couldn't stay away from there ... I'd always seem to gravitate back to the house ... It was Maine." The house is administered by the Farnsworth Art Museum and is open, in season, to the public.

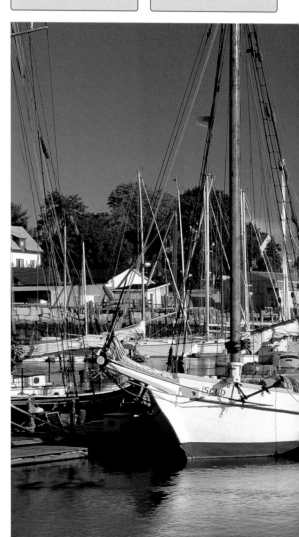

⑩ Rockport

The tiny village of Rockport has a tiny harbor with lots of cultural activities. The musically minded book into chamber music and jazz concerts at the opera house. Photographers head for the internationally known Maine Photographic Workshop, while the work of local artists and craftsmen is displayed in the many galleries. These include Maine Coast Artists, specializing in upcoming contemporary artists.

In the little park down by the

Below: yachts at rest in Camden Harbor
Right: lobsters at Boothbay Harbor

harbor is a statue of André the Seal. A children's book and film were based on the story of André, who lived here for 20 years.

▶ *Leave Rockport on scenic Russell Avenue, going north, with sudden glimpses of the Camden Hills and Penobscot Bay. This becomes Chestnut Street in Camden.*

⑪ Camden

*"All I could see from where I stood Was three long mountains and a wood;
I turned and looked another way, and saw three islands in a bay."*
The panorama from the top

of Mount Battie inspired Maine poet Edna St. Vincent Millay to compose this poem in 1917. The views today are still the same of the Camden Hills, Penobscot Bay, and, on a clear day, Monhegan Island.

In the town, below the hill, Millay's statue stands by the harbor in what is, arguably, the state's most popular year-round resort. Conway Farm House, dating from 1770, is one of the oldest houses in the area. It is now a museum which includes the house, barn, smithy, maple sugar house and modern museum building.

ⓘ *Public Landing*

SPECIAL TO...

Lobsters, the specialty of Maine, are caught in the millions of traps set in the cold waters offshore. Traditionally, these box-like contraptions consist of an oak frame with cotton netting. Many visitors take them as souvenirs. However, don't be tempted to pick up any washed on to a beach by the tide: that counts as "molesting a trap" and carries a fine. Buy one from a road-side stand or, better still, stop at a fishing village, look for a pile on the dock or by a house, and make an offer to the owner.

The Wadsworth-Longfellow House was the first brick house to be built in Portland

i *Convention and Visitors Bureau of Greater Portland, 305 Commercial Street*

▶ *Start at Congress Square.*

❶ Congress Square

This busy five-street intersection is the scene of many summer events, including concerts. On the corner of Congress and Free streets is the Hay Building, described as a flatiron building because of its wedge-shape. Built in 1826, it is one of the recognized icons of Portland.

❷ Portland Museum of Art

The I. M. Pei firm's brick colonnaded building (1983), right on the square, makes an impressive addition to the L. D. M. Sweat Memorial Galleries and rotunda, built in 1911. It houses one of New England's finest art collections and contains pieces by well-known Maine and American painters such as Winslow Homer, Rockwell Kent, Andrew Wyeth and John Singer Sargent. You will also find the Joan Whitney Payson Collection of Impressionist and Postimpressionist works here. One of the best known is Auguste Renoir's *Confidences*. A romantic tête-à-tête, this is a sensitive portrait of one of his favorite models, Margot Legrand.

❸ Children's Museum of Maine

Next door to the art museum, in a former Greek Revival church, is one of the best museums of its kind in New England. The Children's Museum of Maine really is for all ages. Even toddlers have their own play area, and older children can play at pretend in "Our Town," with its market, fire truck, lobster boat, bank, farm and animal hospital. For the technically minded, there are lots of interac-

tive exhibits and other things to fire the imagination, including the star lab, space shuttle and TV studio.

A wonder from the 19th century is a camera obscura, one of only seven in the world. A camera obscura is a dark room where images of objects from outside are projected onto a wall. It may sound simplistic in these days of "virtual reality," but this effective, primitive use of light and lens led to still and motion picture cameras.

▶ *Leave Congress Square and walk north on Congress Street to No. 522.*

❹ Maine College of Art

On the outside, the 1904 Porteous, Mitchell & Braun Building is a beaux arts classic, complete with cherubs. Inside is the Maine College of Art and the ICA, the Institute of Contemporary Art.

▶ *Look across Congress Street.*

❺ Mechanics Hall

This impressive, Italianate, granite-fronted building, with its statues of Archimedes and Vulcan, is the home of the Maine Charitable Mechanic

Association. Dedicated in 1851 to "informing and cultivating the mind and training up a race of mechanics (skilled workmen) of sound moral principle and intellectual power."

▶ *Continue along Congress Street to No. 485.*

❻ Wadsworth-Longfellow House

Three generations of one of the city's most distinguished familes lived here, behind the wrought-iron fence. In 1785, General Peleg Wadsworth, a hero of the Revolution and state senator, built this house, now the oldest surviving residence in Portland, and the first to be constructed of brick. The bricks were shipped in from Philadelphia.

Wadsworth's grandson, the poet Henry Wadsworth Longfellow, grew up here. His childhood flute is on show, and the house is furnished much as he would have remembered it as an adult. "Often I think of the beautiful town that is seated by the sea; often in thought go up and down the pleasant streets of that dear old town, and my youth comes back to me." Next door, the Center for Maine History has changing exhibitions about the state.

SPECIAL TO...

Henry Wadsworth Longfellow (1807–82) is America's best-loved 19th-century poet. *The Battle of Lovell's Pond*, his first published verses, appeared in the *Portland Gazette* when he was only 12 years old. His best-known works tell all-American tales such as *The Song of Hiawatha* and *Paul Revere's Ride*, but his popularity was not limited to the United States. He had a following in England that included Queen Victoria and, after his death, he was the first American to be commemorated with a bust in Poet's Corner at Westminster Abbey.

Portland's impressive City Hall

▶ *Just up Preble Street is the Portland Public Market. Opened in 1998, it is a cornucopia of fresh produce and delicious things to eat. Continue on Congress Street.*

7 Monument Square
This space, originally the town's Market Square, is named for Our Lady of Victories Monument. The monument is a Civil War memorial built in 1891, with money raised by local soldiers and sailors. In recent years, the farmers' market has been revived, with stalls set out on Wednesdays in the summer and fall. Summer brings concerts; in December, the city's Christmas tree lights up the square and on New Year's Eve, crowds gather to watch the fireworks.

▶ *Look across Congress Street.*

8 Maine Bank and Trust
Portland's first skyscraper, built in 1910 in the beaux arts style, was at that time New England's tallest building. Unlike traditional structures of the period, where the exterior walls supported the building, this was constructed with a steel skeleton, allowing greater height. Inside, the marble lobby soars to a ceiling at least three stories high. The impression is of solidity and security – perfect for a bank building.

SPECIAL TO...

Congress Street leads to Munjoy Hill, perhaps a derivation of the French *Mont Joie*. Here, the 221-foot (67m) high Portland Observatory was erected in 1807, as a signal tower. Communication by flags announced the identity of approaching merchant ships and enabled the docks to be prepared for their arrival. Views from the top are spectacular.
Nearby is the Eastern Promenade. Turn right for the bandstand. Here, the panorama encompasses Portland Harbor, the best deep-water port north of New Jersey. Watch for an oil tanker or a cruise ferry coming from Nova Scotia. Don't try to count the islands in Casco Bay; supposedly, there are 365 of them, hence the name, the Calendar Islands.

▶ *Continue on Congress Street to No. 425.*

9 First Parish Church
Founded in 1674, this church predates any other house of worship in Portland. The second building on the site took several hits during the British bombardment of the town in 1775. Inside, a cannon ball still lodges within the chain supporting the magnificent 600-pound (273kg) cut-glass chandelier. The 1794 clock and 1804 bell were saved and incorporated into the present building, rebuilt of granite in 1826.

▶ *Continue on Congress Street.*

10 City Hall
The granite used to build the City Hall was quarried locally in Maine, but the design is based on the classic French *hôtel-de-ville*. Inside is a 3,000-seat auditorium, where the Portland Symphony Orchestra often gives concerts. This is the third municipal headquarters to be located here: the first was destroyed by the Great Fire of 1866; its successor by another blaze in 1908.

▶ *Turn right on Exchange Street.*

11 Exchange Street

Exchange Street leads into the six-square-block Old Port Exchange area, the oldest part of the city. Warehouses and offices have now become boutiques, art galleries, and ethnic restaurants. Look closely and you'll see another reminder of British shelling in 1775: the cannon ball embedded in the Coles-worth building, on the right, just past the entry to the parking garage.

▶ *Continue to the intersection with Middle Street.*

12 Tommy's Park

The *trompe-l'oeil* by two Portland artists on the wall represents architectural elements of the 19th-century marble post office which once stood across the street in what is now the postage-stamp size Post Office Park. In this sunny spot, the granite boulders represent the many islands of Casco Bay, just outside Portland Harbor.

▶ *Turn left on Middle Street and walk two blocks to the intersection with Pearl Street.*

13 F. O. Bailey

Now the home of a well-respected firm of antiques sellers and auctioneers, this was one of the first buildings put up after the Great Fire of 1866. Look for the architect's autograph on the base of the left corner pilaster, on the Middle Street side.

▶ *Continue toward the harbor on Pearl Street. After a block, turn right on cobblestoned Milk Street. Straight ahead is the Regency Hotel.*

14 Milk Street Armory

It is no coincidence that the Regency Hotel, between Silver and Market streets, resembles a fortress. This was originally the armory, and was very active in the late 19th to mid-20th centuries. It also had a tradition of hospitality, as it was the site of musical events and impressive balls. The contemporary dolphin fountain was originally offered to, and rejected by, the city fathers. Shunted around town, it stood on a variety of sites until it was finally bought by the hotel.

▶ *Turn left on Silver Street.*

15 Boothby Square

At the intersection of Silver and Fore streets is Boothby Square. Directly in front is a row of old buildings, including the 1792 Sam Butts House and Store. It is the second-oldest surviving post-revolutionary house in Portland.

On your left is the 1868 granite U.S. Customs House. In the impressive interior, it is easy to imagine merchants sitting down to negotiate the tariffs on a cargo of molasses being unloaded at the wharf, just down the street.

▶ *Turn right on Fore Street, pass the granite-fronted 1828 Mariner's Church and turn left immediately onto cobbled Moulton Street. Turn right on Wharf Street, go right on Union Street, then left at the light on Fore Street. On the*

studios, used and rare book stores, and the Danforth Gallery, exhibiting alternative art.

At the five-street intersection known as Gorham's Corner is a seated statue of John Ford, complete with pipe. He grew up in Portland and the pub owned by this famous Hollywood director's father was here.

▶ *Continue through the five-street intersection onto Pleasant Street. Immediately past the first parking garage, turn right and go up the alley and stairs to Spring Street. On the right is the Civic Center. Cross the street and turn left.*

☷ Clapp House and McLellan House

The Great Fire did not reach this area, so these two impressive merchants' homes still stand. The Maine College of Art has offices in Clapp House, a Greek Revival mansion. Major Hugh McLellan's grand Federal house was given to the Portland Society of Art, in 1908, by Mrs.

Lorenzo de Medici Sweat, along with funds to build a "proper" art museum.

▶ *Turn right on High Street. Across the street is another Federal brick residence, now a private club, built by McLellan's brother, also a successful merchant and auctioneer. Return to Congress Square, at the end of the block.*

corner of Cotton Street is the Tracy-Causer Building.

☷ Tracy-Causer Building
Note the old street sign on this building, one of the few survivors of the Great Fire of 1866. The city's Landmarks Association successfully campaigned for its preservation and restoration in 1996. On the harbor side stand some of the few remaining warehouses from the "Golden Age" of the 19th and early 20th centuries. Straight ahead is Portland's second flat-iron building, now full of artists'

The Portland skyline at dawn, as seen from Back Cove

2 DAYS • 268 MILES • 431KM

Mountains &
Lakes of Maine

Nature lovers and sports fans head for the lakes and mountains, just as vacationers did 150 years ago when they came by railroad to escape the summer heat of more southerly states. Winter also brings visitors, such as downhill and cross-country skiers.

ITINERARY

PORTLAND	▶ Poland Spring (28m–45km)
POLAND SPRING	▶ Trap Corner (25m–40km)
TRAP CORNER	▶ Bethel (16m–26km)
BETHEL	▶ Rangeley (63m–101km)
RANGELEY	▶ Kingfield (35m–56km)
KINGFIELD	▶ Farmington (21m–34km)
FARMINGTON	▶ Portland (80m–129km)

i *305 Commercial Street*

▶ *Leave Portland on I–495 (the Maine Turnpike), turning off on Exit 11 at Gray (18m/29km). Follow Route 26 north for 8 miles (13km) to Sabbathday Lake.*

❶ Sabbathday Lake

A cluster of white buildings plus a large red-brick house mark Sabbathday Lake Village, the home of the Shakers, the religious community founded in 1782 by Mother Ann Lee, who voyaged from Manchester, England. Some 30 years later, the Shaker movement had grown to around 7,000, with settlements in New England, Ohio, and Kentucky.

This is the last remaining group. Less than a dozen men and women live here, following the credo "Put your hands to work and your heart to God." They aim for self-sufficiency through farming, tending the orchards, knitting, and printing. During the summer, outsiders are invited to join the Sunday services at 10am in the Meeting House, with its plain wooden benches. On other days, visitors can tour some of the buildings, including the museum, with examples of ingenious labor-saving inventions.

▶ *Follow Route 26 to Poland Spring.*

❷ Poland Spring

The popularity of bottled mineral waters may seem a recent phenomenon but Poland Spring water has been prized for more than a century. When its "healing" powers became known, the spring attracted visitors, a hotel was built, and the area developed into a summer resort. The hotel is long gone but its "library" building remains. This is now the Maine State Building from the Chicago Expo in 1893, moved and reconstructed here as an attraction for visitors. It is a museum recalling the grand old days when holiday-makers came, complete with their servants, for a month or two in the summer. Poland Spring water is still bottled nearby, but it is now owned by Perrier.

▶ *Continue on Route 26 north for 17 miles (27km) through South Paris, where the Celebration Barn Theater puts on performances of vaudeville, mime, and juggling in the summer. Turn right to Paris.*

❸ Paris

Few Americans remember Hannibal Hamlin, Vice-President during Abraham Lincoln's first term. His home is the most impressive structure in this cluster of pristine white Federal and Victorian houses on the summit of a hill. Admire the vistas across the valley and to the White Mountains to the west, then tour the tiny library in the former jail. Built in 1822, it is constructed entirely of granite, including the floors. Ask to see the jail door keys, and to hear how a fat prisoner became stuck while trying to escape.

▶ *Continue and rejoin Route 26 and drive north to the junction of Routes 26 and 219. On the east side of the road is a turn-off for Snow Falls Gorge, where there is a picturesque waterfall, picnic tables, and nature trails.*

❹ Trap Corner

"Rockhounds" and gemologists from all over New England know Oxford County because it is rich in minerals and gemstones such as tourmaline, amethyst, and quartz.

At the junction of Routes 26 and 219 is Perham's, a landmark since 1919. As well as a shop selling local finds, and the museum, this is where modern-day prospectors can get maps of nearby quarries and information about panning for gold in the Rangeley area.

▶ *Continue on Route 26.*

❺ Bryant Pond

The people of Maine are renowned for their stubbornness. This town enjoyed making telephone calls the old-fashioned way, and made national headlines with its campaign to keep its hand-cranked phone system, the last one in the country. They lost their battle in 1983, but the

Reflections at Bryant Pond

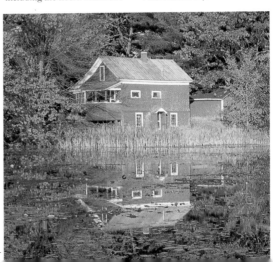

antiquated telephone technology is the focus of what must be one of the smallest museums in New England.

▶ Take **Route 26** to Bethel.

❻ Bethel

Founded on the Androscoggin River, the community nearly died after the Revolution. Railroads brought revitalization in the mid-19th century. As well as benefiting agriculture and timber businesses, the trains

Main picture: the covered bridge at Newry
Inset: one of Bethel's attractive houses; blueberry leaves in Acadia National Park

carried tourists. Now, vacationers come by car to what is a four-season resort. In winter, cross-country and downhill skiers head for Mount Abram and Sunday River, with its 127-trail network over eight different peaks. In summer, the chairlift up the slope provides bird's-eye views of the White Mountains as well as a great hike down. There is also camping, canoeing, mountain biking, fishing, and swimming.

ℹ *Bethel Train Station, 30 Cross Street*

▶ Leave Bethel on **Routes 26 and 2**, and drive 5 miles (8km) north to Newry.

SCENIC ROUTES

About 10m (16km) northwest of Newry is Grafton Notch State Park, where the park road has been designated a "Maine Scenic Highway." Moose can be sighted during dawn and dusk hours, while views of Bald Pate Mountain, plus Screw Augur Falls, epitomize the beauties of the region. The Appalachian Trail crosses the road here. This hiking route starts in Georgia and follows the Appalachian Mountains all the way to Mount Katahdin in northeast Maine.

7 Newry

Just off the road is the Artist's Covered Bridge, much painted and photographed long before the film *The Bridges of Madison County* lent cachet to similar bridges in Iowa. This one was built in 1872, over the Sunday River. More than just a scenic spot, it has popular swimming holes as well.

▶ Continue on scenic **Route 2** north to the papermill town of Rumford and cross the river at the mighty Pennacook Falls to Mexico, where much of the country's paper for books is made. Take **Route 17** north toward Oquossoc, then turn east on **Route 4** to Rangeley.

8 Rangeley

Wilderness and isolation are the hallmarks of the Rangeley region, surrounded by mountains and punctuated by more than 40 bodies of water. The village boasts of being halfway between the North Pole and the equator, but there is nothing halfway about the winters. A dog-sled postal service used to deliver letters to households cut off by snow; now, snowmobiles provide access to homes and businesses, but they are also raced for fun.

Other winter sports include snowshoeing, dog-sledding and ice-fishing, as well as cross-country and downhill skiing. The slopes here are less crowded than at most other resorts. When summer comes, there is fishing for landlocked salmon and trout, canoeing, hiking, and golfing.

There are also two museums. The Rangeley Lakes Region Historical Society, once a jail, recalls the 19th-century era of lake steamers and lodges that catered to New Yorkers escaping the heat of the city. More unusual is the Wilhelm Reich Museum, the home of the controversial Austrian psychoanalyst who studied with, then broke from, Sigmund Freud. Reich emigrated to the U.S.A. and eventually settled in Rangeley, to pursue "orgonomy, the science of the life energy."

His writings and inventions were all to do with sexual energy and personality analysis. In 1956, he was found guilty of violating Food and Drug Administration laws. He died, in prison, a year later. A museum preserves his library, memorabilia, and surviving inventions.

i Rangeley Lakes Region Chamber of Commerce, 6 Park Road

SPECIAL TO...

When shoppers pick up a pack of wild blueberries, they will be taking home some of the 64 million pounds grown every year in Maine. That represents 99 percent of the nation's crop. August is the official month of blueberries, and Rangeley's festival in the middle of the month is a typical celebration, with stalls selling pies and muffins, sauces and ice cream. You can even "pick your own" at the Blueberry Hill Farm outside town.

BACK TO NATURE

At the Hunter Cove Sanctuary, just west of Rangeley, on Route 4, there are marked trails through swamps, meadows, and thickets where bears, moose, and bobcats live. Guides take visitors out for moose-watch canoe trips – as long as they are up by 5am!

▶ *Leave Rangeley via Route 4 south. Note that Smalls Falls, in the Sandy River Gorge, has a good swimming hole, plus a waterfall, picnic site, and hiking trails. At Phillips, take Route 142 northeast to Kingfield.*

❾ Kingfield

What do violins, automobiles, and cameras all have in common? They fascinated the ingenious minds of F. O. and F. E. Stanley, twin brothers who

lived here a century ago. Their most profitable discovery was a photographic process which they sold to a company that later became Kodak. Car fans know them for their Stanley Steamers, made by the Stanley Motor Carriage Company. One of their racing cars set a speed record of 127.66mph (204.3km/h) in 1906, and it remained unbroken for many years. The brothers also made fine violins. The Stanley Museum tells their story and displays their inventions, along with photographs taken by their sister, Chansonetta Stanley Emmons.

▶ *Take Route 27 south through New Portland, stopping to see the amazing 1841 engineering feat, the Fireproof Wire Bridge, suspended across the Carrabassett River. Rejoin Route 4 and head for Farmington.*

❿ Farmington

It is hard to imagine that this agricultural valley produced an international opera star. A simple farmhouse, just outside Farmington, was the birthplace in 1857 of Lillian Norton. As Madame Nordica, she triumphed in Europe and was the first American woman to take Wagnerian roles at the Bayreuth Festival. Returning to the States, her "liquid purity, exceptional range, and magnificent power" charmed New York critics during numerous seasons at the Metropolitan Opera House. The Nordica Memorial Homestead displays her costumes, annotated scores, and other memorabilia.

A branch of the University of Maine is here, continuing a tradition of education dating back to 1788 when the school was founded. The Red School House Museum recalls those days.

i Farmington-Wilton Chamber of Commerce, 575 Wilton Street

▶ *Continue on Route 4 which leads through Dryden, Jay, and*

View over Step Falls, Grafton Notch State Park

SPECIAL TO...

Farmington is the home of Greenwood's Champion Ear Protectors, better-known as ear muffs. They were the brainchild of local teenager Chester Greenwood, whose ears had become painfully cold while ice-skating during the winter of 1873. His prototype was made of wire, covered with fur and velvet, but after improvements, he patented the design and opened a factory in town. Each year, the first Saturday in December is Chester Greenwood Day, complete with a parade.

Livermore Falls, recognized long before arriving by the sulphurous smell of the paper-mills. Take Route 108 east for the Norlands Living History Center.

⓫ Norlands Living History Center

Step into the past at the former home of one of the most fascinating and influential families of 19th-century Maine. The seven Washburn sons included diplomats, congressmen, journalists, businessmen and a navy captain, yet the farm exemplifies the thrifty lifestyle considered to be typical of New England.

On the hour-and-a-half-long guided tour, costumed guides explain the ways of farmers in the 19th century and you see the 1828 church, the family's 1867 mansion, the library, farmhouse and barn on what is now a 445-acre (180-hectare) estate. On special days, there may be cooking on a cast-iron stove, harvesting grain or tending the vegetable garden.

▶ *Follow Route 4 to Auburn and then take I-495 south (Maine Turnpike) for the return to Portland.*

GETTING AROUND

Whether you use your own car or a rental car, driving is perhaps the best way to see New England. The forested hills, winding river valleys, and historic New England towns and villages are most accessible and best appreciated when seen from a car traveling at moderate speed on secondary roads (see **Motoring**, pages 159–60). But other means of transportation are available as well.

By Car

Within New England, you'll normally drive only an hour or two to your next destination. From Boston, it's only an hour's drive to Providence, Plymouth, Manchester, or Portsmouth; about two hours to Hartford, Portland, Mystic, or Cape Cod; about three hours to New Haven, the Berkshires, southern Vermont, Boothbay Harbor, or New Hampshire's White Mountains; and only about four hours to New York City or central Vermont. Five hours takes you from Boston to the resort and national park at Bar Harbor, Maine.

By Recreational Vehicle

Among the most pleasant ways to tour the country is in a recreational vehicle (motor home). RVs come in all sizes and shapes, and usually sleep four to six people comfortably, include a full kitchen (with cooking range, refrigerator, and running water), and are air-conditioned; some even have a shower!

Hundreds of campgrounds in New England can provide electrical, water, and sewer hookups for $15 to $20 per night. Some RVs can operate for several days without hookups. In an RV, you're completely independent, and for families with young children it can be a very cost-effective way to tour New England.

Renting an RV has its disadvantages as well. Rentals are fairly expensive, and you should work out estimated budgets for a trip in an RV versus a trip using a rental car and hotels before making your final decision. When figuring costs, keep in mind that RVs use a lot more fuel than passenger cars. During the busy summer months, many of New England's choicest campgrounds fill up early in the day. You may have to reserve in advance, which takes some of the fun out of footloose travel. Finally, New England is a region with many delightful country inns. If you've gone to the expense of renting an RV, you may not feel that you can pay to stay in an inn very often.

For more information on RVs, contact the Recreation Vehicle Industry Association, 1896 Preston White Drive, PO Box 2999, Reston, Virginia 20195-0999 (tel: 703/620-6003; fax 703/591-0734); for $5 they'll send you a 40-page catalog listing locations, services, and rates of the various RV rental agencies. The Recreation Vehicle Rental Association, 3930 University Drive, Fairfax, Virginia 22030 (tel: 703/591-7130) is another good source. RV America has a comprehensive website (www.rvamerica.com). Call Go Camping America (tel: 800/47-SUNNY) for a very helpful, free 16-page camping vacation planner.

By Plane

The larger cities, such as Boston, Providence, Hartford, Portland, and Burlington, all have good air service provided by the larger domestic airlines. Numerous regional "feeder" airlines fly between the larger and smaller cities, and many regional carriers connect to New York City.

Almost all the small regional airlines operate in conjunction with larger national and international airlines. The regional airlines' flights are included in the flight schedules of such airlines as American, Delta, Continental and USAir. Call these airlines for information on flights, fares, and cities served.

By Train

Amtrak (tel:1–800/USA–RAIL) operates trains connecting Boston with Springfield and Pittsfield, Massachusetts, and Albany, New York; Hartford, New Haven, New London, and Mystic, Connecticut; Providence, Rhode Island; and (via Springfield) Brattleboro, White River Junction, and Montpelier, Vermont; and Montréal, Québec. The Downeaster from Boston to Portland, Maine is the latest expansion, along with the high-speed Acela service to New York City and on to Washington D.C.

Trains on routes between Boston and points south and west are fast and frequent, but to get to points in Vermont from Boston, connections are not good and service is infrequent.

By Bus

Bus services are quite good in New England.

Bonanza Bus Lines (tel: 401/751–8800 or 800/556-3815), South Station Bus Terminal, 700 Atlantic Drive, runs from Boston to Cape Cod (Falmouth and Woods Hole) and Fall River (Massachusetts), and Newport and Providence (Rhode Island). Other routes run from Providence to central and western Connecticut and Massachusetts' Berkshires, and from Providence to Cape Cod.

Concord Trailways (tel: 603/228-3300 or 1-800/639-3317) is the line to take to New Hampshire. Buses start at Logan Airport and the Peter Pan Trailways Terminal in Boston, then head north to Concord, Laconia and North Conway, Plymouth, Waterville Valley, and Franconia. Another route goes to Alton and Wolfboro.

Greyhound (tel: 800/231-2222), with its terminal at South Station in Boston, operates many of the long-distance routes in New England, and connects the region with the rest of the country.

Peter Pan Trailways (tel: 617/426-7838 or 800/343-9999), at the Peter Pan Trailways terminal in Peter Pan Plaza, opposite Amtrak's South Station, runs between Boston and Albany, Amherst, Bridgeport, Danbury, Hartford, Holyoke, Lee, Middletown, New Britain, New Haven, New York City, Northampton, Norwalk, Pittsfield, Springfield, Sturbridge, Waterbury, and Worcester. Other routes connect Springfield, Massachusetts, with Bradley International Airport and Hartford, Connecticut.

Plymouth & Brockton Street Railway Co. (tel: 508/746-0378), Peter Pan Trailways Terminal in Dewey Square, is the one to take from Boston to Plymouth, Sagamore, Hyannis, Barnstable, and Provincetown on Cape Cod.

Vermont Transit Lines (tel: 802/862-9671, or 800/451-3292 in Vermont), Greyhound Terminal, in collaboration with Greyhound Lines, operates a comprehensive network.

HEALTH SERVICES

All New England cities have hospitals; blue signs bearing a white H mark the way. Boston is one of the most renowned medical centers, with dozens of hospitals and medical facilities.

To use most of these facilities, however, you'll need health insurance, since prices for services are astronomical.

HITCHHIKING

Hitchhiking is not a good way to get around New England, either within cities or between cities and towns. It's illegal to hitchhike on expressways. Incidents of robbery and violence by driver or hitcher, though few in number, mean most motorists won't stop.

HOLIDAYS

(LWE = long weekend, including Monday)
1 January – New Year's Day;
Third Monday in January – Martin Luther King Day (LWE);
Second weekend in February – Lincoln's Birthday (LWE);
Third weekend in February – Washington's Birthday (LWE);
(Presidents Week, linking the two weekends, is often a school holiday);
First Tuesday in March – Town Meeting Day (Vermont);
Third Monday in April – Patriots' Day (Massachusetts and Maine, LWE);
Easter;
Last weekend in May – Memorial Day (LWE);
4 July – Independence Day;
Second Monday in August – Victory Day (Rhode I, LWE);
16 August – Bennington Battle Day (Vermont);
First Monday in September – Labor Day (LWE);
Second Monday in October – Columbus Day (LWE);
First Tuesday in November – Election Day (some states);
11 November – Veteran's Day;
Fourth Thursday in November – Thanksgiving Day;
25 December – Christmas Day.

LIQUOR LAWS

The minimum age for drinking varies by state, but in most it's 21 years. A few towns in New England, such as Rockport, Massachusetts, are "dry" (no shop, restaurant, or hotel may sell liquor, but it's not illegal to bring in your own liquor and serve yourself). Restaurants have either a full liquor license (liquor, wine, and beer), a wine and beer license, or no license. Some unlicensed restaurants let you bring your own; others don't. It's illegal to drink alcohol in public areas. Drink/driving laws are very strict.

MOTORING
Driving

In many places outside major cities, cars are permitted to turn right on a red light after stopping, if it is safe to do so.

Freeways and toll roads make travel easy, whereas side roads are often narrow and winding. Use particular care in winter.

You should always have your driving license with you.

Speed limits, licensing of drivers, and all other rules governing automobile use are set by each state's legislature.

Car Rental

To rent a car in New York or New England, you must be at least 21 years of age (though most major agencies require you to be at least 25) and have a valid driver's license. A credit or charge card is almost always a necessity.

Some companies may insist that non-U.S. residents have an International Drivers Permit.

If your own auto insurance covers damage to a rental car, you needn't purchase Collision Damage Waiver (CDW) or Loss Damage Waiver (LDW).

The major New England airports have national car rental chains:
Alamo (tel: 800/GO ALAMO)
Avis (tel: 800/230-4898)
Budget (tel: 800/527-0700)
Dollar (tel: 800/800-3665)
Hertz (tel: 800/654-3131)
National (tel: 800/227-7368)
Thrifty (tel: 800/847-4389).

Breakdowns

Car rental companies will advise drivers of what to do in the case of a breakdown. The American Automobile Association has reciprocal arrangements with many other motoring organizations around the world, so it is worth checking with your own association before leaving home. The AAA nationwide, toll-free number is 800-AAA-HELP. In case of a breakdown, lift up the hood, as a signal, and remain in the car. Only open doors and windows to police in a patrol car.

Accidents

All accidents should be reported to the police. Exchange names, addresses, driver license number, and insurance details.

Non-U.S. residents who have caused, or are held responsible for, an injury, should insist on contacting their embassy or consulate.

Safety Belts

The use of safety belts is required by law. Throughout the United States, infants and small children (under 5) are required by law to be placed in child safety seats secured by seat belts.

Child safety seats are available from car-rental firms at a small extra charge.

Speed Limits

The speed limit in New England is 55 to 65mph (88 to 105km/h). In cities and built-up areas, it is 20 to 40mph (32 to 64km/h), and 15mph (24km/h) in school zones.

Speed limits are strictly enforced. When a school bus stops, all traffic must do the same.

Police use radar to detect speeding drivers.

Road Maps

New England maps are sold in the region's bookstores and gas stations. Maps of each state drawn with greater detail are available, sometimes for free, from official state tourism departments by mail, or from state roadside information centers located on major highways near state borders.

For addresses of the state tourism offices, see **Visitor Information** below.

NEWSPAPERS/ MAGAZINES

Each of the larger cities in New England has its own daily newspaper. The *Boston Globe* and the *Boston Herald* are distributed throughout New England, as is the *New York Times*, and, in most cities, the *Washington Post*.

POST OFFICES

Most post offices are open Monday through Friday from 8am to 5pm and Saturday from 8am to noon or 2pm. A few major post offices stay open until 5.30 or 6pm, and the post office at Boston's Logan Airport stays open until midnight. To receive mail at a post office, have it sent to you c/o General Deliveries (Poste Restante) in the town where you'd like to pick up your mail. Specify the name of the post office where you'd like to pick up your mail; if in doubt, write "Main Post Office." You'll need to show identification, such as a passport or driver's license, to pick up your mail.

SAFETY

Whenever you're traveling in an unfamiliar city or country, stay alert and keep a close eye on your possessions.

TAXES

Taxes on hotel rooms, restaurant meals, some transportation services, and purchases in general are levied by each state and by some cities. Taxes on rooms, meals, and other purchases (which can be as high as 11 or 12 per cent) are not included in the price.

TIPS FOR SPECIAL TRAVELERS
Families

Museums, amusement attractions, whale-watch trips, and most other sights offer reduced admission rates for children or good-value family tickets.

Some attractions (outdoor concerts, state parks, beaches, and so forth) charge admission "per car," so families can pay as little as solo travelers.

A good source of information for family travel is *Frommer's Unofficial Guide to New England and New York with Kids*.

Seniors

Senior discounts are readily available throughout New England at museums, parks, attractions, and some hotels and on Amtrak trains, so make sure to carry some convincing form of photo identification.

It's best to request discounts on hotel rates, train and plane fares, and rental-car fees when you make your reservation, not when you're paying for the services.

For more information about senior discounts in general and for a good-as-gold discount card, contact the American Association of Retired Persons (AARP), 601 E Street, NW, Washington, D.C. 20049 (tel: 1-800/424-3410).

Travelers with Disabilities

All of New England's major hotels and most museums and stores, as well as other large institutions, have, by law, to be accessible to visitors in wheelchairs or on crutches. However, many of the smaller country inns and bed-and-breakfast houses are not accessible or not fully accessible. The best plan is always to call ahead to determine whether the level of accessibility is sufficient for your requirements.

Vermont Department of Tourism and Marketing and the New Hampshire Office of Travel and Tourism (see **Visitor Information** below) offer information about accessible facilities and events.

Amtrak trains are accessible to travelers with disabilities, but not all Amtrak stations are; ask about this when you make your train reservations, and also inquire about help with your baggage, special seating, and other assistance. There's a bonus: Amtrak grants discounts of 25 percent (off the normal coach fare) to adult disabled travelers and 50 percent (off normal children's fares) to disabled travelers aged 2 to 12. For full information, ask for a copy of Amtrak's annual Travel Planner from Amtrak, National Railroad Passenger Corp., 400 N. Capitol Street NW, Washington, D.C. 20001 (tel: 800/USA-RAIL).

VISITOR INFORMATION

State tourism offices:
Connecticut Office of

Tourism, 505 Hudson Street, Hartford, CT 06106 (tel: 860/270-8080);

Maine Office of Tourism, 325B Water Street, Hallowell, ME 04347 (tel: 207/623-0363);

Massachusetts Office of Travel & Tourism, 10 Park Plaza, Suite 4510, Boston, Massachusetts 02116 (tel: 617/973-8500;

New Hampshire Office of Travel & Tourism, 172 Pembroke Road (P.O. Box 1856), Concord, New Hampshire 03302 (tel: 603/271-2343);

Rhode Island Tourism Division, 1 West Exchange Street, Providence, Rhode Island 02903 (tel: 401/222-2601 or 800/556-2484);

Vermont Department of Tourism and Marketing, 6 Baldwin Street, 4th Floor, Drawer 33, Montpelier, Vermont 05633 (tel: 802/828-3237).

WEBSITES
Discover New England
www.discovernewengland.org
Connecticut
www.ctbound.com
Maine
www.visitmaine.com
Massachusetts
www.massvacation.com
New Hampshire
www.visitnh.gov
Rhode Island
www.visitrhodeisalnd.com
Vermont
www.1-800-vermont.com

WHEN TO GO
Climate
Without doubt, the best times to tour New England are summer (June through August), and fall (September and October), unless you're coming for skiing.

ACCOMMODATIONS & RESTAURANTS
Following is a selection of hotels and bed-and-breakfasts (🏨) which can be found along the routes of each tour, along with suggestions for restaurants (🍴) to take a break.

Accommodations prices
Accommodations are divided into four prices based on the cost of a double room per night. When hotels have a restaurant, prices are in relation to the cost of the bedrooms:

$	under $70
$$	$70–$110
$$$	$110–$150
$$$$	over $150

Restaurant prices
Restaurants are divided into three price categories based on the cost of a three-course meal for one, excluding drinks:

$	under $20
$$	$20–$40
$$$	over $40

TOUR 1
CONCORD
🏨 **Best Western at Historic Concord $$**
740 Elm Street, Concord MA 01742. Tel: 978/369-6100 or 800/528-1234.

🏨 🍴 **Colonial Inn $$–$$$$**
48 Monument Square, Concord MA 01742. Tel: 978/369-9200 or 800/370-9200.

🍴 **Aigo Bistro $–$$**
48 Monument Square, Concord MA. Tel: 978/371-1333. *Mediterranean cuisine.*

🍴 **Walden Grille $–$$**
24 Walden Street, Concord MA. Tel: 978/371-2233. *Modern American cuisine.*

TOUR 2
ROCKPORT
🏨 **Yankee Clipper Inn $$$–$$$$**
127 Granite Street, Rockport MA 01966. Tel: 978/546-3407 or 800/545-3699. *Closed Jan, Feb.*

🍴 **Grand Café $$**
Emerson Inn, I Cathedral Avenue, Rockport MA. Tel: 978/546-6321. *Modern versions of New England dishes.*

ESSEX
🍴 **Tom Shea's $–$$**
122 Main Street, Essex MA. Tel: 978/768-6931. *Seafood; good sea views.*

IPSWICH
🏨 **Inn at Castle Hill $$$–$$$$**
280 Argilla Road, Ipswich MA 01938. Tel: 978/412-2555. *Closed Jan.*

NEWBURYPORT
🏨 **Clark Currier Inn $$–$$$$**
45 Green Street, Newburyport MA 01950. Tel: 978/465-8363 or 800/360-6582.

TOUR 3
SANDWICH
🏨 **Dan'l Webster Inn $$$–$$$$**
149 Main Street, Sandwich MA 02563. Tel: 508/888-3622.

YARMOUTH PORT
🏨 **Wedgewood Inn $$$–$$$$**
83 Main Street, Yarmouth Port MA 02675. Tel: 508/362-5157.

WELLFLEET
🍴 **Aesop's Tables $$–$$$**
316 Main Street, Wellfleet MA. Tel: 508/349-6450. *Modern cooking; seafood. Closed mid-Oct–mid-May.*

PROVINCETOWN
🏨 **Copper Fox $$–$$$$**
448 Commercial Street, Provincetown MA 02657. Tel: 508/487-8583.

🍴 **Ross' Grill $$**
Whalers' Wharf, Commerical Street, Provincetown MA. Tel: 508/487-8878. *Bar–bistro on water. Closed Tue.*

CHATHAM
🍴 **Christian's $$**
443 Main Street, Chatham MA. Tel: 508/945-3362. *Seafood.*

TOUR 4
STOCKBRIDGE
🏨 🍴 **Red Lion $$–$$$$**
Main Street, Stockbridge MA 01262. Tel: 413/298-5545.

LENOX
🏨 🍴 **Apple Tree Inn $$–$$$**
10 Richmond Mountain Road, Lenox MA 01240. Tel: 413/637-1477. *Situated opposite Tanglewood. Continental cuisine. Restaurant closed Mon–Wed out of season.*

NORTH ADAMS
🏨 **The Porches Inn at MASSMoCA $$$**
231 River Street, North Adams MA 01247. Tel: 413/664-0400.

🍴 **eleven $$**
Building 11, MASS MoCA, Marshall Street, North Adams MA. Tel: 413/662-2004. *Global contemporary cuisine.*

DEERFIELD
🏨🍴 **Deerfield Inn $$$–$$$$**
81 Old Main Street, Deerfield MA 01342. Tel: 413/774-5587 or 800/926-3865.

TOURS 5 and 6
BOSTON
🏨🍴 **Harborside Inn $$$**
185 State Street, Boston MA 02109. Tel: 617/723-7500 or 888/723-7565.

🏨 **Newbury Guesthouse $$$–$$$$**
261 Newbury Street, Boston MA 02116. Tel: 617/437-7666.

🏨🍴 **Ritz-Carlton, Boston Common $$$–$$$$**
10 Avery Street, Boston Common MA 02111. Tel: 617/574-7100 or 800/241-3333.

🏨🍴 **Westin Copley Plaza $$$$**
10 Huntington Avenue, Boston MA 02116. Tel: 617/262-9600 or 888/625-5144.

🍴 **Antico Forno $–$$**
93 Salem Street, Boston MA. Tel: 617/723-6733. *Rustic Italian cuisine.*

🍴 **Figs $–$$**
42 Charles Street, Boston MA. Tel: 617/742-3447. *Gourmet, pizza.*

🍴 **Legal Seafoods $–$$**
100 Huntington Avenue, Copley Place, Boston MA. Tel: 617/266-7775. *Seafood. Several branches.*

🍴 **Sel de la Terre $$–$$$**
255 State Street, Boston MA. Tel: 617/720-1300. *Provençal cuisine.*

TOUR 7
CAMBRIDGE
🏨🍴 **Inn at Harvard $$–$$$$**
1201 Massachusetts Avenue, Cambridge MA 02138. Tel: 617/491-2222 or 800/458-5886.

🏨🍴 **Sheraton Commander Hotel $$$$**
16 Garden Street, Cambridge MA 02138. Tel: 617/547-4800 or 800/228-1169.

🏨 **A Cambridge House Bed and Breakfast Inn $$$**
2218 Massachusetts Avenue, Cambridge MA 02138. Tel: 617/491-6300 or 800/232-9989.

🍴 **East Coast Grille $$–$$$**
1271 Cambridge Street, Cambridge MA. Tel: 617/491-6568. *Fish and BBQ. Closed lunch Mon–Sat.*

🍴 **Rialto $$$**
Charles Hotel, 1 Bennett Street, Cambridge MA. Tel: 617/661-5050. *Eclectic; top chef. Closed lunch.*

TOUR 8
HARTFORD
🏨 **Goodwin Hotel $$**
Goodwin Square, 1 Haynes Street, Hartford CT 06103. Tel: 860/246-7500 or 888/212-8380.

🏨 **Hastings Hotel $$–$$$$**
85 Sigourney Street, Hartford CT 06103. Tel: 860/727-4200 or 800/777-7803.

🍴 **Max Downtown $$–$$$**
185 Asylum Street, Hartford CT. Tel: 860/522-2530. *Stylish, contemporary cooking.*

🍴 **Trumbull Kitchen $$**
150 Trumbull Street, Hartford CT. Tel: 860/493-7417. *Fusion style.*

TOUR 9
NEW HAVEN
🏨 **New Haven Hotel $$–$$$**
229 George Street, New Haven CT 06510. Tel: 203/498-3100 or 800/644-6835.

🏨 **Three Chimneys $$$–$$$$**
1201 Chapel Street, New Haven CT 06511. Tel: 203/789-1201 or 800/443-1554.

🏨 **Three Judges Motor Lodge $**
1560 Whalley Avenue, New Haven CT 06515. Tel: 203/389-2161.

🍴 **Roomba $$**
1044 Chapel Street, Hartford CT. Tel: 203/562-7666. *Nuevo Latino cuisine.*

🍴 **500 Blake Street Café $$–$$$**
500 Blake Street, Hartford CT. Tel: 203/387-0500. *Modern Italian.*

TOUR 10
LITCHFIELD
🏨🍴 **Tollgate Hill Inn $$–$$$$**
Route 202, Litchfield CT 06759. Tel: 860/567-4545.

🍴 **West Street Grill $$–$$$**
43 West Street, Litchfield CT. Tel: 860/567-3885. *Contemporary American cuisine; seafood. Fashionable, expensive.*

KENT
🍴 **Bull's Bridge Inn $$**
333 Kent Road, Kent CT. Tel: 860/927-1000. *Classic grills.*

SALISBURY
🏨 **The Under Mountain Inn $$$$**
482 Undermountain Road, Salisbury CT 06068. Tel: 860/435-0242.

🍴 **White Hart $$**
Village Green, Salisbury CT. Tel: 860/435-0030. *Modern New England cooking.*

NORFOLK
🏨 **Greenwoods Gate Inn $$$$**
105 Greenwoods Road, Norfolk CT 06058. Tel: 860/542-5439.

TOUR 11
OLD SAYBROOK
🍴 **Old Saybrook Diner $–$$**
809 Boston Post Road, Old Saybrook CT. Tel: 860/395-1079. *Classic diner.*

ESSEX
🏛 ¶¶ **Griswold Inn $$$–$$$$**
36 Main Street, Essex CT
06425. Tel: 860/767-1776.

OLD LYME
🏛 **Bee & Thistle Inn $$–$$$**
100 Lyme Street, Old Lyme
CT 06371. Tel: 860/434-1667 or
800/622-4946.

¶¶ **Old Lyme Inn $$–$$$**
85 Lyme Street, Old Lyme CT.
Tel: 860/434-2600.
Contemporary.

NOANK
¶¶ **Abbott's Lobster in the
Rough $–$$**
117 Pearl Street, Noank CT.
Tel: 860/536-7719. *Lobster
dishes.*

MYSTIC
🏛 **Old Mystic Inn $$**
52 Main Street, Mystic CT
06372. Tel: 860/572-9422.

**TOUR 12
PROVIDENCE**
🏛 **Day's Hotel on the Harbor
$$**
220 India Street, Providence
RI 02903. Tel: 401/272-5577.

🏛 **Old Court $$–$$$**
144 Benefit Street, Providence
RI 02903. Tel: 401/751-2002.

🏛 ¶¶ **Providence Biltmore
$$$**
Kennedy Plaza, Providence RI
02303. Tel: 401/421-0700 or
800/294-7709.

¶¶ **Eclectic Grille $$**
245 Atwells Avenue,
Providence RI. Tel: 401/831-
8010. *Modern Italian cuisine.
Closed lunch.*

¶¶ **XO Café $$**
125 North Main Street,
Providence RI. Tel: 401/273-
9090. *Fusion cuisine. Closed lunch.*

**TOUR 13
NEWPORT**
🏛 **Cliffside Inn $$–$$$**
2 Seaview Avenue, Newport
RI 02840. Tel: 401/847-1811 or
800/845-1811.

🏛 **Francis Malbone House
$$–$$$**
392 Thames Street, Newport
RI 02840. Tel: 401/846-0392 or
800/846-0392.

🏛 **Adele Turner Inn $$–$$$$**
93 Pelham Street, Newport
RI 02840. Tel: 401/847-1811 or
800/845-1811.

¶¶ **Tucker's Bistro $$**
150 Broadway, Newport RI. Tel:
401/846-3449. *Modern American
cuisine. Closed Sun in winter.*

¶¶ **White Horse Tavern $$$**
26 Marlborough Street,
Newport RI. Tel: 401/849-3600.
*America's oldest pub. Seafood a
specialty.*

**TOUR 14
BENNINGTON**
🏛 **Molly Stark Inn $–$$**
1067 Main Street, Bennington
VT 05201. Tel: 802/442-9631
or 1-800/356-3076.

🏛 **South Shire Inn $$$**
124 Elm Street, Bennington
VT 05201. Tel: 802/447-3839.

¶¶ **Blue Benn $–$$**
102 Hunt Street, Bennington
VT. Tel: 802/442-5140.
American/vegetarian. Diner.

¶¶ **Paradise $$**
141 Main Street, Bennington
VT. Tel: 802/442-5418. *Steak
and seafood.*

**TOUR 15
MANCHESTER**
🏛 **Manchester Highlands
Inn $$**
216 Highland Avenue,
Manchester VT 05255. Tel:
802/362-4565 or 800/743-4565.

🏛 ¶¶ **The Marsh Tavern at
The Equinox Resort $$–$$$**
3567 Main Street, Manchester
Village VT 05254. Tel: 802/362-
4700. *Regional cuisine.*

WESTON
🏛 ¶¶ **Inn at Weston $$–$$$**
Route 100, Weston VT 05161.
Tel: 802/824-5804. *International
cuisine.*

CHESTER
🏛 **Stone Hearth Inn $–$$$**
698 Route 11 West, Chester VT
05143. Tel: 802/875-2525.

NEWFANE
🏛 ¶¶ **Four Columns Inn $$$**
On the Green, Newfane VT
05345. Tel: 802/365-7713 or
800/787-6633. *Award-winning
gourmet food. Distinctive blend of
New American, Asian and French
cuisine.*

**TOUR 16
RUTLAND**
🏛 **The Inn at Rutland
$$–$$$$**
70 North Main Street, Rutland
VT 05701. Tel: 802/773-0575.

MENDON
🏛 ¶¶ **Red Clover Inn $$$**
7 Woodward Road, Mendon VT
05701. Tel: 802/775-2290.
*Modern American cuisine. Closed
lunch and Sun out of season.*

QUECHEE
🏛 **Quechee Inn $$–$$$$**
Mashland Farm, Main Street,
Quechee VT 05059.
Tel: 1-800/235-3133.

¶¶ **Simon Pearce Restaurant
$$$**
At the Mill, Quechee VT. Tel:
802/295-1470. *Contemporary New
England with international twist.*

WOODSTOCK
🏛 ¶¶ **Woodstock Inn $$$**
14 The Green, Woodstock
VT 05091. Tel: 802/457-1100
or 800/448-7900.

¶¶ **Bentleys Restaurant $$**
3 Elm Street, Woodstock VT.
Tel: 802/457-3232. *Contemporary
cuisine.*

**TOUR 17
BURLINGTON**
🏛 ¶¶ **Inn at Essex $$–$$$**
70 Essex Way, Essex Junction
VT 05452. Tel: 802/878-1100 or
800/727-4295.

¶¶ **NECI Commons $–$$**
25 Church Street, Burlington
VT. Tel: 802/862-6324. *Bistro
with flair.*

MIDDLEBURY
🏨 🍴 **Old English Carvery**
$–$$
Middlebury Inn, 14 Court
House Square, Middlebury VT.
Tel: 802/388-4961. *Roasts and
grills.*

STOWE
🏨 🍴 **Stoweflake Mountain
Resort and Spa $$$$**
1746 Mountain Road, Stowe VT
05672. Tel: 802/253-7355 or
800/253-2232.

🏨 🍴 **Whip Bar and Grill $–$$**
Green Mountain Inn, 18 South
Main Street, Stowe VT. Tel:
802/253-7301. *Stylish tavern fare.*

TOUR 18
PORTSMOUTH
🏨 **The Sise Inn $$$–$$$$**
40 Court Street, Portsmouth
NH 03801. Tel: 603/433-1200.

🏨 **Inn at Strawbery Banke
$$–$$$**
314 Court Street, Portsmouth
NH 03801. Tel: 603/436-7242 or
800/428-3933.

🍴 **Portsmouth Brewery $–$$**
56 Market Street, Portsmouth
NH. Tel: 603/431-1115. *Casual;
hamburgers and more.*

🍴 **Rosa Restaurant $–$$**
80 State Street, Portsmouth
NH. Tel: 603/436-9715.
*Traditional Italian cuisine in an
historic setting.*

TOUR 19
BRETTON WOODS
🏨 **Bretton Arms Country
Hotel $$$–$$$$**
US Route 302, Bretton Woods
NH 03575. Tel: 603/278-1000.

JACKSON
🏨 🍴 **Inn at Thorn Hill $$$**
Thorn Hill Road, Jackson NH
03846. Tel: 603/383-4242 or
800/289-8990. *Gourmet dining
room.*

NORTH CONWAY
🍴 **1785 Inn Restaurant $$**
North Conway NH 03860. Tel:
603/356-9025 or 800/421-1785.
Traditional fine dining.

🍴 **Horsefeathers $**
Center of village, North
Conway NH. Tel: 603/356-2687.
Pasta and burgers.

TOUR 20
HOLDERNESS
🏨 🍴 **The Manor on Golden
Pond $$$$**
Shepard Hill Road, Holderness
NH 03245. Tel: 603/968-3348.

🍴 **Walters Basin $$**
By the bridge, Holderness NH.
Tel: 603/968-4412. *American
cuisine.*

CENTER SANDWICH
🏨 🍴 **Corner House Inn $$**
Main Street, Center Sandwich
NH 03227. Tel: 603/284-6219.
New England country dining.

WOLFEBORO
🍴 **Wolfe's Tavern $–$$**
90 North Main Street,
Wolfeboro NH. Tel: 603/9569-
3016. *Pub and steak house.*

MEREDITH
🏨 **Nutmeg Inn $$**
80 Pease Road, Meredith
NH 03253. Tel: 603/279-8811.

TOUR 21
WISCASSET
🍴 **Sarah's Café $**
Main Street, Wiscasset ME.
Tel: 207/882-7504. *Mexican style
cuisine.*

ROCKLAND
🏨 **Lime Rock Inn $$**
96 Lime Rock Street, Rockland
ME 04841. Tel: 207/594-2257.

🍴 **Café Miranda $$**
15 Oak Street, Rockland ME.
Tel: 207/594-2034. *Fun bistro.*

ROCKPORT
🏨 🍴 **Samoset Resort
$$$–$$$$**
220 Warrenton Street, Rockport
ME 04856. Tel: 207/594-2511 or
800/341-1650.

CAMDEN
🍴 **Sea Dog Brewing Co. $**
43 Mechanic Street, Camden
ME. Tel: 207/236-6863. *Hearty
pub fare; on water.*

TOUR 22
PORTLAND
🏨 **The Danforth $$$**
163 Danforth Street, Portland
ME 04102. Tel: 207/879-8755 or
800/991-6557.

🏨 🍴 **Portland Regency Hotel
$$$**
20 Milk Street, Portland ME
04101. Tel: 207/774-4200 or
800/727-3435.

🍴 **Back Bay Grill $$**
65 Portland Street, Portland
ME. Tel: 207/772-8833. *Modern
New England cuisine; innovative
appetizers; extensive wine list.*

🍴 **Fore Street Restaurant $$**
288 Fore Street, Portland ME.
Tel: 207/775-2717. *Trendy, state-
of-the-art modern American
cuisine.*

TOUR 23
BETHEL
🏨 🍴 **Bethel Inn and Country
Club $$$–$$$$**
On the Green, Bethel ME
04217. Tel: 207/824-2175 or
800/654-0125.

NEWRY
🏨 **Black Bear B&B $$**
829 Sunday River Road, Newry
ME 04261. Tel: 207/824-0908.

RANGELEY
🏨 **Rangeley Inn $$**
Main Street, Rangeley ME
04970. Tel: 207/864-3341 or
800/666-3687.

🍴 **The Red Onion $**
Main Street, Rangeley ME.
Tel: 207/864-5022. *Pizzas, steaks;
casual.*

KINGFIELD
🍴 **Longfellow's Restaurant
$–$$**
Main Street, Kingfield ME.
Tel: 207/265-4394. *Casual dining
in a tavern overlooking the
Carrabassett River.*

FARMINGTON
🍴 **Homestead Bakery $**
186 Broadway Street,
Farmington ME. Tel: 207/778-
6162. *Down-home dishes.*

Practical Information

The addresses, telephone numbers and opening times of the attractions mentioned in the tours, including the telephone numbers of the Tourist Information Offices are listed below tour by tour.

TOUR I

|i| Cambridge Visitor Information Booth, Harvard Square, Cambridge MA 02138. Tel: 617/441-2884.

|i| Lexington Visitor Center, 1875 Massachusetts Avenue, Lexington MA 02473. Tel: 781/862-1450.

|i| Minute Man Visitor Center, Route 2A, Lexington MA 02473. Tel: 978/369-6993.

|i| Concord Chamber of Commerce, 58 Main Street, Concord MA 01742. Tel: 978/369-3120.

|i| North Bridge Visitor Center, 174 Liberty Street, Concord MA 01742. Tel: 978/369-6993.

1 Museum of Our National Heritage
33 Marrett Road (Route 2A), Lexington. Tel: 781/861-6559. *Open Mon–Sat 10–5, Sun 12–5.*

2 Munroe Tavern
1322 Massachusetts Avenue. Lexington. Tel: 781/862-1703. *Open Apr–Oct daily for tours.*

3 Lexington
Buckman Tavern
1 Bedford Street.
Tel: 781/862-5598. *Open Mar–early Dec, Mon–Sat 10–4, Sun 1–4.*

Hancock-Clarke House
36 Hancock Street.
Tel: 781/861-0928. *Open Apr–Oct daily for tours.*

4 Minute Man National Historical Park
Route 2A, Lexington.
Tel: 978/369-6993.

5 Concord
The Wayside
455 Lexington Road. Tel: 978/369-6975. *Open Apr–Oct. Tours Tue–Sun 1, 2.30 ,4.*

Orchard House
399 Lexington Road.
Tel: 978/369-4118. *Open Mon–Sat 10–4.30, Sun 1–4.30; shorter hours on winter weekdays. Closed first 2 weeks Jan.*

Concord Museum
200 Lexington Road.
Tel: 978/369-9763. *Open Mon–Sat 9–5, Sun noon–5. Shorter hours in winter.*

Ralph Waldo Emerson House
23 Cambridge Turnpike.
Tel: 978/369-2236. *Open mid-Apr–mid-Oct, Thu–Sun 10–4.30.*

Sleepy Hollow Cemetery
Route 62/Bedford Street, Concord. Tel: 978/318-3233.

Old Manse
269 Monument Street.
Tel: 978/369-3909. *Open mid-Apr–Oct, 10–5.*

6 Walden Pond
Walden Pond State Reservation, Route 126/Walden Street.
Tel: 978/369-3254.

7 Gropius House
68 Baker Bridge Road, Lincoln. Tel: 781/259-8098. *Open Jun–mid-Oct, Wed–Sun. Some winter weekends. Phone for hours.*

8 DeCordova Museum and Sculpture Park
51 Sandy Pond Road, Lincoln. Tel: 781/259-8355. *Open Tue–Sun 11–5. Park open to 10pm in summer.*

Recommended Trips
South Bridge Boathouse
496 Main Street, Concord.
Tel: 978/369-9438. *Open Apr–Oct daily.*

TOUR 2

|i| Boston Common Visitor Information Center, 147 Tremont Street. Tel: 617/536-4100.

|i| Marblehead Information Booth, Pleasant and Spring streets, Marblehead MA 01945. Tel: 781/631-2868.

|i| National Park Service Regional Visitor Service, New Liberty and Essex streets, Salem MA 01970. Tel: 978/740-1650.

|i| Stage Fort Park Information Center, Hough Avenue, Gloucester MA 01930. Tel: 978/281-8865 (seasonal) or 33 Commercial Street. Tel: 978/283-1601.

|i| Rockport Chamber of Commerce, Upper Main Street, Rockport MA 01966 (seasonal) or 22 Broadway. Tel: 978/546-6575.

|i| Newburyport Information Kiosk, Merrimac Street, Newburyport MA 01950. Tel: 978/462-9998.

2 Marblehead
Jeremiah Lee Mansion
161 Washington Street.
Tel: 781/631-1069. *Open mid-May–Oct, Mon–Sat 10–4, Sun 1–4.*

3 Salem
Salem Witch Museum
Washington Square North.
Tel: 978/744-1692. *Open daily 10–5 (till 7pm Jul, Aug).*

Salem Witch House
282 Rear of Derby Street.
Tel: 978/740-9229. *Open daily, Apr–Jun and Sep 9–6; Jul–Aug 9–9; Oct 9–midnight; Nov–Apr 10–5.*

Witch House
310½ Essex Street. Tel: 978/744-0180. *Open mid-Mar–Nov 10–4.30 (till 6pm Jul–Oct).*

Pioneer Village
Forest River Park. Tel: 978/744-0991. *Open Apr–Nov, Mon–Sat 10–5, Sun noon–5.*

Peabody Essex Museum
East India Square.
Tel: 978/745-9500. *Open Mon–Sat 10–5, Sun noon–5. Closed Mon Nov–Mar.*

Salem Maritime National Historic Site
174 Derby Street. Tel: 978/740-1680. *Open daily 9–5.*

6 Hammond Castle Museum
30 Hesperus Avenue, Gloucester. Tel: 978/283-2080/7673. *Open. Mon–Fri 10–4.*

7 Gloucester
Cape Ann Historical Museum
27 Pleasant Street.
Tel: 978/283-0455. *Open Tue–Sat 10–5. Closed Feb.*

8 Rocky Neck and Beauport
Sleeper-McCann House Museum
75 Eastern Point Boulevard, Beauport, Gloucester. Tel: 978/283-0800. *Open daily mid-May–mid-Oct.*

9 Rockport
Rockport Art Association Gallery
12 Main Street.
Tel: 978/546-6604.

10 Pigeon Cove
Paper House
52 Pigeon Hill. Tel: 978/546-2629. *Open daily Apr–Oct, 10–5.*

11 Essex
Shipbuilding Museum
28 Main Street. Tel: 978/768-7541. *Open May–Oct, Mon–Sat 10–5, Sun 1–4.*

12 Ipswich
John Whipple House
1 South Village Green.
Tel: 978/356-2811. *Open May–mid-Oct, Wed–Sat 10–4, Sun 1–4 (last tour 3).*

John Heard House
54 South Main Street.
Tel: 978/356-2811. *Open May–mid-Oct, Wed–Sat 10–4, Sun 1–4 (last tour 3).*

Castle Hill/Crane's Beach
290 Argilla Road. Tel: 978/356-4351 (beach) – 4354. *Call for details.*

13 Plum Island and the Parker River National Wildlife Refuge
Northern Boulevard, Plum Island, Newburyport.
Tel: 978/465-5753.

Practical Information

i Tourist Information Office
12 Number on tour

14 Newburyport
Custom House Maritime
Museum
25 Water Street. Tel: 978/
462-8681. *Open Apr–Dec,
Mon–Sat 10–4, Sun 1–4.*

Cushing House Museum
98 High Street. Tel: 978/
462-2681. *Open May–Oct,
Tue–Fri 10–4, Sat 11–2.*

For History Buffs
Abbot Hall
188 Washington Street.
Tel: 781/631-0000. *Open
Jun–Oct, daily 8–6;
Nov–May, weekdays 8–6.*

Special to...
The House of the Seven
Gables
54 Turner Street. Tel: 978/
744-0991. *Open daily 10–5
(Jul–Oct, 10–7).*

Woodmans of Essex
121 Main Street, Essex.
Tel: 978/768-6451 and
800/649-1773. *Open
summer 11–10; closes
8/9pm in winter.*

Recommended Walks
Halibut Point State Park
Off Route 127, Rockport.
Tel: 978/546-2997.

Back to Nature
Wolf Hollow
144 Essex Road, Ipswich.
Tel: 978/356-0216.

For Children
Moby Duck Amphibious
Sightseeing
75 Essex Avenue,
Gloucester. Tel: 978/281-
9565. *Daily from 10am.*

The *Adventure*
Jodrey State Fish Pier,
Route 128. Tel: 508/281-
8079. *Open late May–early
Sep, Thu–Sun 10–4.*

TOUR 3
---

i Cape Cod Chamber of
Commerce, Hyannis MA
02601. Tel: 508/862-0700.

i Cape Cod Canal
Chamber of Commerce,
70 Main Street, Buzzards
Bay MA 02532.
Tel: 508/759-6000.

i Yarmouth Chamber of
Commerce, 657 Route 28,

West Yarmouth MA
02675. Tel: 508/778-1008.

i Dennis Chamber of
Commerce, Routes 134/28,
West Dennis MA 02760.
Tel: 508/398-3568.

i Brewster Chamber of
Commerce, 74 Locust
Lane, Brewster MA 02631.
Tel: 508/255-7045.

i Eastham Information
Center, Route 6, Eastham
MA 02642. Tel: 508/255-
3444.

i Wellfleet Chamber of
Commerce Information
Booth, off Route 6, South
Wellfleet MA 02663.
Tel: 508/349-2510.

i Provincetown
Chamber of Commerce,
307 Commercial Street,
Provincetown MA 02657.
Tel: 508/487-3424.

i Chatham Information
Booth, 533 Main Street,
Chatham MA 02633.
Tel: 508/945-5199.

2 Sandwich
Thomas Dexter Grist Mill
Water Street.
Tel: 508/888-4910 (town
hall). *Open mid-Jun–mid-
Sep, Mon–Sat 10–4.15.*

Hoxie House
18 Water Street. Tel: 508/
888-1173. *Open mid-Jun–
Sep, Mon–Sat 10–5, Sun 1–5.*

Thornton W. Burgess
Museum
4 Water Street (Route
130). Tel: 508/888-4668.
*Open Apr–Oct, Mon–Sat
10–4, Sun 1–4.*

3 Barnstable
Sturgis Library
Route 6A. Tel: 508/362-
6636. *Call for hours.*

4 Yarmouth
Captain Bangs Hallet
House
11 Strawberry Lane.
Tel: 508/362-3021. *Open
Jun–mid-Oct, Thu–Sun.*

Thatcher House and
Winslow-Crocker House
250 Route 6A. Tel: 508/362
-4285. *Open Jun–mid-Oct,
Tue, Thu, Sat, Sun noon–5.*

5 Concord
Josiah Dennis Manse
Museum
Nobscusset Road and
Whig Street, Dennis.
Tel: 508/385-2232. *Open
Jul–Aug, Tue and Thu 2–4.*

Cape Playhouse
Main Street, Dennis.
Tel: 508/385-3838. *Open
summer Mon–Sat evenings,
matinees Wed and Thu.
Children's Theater Fri am.*

Cape Museum of Fine Arts
Route 6A, Dennis.
Tel: 508/385-4477. *Open
Mon–Sat 10–5, Sun 1–5.*

Scargo Tower
Off Route 6A. *Open daily.*

6 Brewster
Brewster Historical
Society Museum
Route 6A, Spruce Hill.
Tel: 508/896-8495.

New England Fire and
History Museum
1439 Main Street, Route
6A. Tel: 508/896-5711.
*Open May–Sep 10–3;
weekends in fall.*

8 Eastham
Captain Edward Penniman
House
Fort Hill Road. Tel: 508/
255-3421. *Tours Mon–Sat;
open Tue–Fri 1–4.*

Cape Cod National
Seashore
Salt Pond Visitor Center,
Route 6. Tel: 508/255-3421.

Oldest Windmill
Opposite Town Hall.
Open Jun–Sep, daily 10–5.

12 Provincetown
Pilgrim Monument and
Provincetown Museum
High Pole Hill. Tel: 508/487-
1310 or 800/247-1620.
Open daily. Closed Jan–Mar.

13 Chatham
Railroad Museum
Depot Road. Tel: 508/945-
2809. *Open mid-Jun–mid-
Sep, Tue–Fri 1–4.*

Special to...
Sandwich Glass Museum
109 Main Street.
Tel: 508/888-0251. *Open
Feb–Mar, Wed–Sun 9.30–4;
Apr–Oct, daily 9.30–5.*

Cranberry World Visitors
Center
225 Water Street,
Plymouth. Tel: 508/747-
2350. *Open daily May–Nov.*

For Children
Heritage Plantation
Pine and Grove streets.
Tel: 508/888-3300. *Open
early May–Oct, daily 10–5.*

Green Briar Nature
Center & Jam Kitchen
6 Discovery Hill Road, East
Sandwich. Tel: 508/888-
6870. *Open Jan–Mar,
Tue–Sat 10–4; Apr–Dec,
Mon–Sat 10–4, Sun 1–4.*

Cape Cod Museum of
Natural History
Route 6A, Brewster.
Tel: 508/896-3867. *Open
Tue–Sat 9.30–4.30, Sun
12.30–4.30.*

Scenic Route
Cape Cod Central
Railroad
252 Main Street, Hyannis.
Tel: 508/771-3800. *Open
late May–Oct, Tue–Sun
10–4 (check last train
times). Also Mon holiday
weekends.*

TOUR 4
---

i Greater Springfield
CVB, PO Box 15589,
Springfield MA 01115.
Tel: 413/787-1548.

i Riverfront Park
Information Center, West
Columbus Avenue,
Springfield MA 01115.

i Stockbridge
Information Booth, Main
Street, Stockbridge
MA 01262.

i Lenox Chamber of
Commerce, 75 Main
Street, Lenox MA 01240.
Tel: 413/637-3646.

i Berkshire Hills Visitors
Bureau, Berkshire
Common Level Plaza,
Pittsfield MA 01201.
Tel: 413/443-9186.

i RSVP Tourist
Information Booth, Park
Square, Pittsfield MA
01201. Tel: 413/443-7477.

i Williamstown
Chamber of Commerce,
Routes 2 and 7,
Williamstown MA 01267.
Tel: 413/458-9077.

i Shelburne Falls Village
Information Center, 75
Bridge Street, Shelburne
Falls MA 01370. Tel: 413/
625-2544.

i Pioneer Valley Tourist
Information Center, Routes
5 and 10, South Deerfield
MA 01342. Tel: 413/665-
7333.

i Northampton Area
Visitors Center, 99 Pleasant
Street, Northampton MA
01060. Tel: 413/584-1900.

2 Great Barrington
Aston Magna Festival
St. James Church. Tel: 413/
528-3595. *Open Jul–Aug.*

5 Stockbridge
Red Lion Inn
Main Street. Tel: 413/298-
5545.

Norman Rockwell
Museum
Route 183. Tel: 413/298-
4100. *Open daily 10–5
(closes 4 winter weekdays).
Studio open May–Oct only.*

Chesterwood
Off Route 183.
Tel: 413/298-3579. *Open
May–Oct, daily 10–5.*

Naumkeag
Prospect Hill Road.
Tel: 413/298-3239. *Open
May–Oct, daily 10–5.*

Berkshire Botanical
Garden
Junction Routes 183 and
102. Tel: 413/298-3926.
Open May–Oct, daily 10–5.

6 Tanglewood
Tanglewood Music Festival
Route 183, Lenox. Tel: 413/
637-5165. *Jul and Aug.*

7 Lenox
The Mount–Edith Warton
Home
Plunkett Street. Tel: 413/
637-1899. *Open late
May–Nov, daily 9–5.*

Shakespeare & Co.
70 Kemble Street, Lennox.
Tel: 413/637-1199. *Season
May–Dec.*

8 Arrowhead
780 Holmes Road,
Pittsfield. Tel: 413/442-
1793. *Open Jun–Oct. Rest of
year by appointment only.*

**9 Hancock Shaker
Village**
Junction Routes 20 and 41,
Pittsfield. Tel: 413/443-
0188. *Open Apr–Nov, daily
9.30–5 (closes 3pm early in
season).*

10 Williamstown
Sterling and Francine
Clark Art Institute
225 South Street. Tel: 413/
458-2303. *Open Tue–Sun
10–5; also Mon Jul and Aug.*

Williams College Museum
of Art
Main Street. Tel: 413/597-
2429. *Open Tue–Sat 10–5,
Sun and holiday Mon 1–5.*

Williamstown Theatre
Festival
Williams College. Tel: 413/
597-3400. *Open Jun–Aug.*

11 North Adams
MASS MoCA
87 Marshall Street. Tel:
413/664-4481. *Open Jun–
Oct, daily 10–6; winter,
Tue–Sun 10–4.*

13 Deerfield
The Street (off Routes 5
and 10). Tel: 413/774-
5581. *Open daily 9.30–4.30.*

Emily Dickinson House
280 Main Street, Amherst.
Tel: 413/542-8161. *Limited
opening. Make reservation.*

Special to…
Basketball Hall of
Fame/Naismith Memorial
1150 West Columbus
Avenue, Springfield.
Tel: 413/781-6500. *Open
daily 10–5.*

For Children
Six Flags New England
Route 159, Agawam. Tel:
413/786-9300. *Open
May–Oct, daily 10–10 or
11; winter weekends, times
vary.*

Magic Wings Butterfly
Conservatory and Garden
Routes 5 and 10, South
Deerfield. Tel: 413/665-
2805. *Open all year daily.*

For History Buffs
Colonel John Ashley
House
Cooper Hill Road, Ashley
Falls. Tel: 413/229-8600.
*Open May–mid-Oct, 10–5;
Sat, Sun and holidays 1–5.*

Back to Nature
Barthlomew's Cobble
Weatogue Road off Route
7A, Ashley Falls. Tel: 413/
229-8600. *Open daily
sunrise–sunset. Museum
8.30–4.30, closed holidays.*

Pleasant Valley Wildlife
Sanctuary
472 West Mountain Road.
Tel: 413/637-0320.

TOUR 5

i Boston Common
Visitor Information Center,
147 Tremont Street.
Tel: 617/536-4100.

i Boston National
Historical Park Visitor
Center, 15 State Street.
Tel: 617/242-5642.

i Charlestown Navy Yard
Visitor Center. Constitution
Road, Charlestown.
Tel: 617/242-5601.

2 State House
Beacon Street. Tel: 617/
727-3676. *Tours weekdays
and Sats 10–4.*

**8 Old Corner
Bookstore/Boston
Globe Store**
1 School Street.
Tel: 617/367-4004.

**9 Old South Meeting
House**
310 Washington Street.
Tel: 617/482-6439. *Open
daily.*

10 Old State House
Corner of State and
Washington streets.
Tel: 617/720-3290/3285.
Open daily 9.30–5.

11 Faneuil Hall
Merchants Row. Tel: 617/
242-5675/5642. *Open daily
9–5.*

**12 Union Oyster
House**
41 Union Street.
Tel: 617/227-2750.

15 Paul Revere's House
19 North Square. Tel:
617/523-2338. *Open daily
9.30–4.15 (5.15 summer).*

18 USS Constitution
Pier 1, Charlestown Navy
Yard. Tel: 617/242-5670/
5671. *Open daily 10–4.*

**19 Bunker Hill
Monument**
Monument Square,
Charlestown. Tel: 617/242-
5641. *Open daily 9–4.*

Special to…
Omni Parker House
60 School Street.
Tel: 617/227-8600 or
800/THE OMNI.

TOUR 6

i Boston Common
Visitor Information Center,
147 Tremont Street.
Tel: 617/536-4100.

i Boston National
Historical Park Visitor
Center, 15 State Street.
Tel: 617/242-5642.

**1 New England
Aquarium**
Central Wharf. Tel: 617/
973-5200. *Open daily 9–5
(later some evenings).*

3 Faneuil Hall
See Tour 5.

**6 The Harrison Gray
Otis House**
141 Cambridge Street.
Tel: 617/227-3956.
Open Wed–Sun 11–5.

7 Black Heritage Trail
Abiel Smith School
46 Joy Street. Tel: 617/725-
0022. *Open daily 10–4.
Closed Sun in winter.*

African Meeting House
8 Smith Court.
Tel: 617/725-0022. *Open
daily 10–4.*

**8 Nichols House
Museum**
55 Mount Vernon Street.
Tel: 617/227-6993. *Call for
opening hours.*

Special to…
Durgin-Park
340 Faneuil Hall Market-
place. Tel: 617/227-2038.

Practical Information

ⓘ Tourist Information Office

⓬ Number on tour

Scenic Routes
Boston Duck Tours
Depart from Prudential
Center, Boylston Street.
Tel: 617/227-5296. *Apr–
Nov, half-hourly from 9am.*

TOUR 7

ⓘ Cambridge Visitor
Information Booth,
Harvard Square,
Cambridge MA 02139.
Tel: 617/441-2884.

ⓘ Harvard University, 26
Oxford Street, Cambridge
MA 02138. Tel: 617/495-
3045. Museums and tours.

ⓘ Harvard Information
Center, Holyoke Center
Arcade, 1350
Massachusetts Avenue,
Cambridge MA 02138.
Tel: 617/495-1573.

**⓺ Carpenter Center
for the Visual Arts**
24 Quincy Street. Tel: 617/
495-4700 for film times.

**⓻ Fogg and Busch-
Reisinger Art
Museums**
32 Quincy Street.
Tel: 617/495-9400. *Open
Mon–Sat 10–5, Sun 1–5.*

**⓼ Arthur M. Sackler
Museum**
485 Broadway. Tel:
617/495-9400. *Open
Mon–Sat 10–5, Sun 1–5.*

⓽ Memorial Hall
45 Quincy Street. Tel: 617/
496-2222. *Opening very
limited; phone for details.
Transepts open daily noon–6.*

**⓾ Museums of
Natural History**
26 Oxford Street.
Tel: 617/495-8206. *Open
Mon–Sat 9–5, Sun 1–5.*

⓭ Brattle Street
Cambridge Historical
Society
Hooper-Lee Nichols
House, 159 Brattle Street.
Tel: 617/547-4254. *Open
Tue and Thu 2–5.*

**⓮ Longfellow House
National Historic Site**
105 Brattle Street. Tel: 617/
876-4491. *Open Wed–Sun
10–4.30.*

TOUR 8

ⓘ Hartford Civic Center,
1 Civic Center Plaza,
Hartford CT 06103.
Tel: 860/249-6333.

⓶ Old State House
800 Main Street. Tel:
860/522-6766. *Open
Mon–Fri 10–4, Sat 10–3.
Closed last 2 weeks Aug.*

⓷ Travelers Tower
1 Tower Square Tel: 860/
277-4208. *Tours mid-May–
Oct, Mon–Fri 10–3.*

**⓸ Wadsworth
Atheneum**
600 Main Street. Tel: 860/
278-2670. *Open Tue–Fri
11–5, Sat and Sun 10–5.*

**⓺ Bushnell Park
Carousel**
Jewell Street. Tel: 860/987-
5900. *Open mid-Apr–mid-
May, Sat–Sun 11–5; mid-
May–Aug, Tue–Sun 11–5.*

⓼ State Capitol
210 Capitol Avenue. Tel:
860/240-0222. *Tours
Mon–Fri 9.15–1.15
(2.15 Jul–Aug); also Sat
10.15–2.15 Apr–Oct.*

**⓽ Museum of
Connecticut History**
231 Capitol Avenue.
Tel: 860/566-3056. *Open
Mon–Fri 9.30–4.*

⓾ Mark Twain House
351 Farmington Avenue.
Tel: 860/247-0998. *Open
Mon–Sat 9.30–4, Sun
noon–5. Closed Tue Jan–Apr
and mid-Oct–Nov.*

**⓫ Harriet Beecher
Stowe House**
Farmington Avenue at
Forest Street. Tel: 860/525-
9258. *Open daily,
9.30–4.30, closed Mon, mid-
Oct–Nov and Jan–May.*

**⓬ Connecticut
Historical Society**
1 Elizabeth Street.
Tel: 860/236-5621.
*Open Tue–Sun, noon–5;
Library Tue–Sat 10–5.*

**⓭ Noah Webster
House**
227 South Main Street,

West Hartford. Tel:
860/521-5362. *Open
Thu–Mon 1–4; extended
hours in summer.*

Back to Nature
Elizabeth Park Rose
Garden
Prospect Avenue.
Tel: 860/242-0017. *Open
daily dawn–dusk.*

For Children
Science Center of
Connecticut
950 Trout Brook Drive,
West Hartford.
Tel: 860/231-2824. *Open
Tue–Sat 10–5, Sun noon–5.*

TOUR 9

ⓘ Greater New Haven
Convention and Visitors
Bureau, 59 Elm Street,
New Haven CT 06510.
Tel: 203/777-8550.

ⓘ Yale University Visitor
Information Center, 149
Elm Street, New Haven CT
06520. Tel: 203/432-2300.

**⓹ Yale University Art
Gallery**
1111 Chapel Street at York
Street. Tel: 203/432-0600.
*Open Tue–Sat 10–5, Sun
noon–6. Closed major
holidays.*

**⓺ Yale Center for
British Art**
1080 Chapel Street.
Tel: 203/432-2800. *Open
Tue–Sat 10–5, Sun noon–5.
Closed major holidays.*

**⓻ Yale Repertory
Theatre**
Corner of Chapel and York
streets. Tel: 203/432-1234.
Open Sep–May.

**⓫ Beinecke Rare
Book Library**
121 Wall Street
Tel: 203/432-2977. *Open
Mon–Fri 8.30–5, Sat 10–5.
Closed holidays and Sat in
Aug.*

TOUR 10

ⓘ Hartford Civic Center,
1 Civic Center Plaza,
Hartford CT 06103.
Tel: 860/249-6333.

ⓘ Litchfield Hills
Information Booth, Route
202, On-the-Green, Litch-
field CT 06759. Tel:
860/567-4506.

ⓘ Chamber of
Commerce, Main Street,
Salisbury CT 06068.
Tel: 860/435-0740.

⓵ Litchfield
Tapping Reeve House and
Law School
Route 63 South.
Tel: 860/567-4501. *Open
Tue–Sat 11–5, Sun 1–5.*

Litchfield Historical
Society Museum
7 South Street.
Tel: 860/567-4501. *Open
mid-Apr–mid-Nov, Tue–Sat
11–5, Sun 1–5.*

⓷ Lake Waramaug
Hopkins Vineyard
25 Hopkins Road, New
Preston. Tel: 860/868-7954.
*Open May–Dec, Mon–Sat
10–5, Sun 9–5; Jan–Feb,
Fri–Sat 10–5, Sun 11–5;
Mar–Apr, Wed–Sat 10–5,
Sun 11–5.*

⓺ Kent
Sloane-Stanley Museum
and Kent Furnace
Route 7. Tel: 860/927-3849.
*Open mid-May–Oct,
Wed–Sun 10–4.*

Connecticut Antique
Machinery Association
Museum
Route 7. Tel: 860/927-0050.
*Open May–Sep, Sat–Sun
10–5.*

**⓼ Cornwall Bridge to
West Cornwall**
Clarke's Outdoors
163 Route 7, West
Cornwall. Tel: 860/672-
6365. *Open mid-Mar–Dec.*

⓽ Lime Rock Park
Routes 7 and 112, Lake-
ville. Tel: 860/435-5000.
Regular meets Apr–Nov.

⓫ Salisbury
Chaiwalla
1 Main Street. Tel: 860/
435-9758. *Open Mon–Sat.*

Harney & Sons
23 Brook Street, Lakeville.
Tel: 800-TEATIME. *Open
Mon–Sat.*

Special to...
White Flower Farm
Route 63. Tel: 860/567-
8789. *Open daily 9–6;
Nov–Mar 10–5.*

The Silo
44 Upland Road, New
Milford. Tel: 860/355-0300.
Open Wed–Mon 10–5.

Cornwall Bridge Pottery
Route 7, between junc-
tions with Routes 45 and
4. Tel: 860/672-6545. *Open
daily 9–5.*

Recommended Walks
Kent Falls State Park
Route 7. Tel: 860/927-3238.
Open daily 8am–dusk.

TOUR 11

[i] Greater New Haven
Convention and Visitors
Bureau, 59 Elm Street,
New Haven CT 06511.
Tel: 203/777-8550.

[1] Branford
Nathaniel Harrison House
124 Main Street. Tel: 203/
488-4828. *Phone for hours.*

[3] Guilford
Henry Whitfield State
Museum
248 Old Whitfield Street.
Tel: 203/453-2457. *Open
Feb–mid-Dec, Wed–Sun
10–4.30, or by appointment.*

Hyland House
84 Boston Street.
Tel: 203/453-9477. *Open
Jun–Sep, Tue–Sun 10–4.30;
Sep–mid-Oct, weekends only
10–4.*

Thomas Griswold House
171 Boston Street. Tel:
203/453-3176. *Open mid-
Jun–mid-Sep, Tue–Sun 11–4
or by appointment.*

[4] Madison
Hammonasset Beach
State Park
Route 1. Tel: 203/245-2785.
Open daily 8–sunset.

[5] Old Saybrook
General William Hart
House
350 Main Street. Tel: 860/
388-6148. *Open mid-
Jun–mid-Sep, Fri–Sun
12.30–4.*

[6] Essex
Griswold Inn
36 Main Street.
Tel: 860/767-1776.

Connecticut River
Museum
67 Main Street, Steamboat
Dock. Tel: 860/767-8269.
Open Tue–Sun 10–5.

Pratt House
19 West Avenue.
Tel: 860/767-0681. *Open
Jun–early Sep, Sat–Sun 1–4.*

[7] East Haddam
Goodspeed Opera House
Route 82. Tel: 860/873-
8664. *Open Apr–Dec,
Wed–Sun.*

Nathan Hale Schoolhouse
Main Street. Tel: 860/873-
3399. *Open Sat, Sun, holidays 2–4.*

[8] Gillette Castle
Gillette Castle State Park
67 River Road. Tel:
860/526-2336. *Open daily,
end May–mid-Oct, 10–5.*

[9] Old Lyme
Florence Griswold
Museum
96 Lyme Street. Tel: 860/
434-5542. *Open Nov–May,
Wed–Sun 1–5; Jun–Oct,
Tue–Sat 10–5, Sun, 1–5.*

Lyme Academy of Fine
Art
84 Lyme Street.
Tel: 860/434-5232. *Open
Tue–Sat 10–4, Sun 1–4.*

[10] New London
Hempsted House
11 Hempsted Street. Tel:
860/443-7949 or 247-
8996. *Open mid-May–mid-
Oct, Thu–Sun noon–4.*

US *Eagle*
US Coast Guard Academy,
Mohegan Avenue. Tel: 860/
444-8270. *Open Fri–Sun
1–5 when in port. Museum
May–Oct, daily 1–5.*

Lyman-Allyn Art Museum
625 Williams Street.
Tel: 860/443-2545. *Open
Tue–Sat 10–5, Sun 1–5.*

Monte Cristo Cottage
325 Pequot Avenue. Tel:
860/443-0051. *Open Jun–
Sep, Tue–Sat 10–5, Sun 1–5.*

Eugene O'Neill Theater
305 Great Neck Road,
Waterford. Tel: 860/443-
5378.

[11] USS *Nautilus*
Naval Submarine Base, 1
Crystal Lake Road, Groton.
Tel: 860/694-3174 or 800/
343-0079. *Open daily 9–5,
Tue 1–5; Nov–mid-May
9–4, closed Tue.*

[12] Noank
Abbott's Lobster-in-the-
Rough
117 Pearl Street. Tel: 860/
536-7719. *Open Apr–Aug,
daily; weekends to mid-Oct.*

[13] Mystic
Mystic Seaport
75 Greenmanville Avenue.
Tel: 860/572-5315. *Open
daily 9–5, winter 10–4.*

Mystic Aquarium
55 Coogan Boulevard.
Tel: 860/572-5955. *Open
daily 9–5 (6pm Jul–Sep).*

Olde Mistick Village
Coogan Boulevard (Route
27). Tel: 860/536-4941.
*Open Mon–Sat 10–6 (8pm
in summer), Sun noon–5.*

[14] Stonington
Old Lighthouse Museum
7 Water Street. Tel: 860/
535-1440. *Open May–Oct,
Tue–Sun 10–5; Jul–Aug
daily.*

Scenic Routes
The Essex Steam Train
and Riverboat Ride
Valley Railroad, 1 Railroad
Avenue (off Route 9).
Tel: 860/767-0103. *Open
May–Dec; call for schedule.*

Special to...
Pequot Museum and
Research Center
110 Pequot Trail, Mashan-
tucket. Tel: 800/411-9671.
Open Wed–Mon 10–6.

For History Buffs
Fort Griswold State Park
57 Fort Street, Groton.
tel: 860/445-1729. *Open
daily, 8am–sunset.*

For Children
Science Center of East
Connecticut
33 Gallows Lane, New
London. Tel: 860/442-0391·

*Open Tue–Sat 10–6, Sun
1–5.*

Ocean Beach Park
1225 Ocean Avenue, New
London. Tel: 860/447-3031.
*Open late May–early Sep,
daily 9am–11pm.*

TOUR 12

[i] Convention Center, 1
West Exchange Street,
Providence, RI 02903.
Tel: 401/274-1636 or
800/233-1636.

**[3] Rhode Island School
of Design**
Museum of Art
224 Benefit Street.
Tel: 401/454-6500. *Open
Tue–Sun 10–5 (8pm Fri).*

Woods-Gerry Gallery
62 Prospect Street.
Tel: 401/454-6141. *Open
Mon–Sat 10–4, Sun 2–5;
closed Mon Feb 21–Jun 1.*

**[4] Providence
Athenaeum**
251 Benefit Street. Tel: 401/
421-6970. *Open Mon–Thu
9–7, Fri, Sat 9–5, Sun 1–4.*

**[5] David Winton Bell
Gallery**
264 College Street.
Tel: 401/863-2952. *Open
Mon–Fri 11–4, Sat and Sun
1–4.*

[6] Libraries
John Hay Library
Prospect and College
streets. Tel: 401/863-3725.
Open Mon–Fri 9–5.

[7] Brown University
45 Prospect Street,
College Hill. Tel: 401/863-
1000. *Tours Mon–Fri at 10,
11, 1, 3 and 4 (from
Admissions Office); Sat 10,
11 and noon during fall.*

[8] Benefit Street
Governor Stephen
Hopkins House
Benefit/Hopkins streets.
Tel: 401/741-7067. *Open
Apr–Dec, Wed and Sat 1–4.*

[10] John Brown House
52 Power Street.
Tel: 401/331-8575. *Open
Tue–Sat 10–5, Sun noon–4.
Closed Mon, except holidays.*

13 The Arcade
65 Weybosset Street.
Tel: 401/598-1199. *Open
Mon–Fri 10–6, Sat 10–4.*

TOUR 13

i Gateway Information
Center, 23 America's Cup
Avenue, Newport RI
02840. Tel: 401/849-8048.

**1 Brick Market
Building**
Museum of Newport
History
Thames Street/Washington
Square. Tel: 401/841-8770.
*Open Apr–Sep, daily 10–5,
Sun 1–5; closed Tue;
Oct–Mar, Fri–Sun 10–5.*

**4 Wanton-Lyman-
Hazard House**
17 Broadway.
Tel: 401/846-0813. *Open
Thu–Sat, 11–3 in season.*

5 Touro Synagogue
85 Touro Street. Tel: 401/
847-4794. *Open May–Jun
and early Sep–mid-Oct,
Mon–Thu 1–3; Jul–early Sep,
Sun–Fri 10–5, Nov–Apr, Sun
1–3.*

**6 The Newport
Historical Society**
82 Touro Street. Tel: 401/
846-0813. *Open mid-Jun–
Aug, Tue–Sat 9.30–4.30;
Sep–mid-Jun, Tue–Fri
9.30–4.30, Sat 9.30–noon.*

**10 The Redwood
Library and
Athenaeum**
50 Belleville Avenue.
Tel: 401/847-0292. *Open
Tue–Thu 9.30–8; Mon, Fri,
Sat 9.30–5.30; Sun 1–5.*

**11 Newport Art
Museum**
76 Bellevue Avenue.
Tel: 401/848-8200. *Open
Jun–Aug, daily 10–5; Sep–
May, Tue–Sun, shorter hours.*

**12 Newport Casino
and the International
Tennis Hall of Fame**
194 Bellevue Avenue.
Tel: 401/849-3990. *Open
daily 10–5. Call for details
during tournaments.*

13 Kingscote Mansion
Bellevue Avenue.

Tel: 401/847-1000. *Open
May–Oct daily 10–5.*

14 The Elms
Bellevue Avenue. Tel: 401/
847-1000. *Open daily 10–5.*

Chepstow
Narragansett Avenue. Tel:
401/847-1000. *Open in
season, by reservation only.*

15 Château-sur-Mer
Bellevue Avenue.
Tel: 401/847-1000. *Open
May–Oct daily 10–5.*

16 Vernon Court
National Museum of
American Illustration
Bellevue Avenue.
Tel: 401/851-8949. *Open
by reservation only.*

17 The Breakers
Ochre Point Avenue.
Tel: 401/847-1000. *Open
late Mar–Dec, daily 10–5
(stables May–Oct).*

18 Rosecliff
Bellevue Avenue.
Tel: 401/847-1000. *Open
May–Oct, daily 10–5.*

**19 The Astors'
Beechwood Mansion**
580 Bellevue Avenue. Tel:
401/846-3772. *Open mid-
May–Oct, daily 10–5;
Nov–Dec 19 closes at 4;
Feb–mid-May, weekends
only.*

20 Marble House
Bellevue Avenue.
Tel: 401/847-1000. *Open
late Mar–Dec, daily 10–5.*

21 Belcourt Castle
657 Bellevue Avenue. Tel:
401/846-0669. *Open most
of year; phone for details.*

22 Rough Point
Bellevue Avenue.
Information and tickets
from the Gateway
Information Center.
Tel: 401/841-8770.

Special to…
Fort Adams State Park
Ocean Drive.
Tel: 401/847-2400. *Open
daily dawn–dusk.*

Museum of Yachting
Tel: 401/847-1018. *Open
mid-May–Oct, daily 10–5,
winter by appointment.*

Scenic Routes
Cliff Walk
Memorial Bouelvard.
Tel: 401/849-8048. *Open
all year.*

TOUR 14

i Veterans Memorial
Drive, Route 7, Bennington
VT 05201. Tel: 802/447-
3311.

**1 The Bennington
Museum**
West Main Street. Tel: 802/
447-1571. *Open daily Jun–
Oct 9–6; Nov–May 9–5.*

**4 Bennington Battle
Monument**
Monument Circle, Old
Bennington, off Route 9.
Tel: 802/447-0550. *Open
mid-Apr–Oct, daily 9–5.*

**5 Hemming's Sunoco
Station**
Tel: 802/447-9652. *Open
daily 7am–10pm.*

**6 Historic Bennington
Railroad Station**
Bennington Station Restau-
rant. Tel: 802/447-1080.

8 Potters' Yard
324 County Street.
Tel: 802/447-7531.

**11 Park-McCullough
House**
Park and West streets,
North Bennington. Tel:
802/442-5441. *Open late
May–Oct, Thu–Mon,
tours on the hour 10–3.*

TOUR 15

i Veterans Memorial
Drive, Bennington VT
05201. Tel: 802/447-3311.

i The Green, Chester.

1 Arlington
Norman Rockwell
Exhibition
Route 7A. Tel: 802/375-
6423. *Open May–Oct, daily
9–5; Nov–Apr, daily 10–4.*

2 Mt Equinox
Equinox Mountain Inn
Skyline Drive, Manchester.
Tel: 802/362-1113 or
800/868-6843. *Open
May–Oct 8am–10pm.*

American Museum of Fly
Fishing
Route 7A, Manchester.
Tel: 802/362-3300. *Open
daily 10–4.*

3 Hildene
Robert Todd Lincoln's
Hildene
Route 7A, Manchester.
Tel: 802/362-1788. *Open
mid-May–Oct, 9.30–5.30.*

**6 Bromley Mountain
Ski Area**
Bromley Mountain, Route
11. Tel: 802/824-5522.

8 Weston
Vermont Country Store
Route 100. Tel: 802/824-
3184. *Open Mon–Sat 9–5
(6pm Jul–Oct).*

Weston Village Store
Route 100. Tel: 802/824-
5477.

Weston Playhouse
On the Green. Tel: 802/
824-5288. *Open late
Jun–mid-Oct.*

9 Ludlow
Okemo Mountain Resort
77 Okemo Ridge Road.
Tel: 802/228-4041.

10 Chester
Fullerton Inn
40 Common, Chester.
Tel: 802/875-2444.

Green Mountain Railroad
54 Depot Street, Bellows
Falls. Tel: 800/707-3530.
*Open late Jun–mid-Oct, daily
9–5.*

11 Grafton
Grafton Village Cheese
Company
Tel: 800/472-3866. *Open
Mon–Fri 8.30–4.30,
weekends and holidays
10–4.30.*

Village Store
Tel: 802/843-2348. *Open
Mon–Sat.*

12 Newfane
Historical Society
Museum of Windham
County
Tel: 802/365-4148. *Open
Wed–Sun noon–5.*

13 Brattleboro
Museum and Art Center
Tel: 802/257-0124. *Open*

*mid-May–Nov, Tue–Sun
noon–6.*

Naulakha
Dummerston. Tel: 802/254-6868 for rental details.

Special to…
Orvis
Route 7A. Tel: 802/362-3750. *Open daily.*

TOUR 16

ⓘ Central Vermont Chamber of Commerce, PO Box 336, Barre VT 05641. Tel: 802/229-5711.

ⓘ Rutland Chamber of Commerce, at Routes 4B and 7, Rutland VT 05701. Tel: 802/775-0831.

❶ Norman Rockwell Museum
Route 4E. Tel: 802/773-6095. *Open daily 9–6.*

❷ Bethel
White River National Fish Hatchery
Route 107, Gaysville. Tel: 802/234-5400. *Open daily 8–3.*

❸ Quechee and Quechee Gorge
Simon Pearce Glass
Main Street. Tel: 802/295-2711. *Open daily 9–9.*

❹ Woodstock
Marsh-Billings-Rockefeller National Historic Park
Route 12. Tel: 802/457-3368. *Open late May–Oct, daily 10–5.*

Billings Farm Museum
Route 12. Tel: 802/457-2355. *Open late May–Oct, daily 10–5; Nov, Dec weekends.*

❻ Plymouth
Coolidge Homestead and the Wilder House
Tel: 802/672-3772. *Open daily 9.30–5 (weekdays only during off season).*

Plymouth Cheese Factory
Tel: 802/672-3650. *Open daily 9.30–5.*

Green Mountain Sugar House
Echo Lake, Route 100N, Ludlow. Tel: 800/643-9338. *Open daily 9–6.*

Special to…
Crowley Cheese
Healdville. Tel: 802/259-2340. *Cheese shop open daily; factory open Mon–Fri.*

Recommended Walks
Green Mountain Club
Route 100 between Stowe and Waterbury. Tel: 802/244-7037. *Open daily 9–5.*

For History Buffs
Joseph Smith Birthplace Memorial
Dairy Hill Road. Tel: 802/763-7742. *Open daily 9–5.*

TOUR 17

ⓘ Lake Champlain Regional Chamber of Commerce, 60 Main Street, Burlington VT 05401. Tel: 802/863-3489.

ⓘ Addison County Chamber of Commerce, 2 Court Street, Middlebury VT 05753. Tel: 802/388-7951 or 800/733-8376.

ⓘ Stowe Area Association, Main Street, Stowe VT 05672. Tel: 802/253-7321 or 877/GO STOWE.

❶ Shelburne
Shelburne Farms
1611 Harbor Road. Tel: 802/985-8686. *Open mid-May–mid-Oct, daily 10–5.*

Shelburne Museum
Route 7. Tel: 802/985-3346. *Open daily 10–5 (in winter reservations recommended).*

Vermont Teddy Bear Company
Route 7. Tel: 802/985-3001, ext.1800). *Tours Mon–Sat 9.30–4, Sun 10.30–4.*

❷ Charlotte
Vermont Wildflower Farm
4750 Shelburne Road. Tel: 802/985-9455. *Open May–late Oct, daily 10–5.*

❸ Ferrisburgh
Rokeby Museum
4334 Route 7. Tel: 802/877-3406. *Open mid-May–mid-Oct, Thu–Sun.*

❹ Vergennes
Lake Champlain Maritime Museum
4472 Basin Harbor Road.

Tel: 802/475-2022. *Open mid-May–mid-Oct, daily 10–5.*

❺ Middlebury
Sheldon Museum
1 Park Street. Tel: 802/388-2117. *Open Mon–Fri 10–5; May–Oct also Sat 10–4.*

Vermont State Craft Center at Frog Hollow
1 Mill Street, Frog Hollow. Tel: 802/388-3177. *Open summer Mon–Sat 9.30–5.30, Sun 11–5; winter, Mon–Sat 10–5.*

❻ East Middlebury
Waybury Inn
Route 125. Tel: 802/388-4015 or 800/348-1810.

❽ Warren
Sugarbush Resort
Tel: 802/583-6300.

❾ Waitsfield
Vermont Icelandic Horse Farm
The Common Road. Tel: 802/496-7141. *Open daily.*

❿ Waterbury
Ben and Jerry's Ice Cream Factory
Route 100, Waterbury. Tel: 802/244-5641. *Open Jun–Oct, daily 9–5 (to 8pm Jul–Aug; to 6pm Sep–Oct); Nov–May 10–5.*

Lake Champlain Chocolate Co.
Route 100, Waterbury Center. Tel: 802/244-8356. *Open daily.*

Cold Hollow Cider Mill
Route 100. Tel: 802/244-8771 or 800/327-7537. *Open daily 8–6 (Jul–Oct 8–7).*

⓫ Stowe
Stowe Mountain Resort
5781 Mountain Road. Tel: 802/253-3000.

For Children
Spirit of Ethan Allen II
Burlington Boathouse, Burlington. Tel: 802/862-8300. *Boat trips May–Oct daily.*

Waterfront Boat Rentals
Shelburne. Tel: 802/864-4858.

Special to…
University of Vermont Morgan Horse Farm
74 Battell Drive, Weybridge, off Route 23. Tel: 802/388-2011. *Open May–Oct, daily 9–4.*

TOUR 18

ⓘ 500 Market Street, Portsmouth NH 03802. Tel: 603/436-1118.

❸ John Paul Jones House
Corner Middle and State streets. Tel: 603/436-8420. *Open Jun–mid-Oct, Mon–Sat 10–4, Sun noon–4.*

❺ Rundlet-May House
364 Middle Street. Tel: 603/436-3205. *Open Jun mid-Oct, Wed–Sun 11–5.*

❼ Governor Langdon House
143 Pleasant Street. Tel: 603/436-3205. *Open Jun–mid-Oct, Wed–Sun 11–5.*

❿ Wentworth Gardner House
50 Mechanic Street. Tel: 603/436-4406. *Open Jun–mid-Oct, Tue–Sun 1–4.*

⓬ Strawbery Banke
Marcy Street, On the Waterfront. Tel: 603/433-1106. *Open May–Oct, Mon–Sat 10–5, Sun noon–5.*

⓭ Warner House
Corner of Daniel and Chapel streets. Tel: 603/436-5909. *Open Jun–Oct, Mon–Sat 10–4, Sun 1–4.*

Moffatt-Ladd House
154 Market Street. Tel: 603/436-8221. *Open mid-Jun–mid-Oct, Mon–Sat 11–5, Sun 1–5.*

Recommended Trip
Vaughan Cottage Memorial and Celia Thaxter Museum
Star Island. Tel: 603/430-6272. *Open summer, museum daily 1–3, Vaughan Reading Room 8am–10pm.*

For Children
USS Albacore
Albacore Park, 600 Market Street. Tel: 603/436-3680.

Practical Information

Open May–mid-Oct, daily 9.30–5.30.

TOUR 19

i Chamber of Commerce booth, exit 28, off I-83. Tel: 603/536-1001 or 800/386-3678.

i Visitor Center, North Woodstock NH 03262, exit 32 off I-93. Tel: 603/745-8720 or 800/FIND–MTS.

1 North Woodstock
Clark's Trading Post
Route 3, Lincoln. Tel: 603/745-8913. *Open late Jun–mid-Oct daily; weekends spring and fall.*

2 Franconia Notch
Franconia Notch State Park
Tel: 603/823-8800.

The Flume Visitor Center
Route 3. Tel: 603/745-8391. *Open mid-May–Oct (weather permitting) daily 9–5 or 5.30.*

Cannon Mountain Aerial Tramway
I-93. Tel: 603/823-8800. *Open mid-May–Oct daily.*

3 Franconia
Robert Frost Place
Ridge Road, Franconia. Tel: 603/823-5510. *Open Jun weekends, Jul–mid-Oct, Wed–Mon 1–5. Closed Tue.*

6 Mount Washington
Mount Washington Auto Road at Great Glen
Route 16, Gorham. Tel: 603/466-3988. *Open mid-May–late Oct (weather permitting).*

Great Glen Trails
Tel: 603/466-2333.

Mount Washington State Park
Tel: 603/466-3347. *Open daily May–Oct, 8–8 (weather permitting).*

Mount Washington Museum
Tel: 603/466-3988. *Open daily 8–6.*

8 Glen
Heritage-New Hampshire
Route 16. Tel: 603/383-4186. *Open mid-Jun–mid-Oct 9–6.*

Story Land
Route 16. Tel: 603/383-4293. *Open daily mid-Jun–Sep 9–6 (spring and fall weekends only 10–5).*

9 North Conway
Conway Scenic Railroad
Route 16. Tel: 603/356-5251. *Open daily mid-May–late Oct, weekends, spring, fall.*

Weather Discovery Center
Route 16. Tel: 603/356-2137. *Open daily 10–5.*

11 Lincoln
Whale's Tale
Route 3. Tel: 603/745-8810. *Open early Jun–Sep, daily 10–6.*

Hobo Railroad
Main Street. Tel: 603/745-2135. *Open late Jun–mid-Oct, daily; weekends mid-May–mid-Jun.*

For History Buffs
New England Ski Museum
Franconia Notch Parkway, exit 2. Tel: 603/823-7177, or 800/639-4181. *Open Jun–Oct, daily noon–5; Dec–Mar, Thu–Tue noon–5.*

Scenic Routes
Mount Washington Cog Railway
Route 302, Bretton Woods. Tel: 603/278-5404. *Open May–Oct.*

For Children
Six Gun City
Route 2, Jefferson. Tel: 603/586-4592. *Open mid-Jun–mid-Sep, daily 9–6; weekends 9.30–5 in spring.*

Special to…
The Jackson Ski Touring Foundation
PO Box 216, Jackson. Tel: 603/383-9355.

TOUR 20

i Lakes Region Association, Exit 23 off Route 93. Tel: 603/744-8664 or 800/60-LAKES.

1 Ashland
Pauline Glidden Toy Museum

Pleasant Street. Tel: 603/968-7289 or 7023. *Open afternoons, Jul, Aug.*

4 Moultenborough
Castle in the Clouds
Route 171. Tel: 603/476-2352. *Open weekends in spring; daily Jun–Oct.*

Loon Center and Markus Wildlife Sanctuary
Lees Mill Road. Tel: 603/476-5666. *Open daily Jul–mid-Oct; rest of year, Mon–Sat 9–5.*

5 Wolfeboro
Libby Museum
Route 109. Tel: 603/569-1035. *Open daily Jun–Oct.*

Wentworth State Park
Route 109. Tel: 603/569-3699.

Wright Museum
77 Center Street. Tel: 603/569-1212. *Open May–Oct, daily 10–4; Nov and Feb–Apr, Sat 10–4, Sun noon–4.*

6 Alton Bay
Ellacoya State Beach
Route 11, Gilford. Tel: 603/293-7821.

8 Meredith
Annalee Doll Museum
44 Reservoir Road, off Route 104. Tel: 603/279-6542. *Open late May–mid-Oct, daily 9–5.*

Back to Nature
Squam Lakes Natural Science Center
Route 113, Holderness. Tel: 603/968-7194. *Open daily May–Oct.*

Scenic Rides
Mount Washington Cruises
Weirs Beach. Tel: 603/366-5531. *Cruises late May–late Oct.*

Winnipesaukee Railroad
Tel: 603/279-5253. *Open May–Oct, Mon–Sat 10–4, Sun noon–4; Nov–Apr, Sat 10–4, Sun noon–4.*

TOUR 21

i Convention and Visitors Bureau of Greater Portland, 305 Commercial Street, Portland ME 04101. Tel: 207/772-5800.

i Brunswick Chamber of Commerce, 59 Pleasant Street, Brunswick ME 0411. Tel: 207/725-8797.

i 45 Front Street, Bath ME 04530. Tel: 207/443-0751.

i Damariscotta Region Information Bureau, Route 1, Damariscotta ME 04543. Tel: 207/563-3175 or 3176.

i Harbor Park, Rockland ME 04841. Tel: 207/596-0376.

i Public Landing, Camden ME 04843. Tel: 207/236-4404.

i Main Street, Belfast ME 04915. Tel: 207/338-5900.

1 Brunswick
Peary-MacMillan Arctic Museum
Hubbard Hall, Bowdoin Campus. Tel: 207/725-3416. *Open Tue–Sat 10–5, Sun 2–5.*

Bowdoin College Museum of Art
Upper Park Row, Walker Art Building. Tel: 207/725-3275. *Open Tue–Sat 10–5, Sun 2–5.*

2 Bath
Maine Maritime Museum
243 Washington Street. Tel: 207/443-1316. *Open daily 9.30–5.*

3 Wiscasset
Wizard of Odds and Ends
7 Main Street. Tel: 207/882-7870. *Open Jun–Dec daily.*

Musical Wonder House
18 High Street. Tel: 207/882-7163. *Open May–Oct daily 10–5.*

Castle Tucker
Lee Street at High Street. Tel: 207/882-7364. *Open Jul–mid-Oct. Tours hourly Wed–Sun 11–4.*

Nickels-Sortwell House
Main Street. Tel 207/882-6218. *Open Jun–mid-Oct, Wed–Sun, tours hourly 11–4.*

Lincoln County Museum and Old Jail
Federal Street. Tel: 207/882-6817. *Open Jul–Aug, Tue–Sun 11–4.30.*

4 Damariscotta
Chapman-Hall House
Main Street. Tel: 207/563-
3176. *Open mid-Jun–*
mid–Sep, 1–5. Closed Mon.

5 Colonial
Pemaquid/Fort
William Henry
Off Route 130. Tel: 207/
677-2423. *Open daily late*
May–early Sep, 9.30–5.

6 Pemaquid Light and
Fisherman's Museum
End of Route 130. Tel: 207/
677-2494. *Open Jun–mid-*
Oct, daily 10–5 (11 on Sun).

8 Thomaston
General Henry Knox
Museum
Montpelier; junction
Routes 1/131. Tel: 207/
354-8062. *Open late May–*
Sep, Tue–Sat 10–4, last tour
leaves at 3.

Maine Watercraft Museum
4 Knox Street Landing. Tel:
207/354-0444. *Open late*
May–Oct.

9 Rockland
Farnsworth Art Museum
and Wyeth Centre
352 Main Street. Tel: 207/
596-6457. *Open late*
May–Oct, Mon–Sat 9–5,
Sun 1–5; Nov–late May,
Tue–Sat 10–5, Sun 1–5.

10 Rockport
Opera House
7 Central Street.
Tel: 207/236-2823.

Maine Photographic
Workshop
Central Street. Tel:
207/236-8581.

Maine Coast Artists
Gallery
162 Russell Avenue. Tel:
207/236-2875. *Open*
Tue–Sat 10–5, Sun noon–5.

11 Camden
Conway Farm House
Tel: 207/236-2257. *Open*
Jul–Aug, Tue–Fri 10–4.

13 Pownalborough
Courthouse
Route 128, off Route 27.
Tel: 207/882-6817.

Special to…
L. L. Bean
95 Main Street, Freeport.

Tel: 207/865-4761.

Fat Boy Drive-In
18 Bath Road, Brunswick.
Tel: 207/729-9439.

Moody's Diner
Route 1, Waldoboro.
Tel: 207/832-7785.

Olson House
Hathorn Point Road,
Cushing. Tel: 207/596-6457.
Open Jun–mid-Oct, daily
11–4.

Recommended Trips
Monhegan Island
Maine State Ferry Service,
517A Main Street, Rock-
land. Tel: 207/596-2202.

For Children
Owl's Head
Transportation Museum
Next to Knox County
Airport, off Route 73.
Tel: 207/594-4418. *Open*
daily 10–5 (4 Nov–Mar).
Restoration Shop also Thu
6.30–9pm.

The Riding Centre at
Mount Pleasant Farm
Union. Tel: 207/785-4628.
Open daily in summer,
weekends in spring.

TOUR 22

_i_ Convention and
Visitors Bureau, 305
Commercial Street,
Portland ME 04101.
Tel: 207/772-5800.

2 Portland Museum
Of Art
7 Congress Square. Tel:
207/775-6148. *Open daily*
10–5 (Thu–Fri till 9). Closed
Mon mid-Oct–late May.

3 Children's Museum
of Maine
142 Free Street. Tel: 207/
828-1234. *Open memorial*
Day–Labor Day, Mon–Sat
10–5 , Sun noon–5. Rest of
year, Mon 9–11am, Tue–Sat
10–5, Sun noon–5.

4 Maine College Of
Art
97 Spring Street.
Tel: 207/775-3052.

6 Wadsworth-
Longfellow House
487 Congress Street.

Tel: 207/879-0427. *Open*
Jun–Oct, daily 10–4.

Center for Maine History
485 Congress Street. Tel:
207/879-0427. *Open daily*
10–5/6 (Tue–Sat winter).

9 First Parish Church
425 Congress Street. Tel:
207/773-5747. *Open by*
appointment.

10 City Hall
389 Congress Street.
Tel: 207/874-8300. *Open*
weekdays 8–4.30.

Portland Symphony
Tel: 207/842-0800.

13 F. O. Bailey
141 Middle Street. Tel:
207/774-1479.

14 Milk Street Armory
Portland Regency Hotel,
20 Milk Street.
Tel: 207/774-4200.

15 Boothby Square
U.S. Customs House
312 Fore Street. Tel:
207/780-3326. *Open week-*
days 8–4.30.

16 Tracy-Causer
Building
20–36 Danforth Street.
Tel: 207/775-6245. *Call for*
times.

Special to…
Gritty McDuff's
396 Fore Street.
Tel: 207/772-2739.

Portland Observatory
138 Congress Street. Tel:
207/774-5561. *Open late*
May–mid-Oct, 10–5.

TOUR 23

_i_ Convention and
Visitors Bureau, 305 Com-
mercial Street, Portland
ME 04101. Tel: 207/772-
5800.

_i_ Bethel Area Chamber
of Commerce, 30 Cross
Street, Bethel Train Station,
Bethel ME 04217. Tel:
207/824-2282 or 800/442-
5826.

_i_ Rangeley Lakes Region
Chamber of Commerce, 6
Park Road, Rangeley ME
04970. Tel: 207/864-5364.

_i_ Farmington-Wilton
Chamber of Commerce,
30 Main Street, Farmington
ME 04938. Tel: 207/778-
4215.

1 Sabbathday Lake
Sabbathday Lake Village
Route 26, New Gloucester
Tel: 207/926-4597. *Open*
late May–mid-Oct,
Mon–Sat 10–4.30.

2 Poland Spring
State of Maine Building
Tel: 207/998-4142. *Open*
Jun–Sep, weekends; Jul–Aug,
daily.

4 Trap Corner
Perham's of West Paris
194 Bethel Road, Routes
26 and 219. Tel: 207/674-
2341. *Open daily 9–5.*

8 Rangeley
Rangeley Historical
Society Museum
Main Street. Tel: 207/864-
3317. *Open mid-Jun–mid-*
Sep, Mon–Sat 10–noon.

Wilhelm Reich Museum
Dodge Pond Road, off
Route 4/16. Tel: 207/864-
3443. *Open Jul–Aug, Wed–*
Sun 1–5; Sep, Sun 1–5.

9 Kingfield
Stanley Museum
School Street. Tel: 207/
265-2729. *Open Tue–Sun*
1–4 (Tue–Fri Nov–Apr).

10 Farmington
Nordica Memorial
Homestead
Holley Road. Tel: 207/778-
2042. *Open Jun–early Sep,*
Tue–Sun 10–1, 2–5.

Red School House
Museum
Routes 2 and 4. Tel: 207/
778-4215. *Open Tue–Fri*
9–4.

11 Norlands Living
History Center
290 Norlands Road,
Livermore Falls. Tel: 207/
897-4366. *Open Jul–Aug,*
daily 10–4; Sep–Oct, week-
ends.

Back to Nature
Maine Wildlife Park
Route 26. Tel: 207/657-
4977. *Open mid-Apr–mid-*
Nov, 9.30–5.30.

INDEX

A

Abiel Smith School 48
addresses, useful 5
Adventure schooner 19
African Meeting House 48
Afro–American History,
    Museum of 48
Alcott, Louisa May 7, 13, 14,
    15, 48, 56
Alton Bay 137
American Museum of Fly
    Fishing 105
American War of
    Independence 8–9,
    11–13, 15, 100
Amherst 37
Ancient Burying Ground 63
Ann Treadwell Mansion 126
Annalee Dolls 137
Arlington 105
Arrowhead 35
Arthur M. Sackler Museum
    53
Ashland 135

B

banks 4
Barnstable 24
Basketball Hall of Fame 31
Bath 139, 141
Batten Kill River 105
Beauport 21
Beechwood 94
Beinecke Library 70
Belcourt Castle 95
Belfast 146
Ben and Jerry's 97, 119
Bennington 97, 98–101
Berkshire Botanical Garden 33
Berkshire Hills 7, 30–7
Bethel, Maine 154
Bethel, Vermont 111
Bethlehem 131
Billings Farm Museum 112
Black Heritage Trail 48
Boston 8–9, 38–50
Boston Common 41
Boston City Hall Plaza 46, 48
Bowdoin College 141
Branford 77
Brattleboro 108–9
The Breakers 85, 94
Brewster 25
Bridgewater 112, 114
Bromley Mountain 106
Brown University 85, 88
Brunswick 139, 141
Bryant Pond 153–4
Buckman Tavern 11–12
Bull's Bridge 73

Bunker Hill Monument 44
Busch-Reisinger Museum 53

C

Cambridge 39, 51–5
Camden 139, 145
Cape Cod 7, 23–9
    Canal 24
    Light 28
    National Seashore 7, 26
Cape Playhouse 25
car rental 159
Carpenter Center for the
    Visual Arts 53
Castle Tucker 142
Catamount Tavern 100
Center for Maine History
    148
Center Sandwich 123, 135
Charlotte 117
Château-sur-Mer 85, 94
Chatham 29
Chester 107
Chesterwood 33
Children's Museum, Boston
    46
Children's Museum of
    Maine 148
Clapp House 151
Clark's Trading Post 129
climate 161
Colonial Pemaquid 142–3
Colt Firearms Collection
    64
Concord 7, 9, 10, 13–14
Concord Museum 13
Connecticut 58–81
Connecticut Antique
    Machinery Association
    Museum 74
Connecticut Freedom
    Trail 61
Connecticut Historical
    Society 65
Connecticut River Museum
    77, 78
Conway Farm House 145
Coolidge, Calvin 97, 114
Copp's Hill Burying Ground
    44
Cornwall Bridge 74, 75
credit cards 4
currency 4
Custom House 46
customs regulations 4

D

Damariscotta 139, 142, 143
David Winton Bell Gallery
    88

DeCordova Museum 14–5
Deerfield 7, 36–7
Dennis 25
Dickinson, Emily 37, 56
disabilities, travelers with
    160

E

East Brewster 25
East Dennis 25
East Haddam 79
East Middlebury 117–8
Eastham 26, 27
electricity 4
Elizabeth Park Rose Garden
    65
The Elms 94
emergency numbers 4–5
Emerson House 14
Emerson, Ralph Waldo 7, 14,
    15, 56
Essex, Connecticut 78
Essex, Massachusetts 22
Eugene O'Neill Theater
    Center 59, 80

F

the fall 96, 102–3
families on vacation 160
Faneuil Hall 42, 46
Farmington 156
Ferrisburg 117
First Baptist Meeting House
    87
First Parish Church 149
First Unitarian Church 89
Fogg Museum 53
Fort William Henry 142–3
Franconia 130–1
Franconia Notch 129–30
Frost, Robert 57, 97, 99,
    118, 130–1

G

Gillette Castle 79
Gilmanton 137
Glen 132
Globe Corner Bookstore
    42
Gloucester 19
Gorham 131
Governor Langdon House
    126
Governor Stephen Hopkins
    House 88–9
Grafton 97, 107
Grafton Notch State Park
    154
Grandma Moses 97, 99

Granary Burying Ground 41
Granville Gulf State Park
    117
Great Barrington 31
Great Island Trail 28
Green Mountains 109, 118
Gropius House 14
Guilford 77

H

Halibut Point State Park 22
Hammersmith Farm 95
Hammonasset Beach State
    Park 77
Hammond Castle Museum
    19
Hancock-Clarke House 12
Hancock Shaker Village 35
Harkness Tower 69
Harriet Beecher Stowe
    House 64–5
Harrison Gray Otis House
    48
Hartford 59, 60–5
Harvard 6, 39, 51, 52–4
Hastings House 54
Hawthorne, Nathaniel 7, 13,
    14, 15, 18, 32, 33, 56, 141
Haymarket 43
Healdville 114
health matters 5, 159
Hemming's Sunoco Station
    100
Hempsted House 80
Henry Whitfield State
    Museum 77
Heritage New Hampshire
    132
Heritage Plantation 24
Herreshoff Marine Museum
    83
Hildene 106
Historic Bennington
    Railroad Station 100–1
hitchhiking 159
Holden Leonard Mill 101
Holderness 135
Holley House Museum
    75
hotels 161–4
Housatonic Valley 71–5
Hunter Cove Sanctuary
    156

I

International Tennis Hall of
    Fame 93
Ipswich 22
Ives, Charles 56, 57
Ivoryton 78

J

Jackson 132
John Brown House 89
John Hancock Tower 50
John Harvard Statue 52
John Heard House 22
John Paul Jones House 125
John Peirce Mansion 125
Joseph Nightingale House 89
Josiah Dennis Manse 25

K

Kancamagus Highway 123, 133
Kent 74
Kent Falls State Park 74
Killington 97
Kingfield 156
King's Chapel 41–2
Kingscote Mansion 93
Kipling, Rudyard 102, 108

L

Lake Champlain 96, 97, 116
Maritime Museum 117
Lake Waramaug 73
Lake Winnipesaukee 123, 134–7
Lakeville 59, 75
Lenox 33, 35
Lexington 7, 10, 11–12
Libby Museum 136
Liberty Pole 127
Lime Rock Park 75
Lincoln 133
Lincoln County Museum and Old Jail 142
liquor laws 159
Litchfield 59, 72–3
literature 56–7
L. L. Bean 141
Longfellow, Henry Wadsworth 7, 55, 56, 139, 141, 148
Longfellow House 55
Long Trail Brewing Company 114
Loon Center and Markus Wildlife Sanctuary 136
Louisburg Square 48
Ludlow 97, 107
Lyman-Allyn Art Museum 80

M

Madison 77
Magic Wings Butterfly Conservatory and Garden 37
Maine 138–57
Maine Maritime Museum 141
Maine Photographic Workshop 145

Maine Watercraft Museum 144
Maine Wildlife Park 153
Manchester 97, 106
Manchester-by-the-Sea 18
Marble House 94–5
Marblehead 17
Marblehead Neck 17
Mark Twain House 64
Marlboro 109
Marsh-Billings-Rockefeller National Historical Park 112
Mashantucket Pequot Museum 81
Massachusetts 6–55
Massachusetts Museum of Contemporary Art 35–6
The Mayflower 28
McLellan House 151
Mechanics Hall 148
Melville, Herman 32, 35, 56, 82
Memorial Hall 53–4
Meredith 123, 137
Merrymeeting Bay 146
Middlebury 117
Milk Street Armory 150
Minute Man National Historical Park 12–13
Moby Duck tours 19
Moffatt-Ladd House 127
Mohawk Trail 36
Monhegan Island 143
Monomoy Islands 25
Monte Cristo Cottage 80
Monterey 31
Monument Mountain 32
Morgan Horse Farm 120
Mory's 70
motoring 159–60
Moultonborough 136
The Mount 33, 35
Mount Equinox 105–6
Mount Mansfield 119–20
Mount Washington 123, 131, 132, 133
Cog Railway 131
Mr. Steward's Museum of Art and Curiosities 61
Munroe Tavern 11
Museum of Connecticut History 64
Museum of Our National Heritage 11
Museums of Natural History 54
music 57
Musical Wonder House 142
Mystic 58, 59, 81, 83

N

Nathaniel Palmer Home 81
Nathaniel Harrison House 77
National Heritage Museum 11

Naumkeag 33
Nauset Light Beach 27
Naval War College Museum 83
New England Aquarium 46
New England Fire and History Museum 25
New England Holocaust Memorial 46
New England Ski Museum 129, 130
New Hampshire 122–37
New Harbor 143
New Haven 66–70, 76
New London 80
New Milford 73
New Preston 73
Newburyport 22
Newfane 108
Newport 83, 84, 85, 90–5
Art Museum 92–3
Artillery Company 92
Casino 93
Historical Society 92
Newry 155
Nichols House Museum 48
Noah Webster House 65
Noank 80
Nordica Memorial Homestead 156
Norfolk 75
Norlands Living History Center 156
Norman Rockwell Museums 32, 111
North Adams 35–6
North Conway 132–3
North Woodstock 129
Northampton 37

O

Okemo Mountain 107
Old Colony House 91
Old Corner Bookstore 42
Old First Church 99
Old Lighthouse Museum 81
Old Lyme 79
Old Man of the Mountain 129
Old North Bridge 12, 14
Old North Church 44
Old Saybrook 77
Old South Meeting House 42
Old State House, Boston 42
Old State House, Hartford 61
Old Stone Bank 89
Old Train Station 101
Olde Mistick Village 81
Omni Parker House 41
O'Neill, Eugene 29, 56, 57, 80
Orchard House 13
Orleans 26
Owl's Head Light 144
Owl's Head Transportation Museum 144

P, Q

Paris 153
Park-McCullough House 101
Parker River National Wildlife Refuge 22
Park Street Church 41
passports and visas 5
Paul Revere's House 43
Peabody Museum 18
Peary-MacMillan Arctic Museum 141
Pemaquid Light and Fisherman's Museum 143
Pennysaver Building 101
personal safety 160
Peru 106
Pigeon Cove 21–2
Pioneer Village 17–18
Pleasant Valley Wildlife Sanctuary 35
Plum Island 22
Plymouth 114
Poland Spring 153
Portland 139, 147–51, 152
Portland Harbor 149
Portland Museum of Art 148
Portland Observatory 149
Portsmouth 123, 124–7
post offices 5, 161
Potters' Yard 101
Pownalborough Courthouse 146
Presidential Range 130
Prides Crossing 18
Providence 85, 86–9
Providence Athenaeum 87
Provincetown 7, 28–9
public holidays 159
Quechee and the Gorge 111
Quincy Market 46

R

Radcliffe Yard 55
Railroad Museum 29
Rangeley 139, 155–6
recreational vehicles 158
Red School House Museum 156
Redwood Library 92
restaurants 161–4
Revere, Paul 7, 12–13, 15, 41, 43, 89, 112
Rhode Island 83, 84–95
Rhode Island School of Design 85, 87
Ripton 118
Robert Frost Place 130–1
Robert and Joseph Rogers House 91
Rockland 144
Rockport, Maine 145
Rockport, Massachusetts 21
Rockwell, Norman 7, 32–3, 56, 105, 111
Rocky Neck 21

Index & Acknowledgments

Rosecliff 94
Rough Point 95
Round Pond 143
Rundlet-May House 126
Rutland 110

S

Sabbathday Lake 139, 153
St. John's Church 127
Salem 17–18
Salisbury 75
Salisbury Cannon Museum 75
Sandwich 24
Sandwich Glass Museum 24
Santa's Village 131
Saybrook College 69
Science Center of
    Connecticut 65
Science Center of East
    Connecticut 80
Scroll & Key 70
seniors 160
Shakers 35, 139, 153
Shaw/54th Regiment
    Memorial 41
Sheffield 31–2
Shelburne 97, 116–7
Shelburne Falls 36
Shelburne Museum 116
Shore Village Museum 144
The Silo 73
Six Flags New England 31
Six Gun City 131
Skull and Bones Society 69
Sleepy Hollow Cemetery 14
Sloane-Stanley Museum 74
Springfield 31
Squam Lake 123, 135
Squam Lakes Natural
    Science Center 135

Stanley Museum 156
State Capitol, Hartford 63
State Capitol, Providence 87
State House 41
Sterling and Francine Clark
    Art Institute 35
Stockbridge 7, 32–3
Stonington 81
Stony Creek 77
Story Land 132
Stowe 119–20
Stowe, Harriet Beecher 56,
    59, 64–5, 73, 77
Strawbery Banke 123, 127
Sugarbush 119
Sunday River ski area 139,
    154

T

Tanglewood 33
Tapping Reeve House 72
taxes 160
telephones 5
Thatcher House 25
theater 57
Thimble Islands 77
Thomas Thompson House
    126
Thomaston 144
Thoreau, Henry David
    7, 14, 15, 56
time differences 5
Tommy's Park 150
Touro Synagogue 91
Tracy-Causer building 151
transportation 158–9
Trap Corner 153
Travelers Aid Society 5
Travelers Tower 62
Trinity Church, Boston 50

Trinity Church, Newport 92
Truro 28
Twain, Mark 56–7, 59, 64

U

Union Oyster House 43
USS *Albacore* 126
USS *Constitution* 40, 44
USS *Nautilus* 80

V

Vaughan Cottage Memorial
    and Celia Turner
    Museum 125
Vergennes 117
Vermont 96–121
Vermont Icelandic Horse
    Farm 119
Vermont Wildflower Farm
    117
Vernon Court 94
Vernon House 92
visitor information 160–1

W

Wadsworth Atheneum 62–3
Wadsworth-Longfellow
    House 148
Waitsfield 119
Walden Pond 14
Wanton-Lyman-Hazard
    House 91
Ware Collection of Glass
    Flowers 54
Warner House 127
Warren 119
Washington, George 11,
    41, 54, 55, 73, 92, 126

Waterbury 119
Weather Discovery Center
    133
websites 161
Weir's Beach 137
Wellfleet 27–8
Wentworth Gardner
    House 127
West Cornwall 75
Weston 97, 106–7
whalewatching 21
Whaling Museum 82
Wharton, Edith 7, 33, 35, 57
White Flower Farm 73
White Mountains 123,
    128–33
White River National Fish
    Hatchery 111
Widener Library 52–3
Wilhelm Reich Museum
    155–6
William A. Farnsworth Art
    Museum 144
Williamstown 7, 35
Wilmington 109
Winslow-Crocker House 25
Wireless Telegraph Station
    28
Wiscasset 139, 141–2
Witch Museum 17
Wolf Hollow 22
Wolfeboro 136–7
Woodford 109
Woodstock 96, 97, 112
Wright Museum 137
Wyeth Center 144

Y

Yale 59, 68–70
Yarmouth Port 24–5

The Automobile Association
wishes to thank the following libraries and photographers for their assistance
in the preparation of this book.

MARY EVANS PICTURE LIBRARY 8a, 8b, 56a, 56/7; TOM MACKIE 5, 59, 83, 84, 92, 94/5, 95, 102/3, 103a, 118/9, 120/1, 136/7, 136, 142, 143, 144/5, 153, 154/5, 154b, 157, 165; WIM McELEHOLM 79; MAINE OFFICE OF TOURISM 147, 148, 149; GENE PEACH/THE PICTURE CUBE 51; PICTURES COLOUR LIBRARY LTD 9, 10, 103b; SPECTRUM COLOUR LIBRARY 6, 11, 44, 82/3, 97; THE STOCK MARKET 12 (Michele Burgess 1993), 20 (Kunio Owaki 1988), 26/7 (Jean Miele MCMXCII), 28 (B O Zaunders 1991), 31 (ChromoSohm/Sohm MCMXCIV), 32/3 (Brownie Harris 1992), 33 (Lance Nelson), 58 (O'Rourke 1986), 62b (Ed Bohon 1986), 63 (Audrey Gibson 1986), 72/3 (Lance Nelson), 72 (Sonya Jacobs 1985), 74/5 (Kunio Owaki 1987), 81 (James Marshall), 85 (Craig Hammell 1993), 92/3 (Craig Hammell 1993), 116 (Mark E Gibson 1987), 126 (James Blank), 150/1 (Randy Ury 1992); ZEFA PICTURES LTD 34, 37, 38, 49b, 68, 86/7, 91, 96, 105, 108/9, 111, 138, 139a, 146.

All remaining pictures are held in the Association's own library (AA PHOTO LIBRARY) with contributions from:
CHRIS COE 86; R HOLMES 2, 14/5, 18, 29b, 30, 34/5, 36, 39b, 40, 41, 43, 45, 47, 50a, 53, 54, 55, 60, 61, 62a, 66, 76, 78/9, 122, 123b, 124, 125, 130/1, 132/3, 140; J LYNCH 13, 19a, 19b; M LYNCH 4, 7, 23, 24, 25, 27, 29a, 39a, 49a, 50b, 52, 64, 65, 67, 70, 80, 88, 89, 98, 99, 100, 101, 106, 106/7, 110, 112/3, 113, 114, 115, 117, 120, 123a, 127, 129, 131, 132, 135, 139b, 145, 154a; CLIVE SAWYER 17, 42; J WILLIAMS 57.

Contributors
Copy editors: Larry Dunmire, Karen Bird   **Indexer:** Marie Lorimer
Thanks also to **Kathy Arnold** and **Paul Wade** for their updating work on this book.